Moses Stuart

The Father of Biblical Science in America

SOCIETY OF BIBLICAL LITERATURE

BIBLICAL SCHOLARSHIP IN NORTH AMERICA

Kent Harold Richards, Editor

Frank Chamberlain Porter: Pioneer in American Biblical Interpretation	Roy A. Harrisville
Benjamin Wisner Bacon: Pioneer in American Biblical Criticism	Roy A. Harrisville
A Fragile Craft: The Work of Amos Niven Wilder	John Dominic Crossan
Edgar Johnson Goodspeed: Articulate Scholar	James I. Cook
Shirley Jackson Case and the Chicago School: The Socio-Historical Method	William J. Hynes
Humanizing America's Iconic Book: Society of Biblical Literature Centennial Addresses 1980	Gene M. Tucker and Douglas A. Knight, editors
A History of Biblical Studies in Canada: A Sense of Proportion	John S. Moir
Searching the Scriptures: A History of the Society of Biblical Literature, 1880-1980	Ernest W. Saunders
Horace Bushnell: On the Vitality of Biblical Language	James O. Duke
Feminist Perspectives on Biblical Scholarship	Adela Yarboro Collins, editor
Erwin Ramsdell Goodenough: A Personal Pilgrimage	Robert S. Eccles
The Pennsylvania Tradition of Semitics	Cyrus H. Gordon
The Bible and the University: The Messianic Vision of William Rainey Harper	James P. Wind
Max Leopold Margolis: A Scholar's Scholar	Leonard Greenspoon
A Century of Greco-Roman Philology	Frederick William Danker
Moses Stuart	John H. Giltner

Moses Stuart

The Father of Biblical Science in America

by

John H. Giltner

Scholars Press
Atlanta, Georgia

The Society of Biblical Literature gratefully acknowledges
a grant from the National Endowment for the Humanities
to underwrite certain editorial and research expenses of the
Centennial Publications Series. Published results and interpretations do not necessarily represent the view of the
Endowment.

©1988
Society of Biblical Literature

Library of Congress Cataloguing-in-Publication Data

Giltner, John H.
Moses Stuart

(Biblical scholarship in North America; no. 14)
1. Stuart, Moses, 1780-1852. 2. Biblical scholars —
United States — Biography. 3. Theologians —
United States — Biography. I. Title. II. Series.
BS501.S78G55 1988   220′.092′4   [B]   86-29829
ISBN 1-55540-104-X (alk. paper)
ISBN 1-55540-105-8 (pbk, : alk. paper)

CONTENTS

Moses Stuart
Courtesy of Yale University Art Gallery

PREFACE

In the early spring of 1810, two years after the New England Congregationalists opened their first venture in formal, organized graduate theological education with the seminary at Andover, Massachusetts, they called Moses Stuart, a young pastor from New Haven, Connecticut, to fill the chair of Professor of Sacred Literature. Though but meagerly prepared for the position, he carved a career that was notable in the annals of American Christian scholarship. At his death he was eulogized as the "father of biblical learning in America." The tribute is remembered to our own day, though the life and thought that gave it meaning have been largely forgotten. It is the purpose of this study, therefore, to reexamine Stuart's career and scholarly contribution with this estimate in mind.

Like every mortal, Stuart was a child of his time. Little in his theology was original. The system that he expounded was, for the most part, rooted in the Calvinism of his New England birth and nurture. But in biblical learning he was an authentic pioneer, borrowing early and extensively from the far away, and still very new, German biblical critics and linguists. His singular contribution then was the establishment of standards of responsible, modern biblical investigation within his traditional Puritan constituency, which infused the new learning into the mainstream of American evangelical piety.

Believing that the approach that I have taken strikes closer to the real man and at the same time better highlights the religious and social concerns of the period in which he lived, I have written more of an intellectual history than a strict biography. Hence, with the exception of the biographical summaries of the first and last chapters, the main body of the study is arranged topically rather than chronologically. Here I have been consciously, but I believe not unfairly, selective, treating the writings on issues that seemed most to interest Stuart and at the same time best to illuminate his distinctive contributions as teacher, theologian, critic, and commentator.

My indebtedness to a number of kind friends and colleagues who have aided in the preparation of this study is very great. I should like especially to mention the late Professor Sydney Ahlstrom for his wise guidance and critical comments; Barbara Millisor, who prepared the typescript with infinite patience and diligence; Cecelia Reed who compiled the index; and my wife, Fern Mollohan Giltner, for her help in research and editing, as well as for her constant interest and encouragement. I naturally add the remark, circumscribed but true, that I alone am responsible for shortcomings and errors.

Portions of chapters 5 and 9 originally appeared in the *Journal of Religious Thought* (18 [Winter–Spring 1961] 27–39; 23 [1966–67] 3–13) and are used here with the kind permission of the Howard University Press.

I

THE EARLY YEARS AT ANDOVER

Moses Stuart, proclaimed by his contemporaries as well as by later observers as "the father of biblical science in America," was born of humble farmer parents in Wilton, Connecticut, in 1780. Though Stuart was precocious in his grammar school studies and was profoundly shaped by the rigors of his New England farm upbringing, it is his entrance into the sophomore class at Yale College in May 1797 with which we begin our account of his career.

Timothy Dwight had been president of Yale for two years prior to Stuart's arrival, time enough to impress upon the college his keen Puritan intellect, conservative Federalist politics, and ardent Edwardsean revivalist theology. In each of these, Dwight was Stuart's most formative and abiding mentor. Stuart's primary academic interest as an undergraduate was mathematics, but he excelled in all his studies, was inducted into Phi Beta Kappa, and graduated at the head of his class in 1799, at which time he gave the salutatory oration, which was then considered to be the first honor.[1]

Upon graduation Stuart first tried schoolteaching, successively in Easton and Danbury. In 1801 he left teaching to devote full time to preparation for a career in law, moving to Newton, where he studied privately under a local judge. He was admitted to the bar in Danbury in the autumn of 1802. In the meantime he was invited back to Yale to give the master's oration at the September commencement and to become tutor in the college with freedom to pursue private legal studies in New Haven. The appointment was a prestigious recognition of Stuart's promise as a scholar, but more important for him it placed him again under the influence of Dwight at a time when the religious currents set in motion by Dwight's constant evangelical preaching were about to reach flood tide. An earnest revival began at Yale College in the spring of 1802. Stuart returned in September; by October he too had been converted, and in January 1803 he formally joined the Church of Christ in Yale College.[2]

Shortly thereafter he abandoned his legal studies and placed himself under the instruction of Dwight as a student for the ministry, there being

[1] Leonard Bacon, "Moses Stuart," *New Englander* 10 (February 1852) 42.
[2] Ibid., 21.

1

as yet no separate divinity department at the college. Stuart remained at Yale for two years in the dual role of tutor and divinity student. As tutor he conducted daily recitations in Latin and Greek and also served as a dormitory proctor. As a scholar in theology he read Edwardsean New Divinity from the patriarch Edwards himself; from Edwards's disciples, Joseph Bellamy and Samuel Hopkins; and, not the least, from Edwards's grandson, Timothy Dwight, who was still polishing his own notable system in weekly sermon-lectures at the college church. He also participated in the debates that Dwight regularly scheduled on practical theology and applied Christianity. This was supplemented by readings in other standard Calvinist works — all British publications — the theological treatises of Andrew Fuller, Thomas Ridgley's *Body of Divinity*, and Humphrey Prideaux's *Old and New Testament Connected in the History of the Jews and Neighboring Nations*. Church history was introduced through Mosheim's *Ecclesiastical History*.[3]

Stuart was already competent in classical Greek and had had some exposure to New Testament Greek in his undergraduate studies. Hebrew had been offered at Yale while Stuart was an undergraduate, but apparently he did not take the course. It was not taught at all during his second stay at the college, nor does it seem that he received any advanced training in biblical Greek.[4] Stuart's career was to have several ironies, but none was more fascinating than this, that his knowledge of the biblical languages, the disciplines in which he was later to make his most important pedagogical and scholarly contributions, was largely self-taught — and this after he was appointed to his chair at Andover.

Stuart resigned as tutor in September 1804. After a brief period of travel in Vermont he returned to New Haven, where he was invited to assist, as supply preacher, the ailing Dr. James Dana, pastor of the prestigious Center Congregational Church. While still tutor at Yale, Stuart had begun a courtship with Abigail Clark of Danbury, Connecticut. The two were wed on 1 January 1805, the date coincident with his first weeks at Center Church.

Things did not go well between the senior pastor and his assistant. In fact, the relationship between Stuart and Dana soured from the start. Stuart's youth inevitably placed the aged Dr. Dana at a disadvantage. More damaging to the old man was Stuart's popular articulation of the Dwight

---

[3] Charles E. Cunningham, *Timothy Dwight, 1752–1817* (New York: Macmillan, 1942) 228; Roland Bainton, *Yale and the Ministry* (New York: Harper & Brothers, 1957) 77–78; Edwards A. Park, *A Discourse Delivered at the Funeral of Professor Moses Stuart* (Boston: Tappan & Whittemore, 1852) 21.

[4] Ebeneezer Grant Marsh was appointed instructor in Hebrew in 1798, but he fell ill in March 1803 and died the following November. See Franklin B. Dexter, *Biographical Sketches of Yale College with Annals of the College History* (New Haven: Henry Holt, 1885–1912) 5:153–54.

variety of Edwardsean evangelicalism, a theology which Dana, the conservative Old Divinity stalwart, held in contempt, but which the Center Church congregation found considerably more attractive than the lifeless dogmas they had long been served. Center Church was completely taken with the young preacher, and, as Dana's health continued to decline, the congregation moved to force the older man's resignation—this over his bitter protest. Stuart was formally installed as pastor on 4 March 1806, and Timothy Dwight was the ordination preacher.[5]

Stuart's ministry at Center Church, though brief, marked a significant chapter in the history of the church and indeed of the broader movement known as the Second Great Awakening. His preaching was vigorously evangelical. The result was an energized, enlarged congregation whose pastor quickly gained a reputation as one of the bright young stars of New England Calvinist evangelicalism. It is not surprising that the trustees of Andover Seminary, a school but recently organized on just such a theological position as Stuart was popularizing, should take favorable note of his activities. Andover was founded in 1807 by a union of Old Calvinists and Edwardseans precisely to train an orthodox evangelical ministry in the face of ever-growing defections to Unitarianism within New England Congregationalism. Even as the school was being formed, Stuart figured as a potential faculty member, possibly in Christian or natural theology. But funds were available for only three chairs, and these went to more experienced scholars. The seminary opened in May 1808. The following year Eliphalet Pearson, Andover's first professor of Sacred Literature, abruptly resigned. This unexpected circumstance again brought Stuart into consideration. This time the trustees found no obstacles to his being hired, apart from Stuart's own half-hearted but honest protestations about his scholarly deficiencies and Center Church's genuine reluctance to release their popular preacher. Andover extended a formal call in the fall of 1809. Stuart accepted at an annual salary of one thousand dollars plus housing, and by a vote of both the church and a select ecclesiastical council of the New Haven Consociation of Congregational Churches the pastoral relationship between Stuart and the Center Church came to an end.

The Professor of Sacred Literature

Stuart moved to Andover during the winter of 1810. William Bartlet, a wealthy merchant of Salem and a generous benefactor of the seminary, had purchased six acres of land on the west side of Andover Common, and, when Stuart was appointed, Bartlet gave him carte blanche to build the kind of house he desired. Here Stuart raised a "perfectly simple" though

[5] Stuart's relationship to Dana and the account of his call to Center Church is given in detail in John H. Giltner, "Moses Stuart, 1780–1852" (Ph.D. diss., Yale University, 1956) chap. 3.

"large and commodious" building in the prevailing Georgian style.[6] When the Stuart family occupied the new house in 1810, there were two children. Seven others followed, and of the nine, seven survived childhood.[7]

Stuart was just approaching his thirtieth birthday when he met his first class at the seminary. Except for frequent trips to nearby Boston, occasional excursions during the summer recesses to New York, Philadelphia, or northern New England, and one sick leave during the summer of 1822 to Charleston, South Carolina, he spent the rest of his life at Andover.

Essential to the apologetic aims of Andover's founders was the public articulation of the strict Calvinist orthodoxy of the Westminster Shorter Catechism, which represented the views of the Old Calvinists within the Andover circle, and a new theological symbol, the so-called Andover Creed. The creed had been drawn up by founders loyal to the strict Calvinist views of the late Samuel Hopkins, protégé of Jonathan Edwards and for many years pastor in Newport, Rhode Island. Although later there was some ambiguity about enforcement, in general each of the professors was required at five-year intervals to make a public subscription to the Westminster statement, and those professors who were on the "Associate Foundation," the legal designation for the funds from the Hopkinsian founders, were required to subscribe to both creeds at the five-year intervals. Stuart's chair was in this latter category. Yet despite the creedal strictures, the founders did allow the faculty considerable freedom in determining the curriculum. It was urged, for instance, that each instructor "mark out the course to be pursued in his own department, both in public and private lectures" and that together the faculty "determine what proportion of the time should be occupied with study in each department."[8] Thus, experimentation was in order. For a time the curriculum combined private tutoring with public lectures, the three classes devoting one year to private study and recitation in each department: theology, sacred rhetoric (homiletics), and sacred

---

[6] Sarah Stuart Robbins, *Old Andover Days* (Boston: Pilgrim Press, 1908) 14.

[7] With the exception of Moses Brown (1813–1835), who died suddenly at the age of twenty-two, the other surviving Stuart children lived out useful careers, though none followed his or her father's profession. Isaac William (1809–1861) patterned his career after his father's. A graduate of Yale, he served for a time as professor of Greek and Latin in the College of South Carolina in Columbus. He later settled in Hartford, where he pursued a private career writing on local Connecticut history. James Clark (1812–1870), also a Yale graduate, became a successful physician in Syracuse, New York. Each of the daughters married clergymen or theological professors. Writing under the pseudonym H. Trusta, Elizabeth Stuart Phelps (1815–1852) achieved extraordinary popular fame as an author of religious novels. Sarah Stuart Robbins (1817–1910) also was a well-known author. Her specialty was children's literature, though she is remembered now for her fascinating nostalgic account of her childhood and youth in *Old Andover Days*. The other two daughters were Mary Stuart Phelps (1821–1856) and Abbe Stuart Anthony (1823–1876). For more details on the Stuart children, see Giltner, "Moses Stuart," 283–88.

[8] Leonard Woods, *History of Andover Theological Seminary* (Boston: J. R. Osgood, 1885) 186.

literature. Throughout the three years, the students also listened to public lectures delivered by the three professors. The pioneer institution thus relied on traditional eighteenth-century instruction for the ministry, a combination of collegiate education and advanced private tutoring under a prominent local pastor. The disadvantages of this first plan, whereby the student had to assimilate lecture material often wholly removed from his private studies, became apparent soon enough, and the faculty decided that the public and private instruction should coincide, each professor spending a full year lecturing and tutoring one of the classes at a time. This solution, however, raised the problem of logical order in the curriculum. The final settlement was that sacred literature and the languages would fall to the junior class, theology to the middlers, and sacred rhetoric to the seniors. With minor exceptions this plan remained in effect throughout Stuart's teaching career. It was through his courses, then, that the successive generations of Andover students were introduced to higher theological education.

Although the Andover Constitution offered sufficient latitude to work out the overall course of study, nothing was left unsettled about what subjects were to be taught. The sixth and tenth articles list the duties of Stuart's department:

> Under the head of *Sacred Literature* shall be included Lectures on the formation, preservation, and transmission of the Sacred Volume; on the languages in which the Bible was originally written; on the Septuagint version of the old Testament, and on the peculiarities of the language and style of the new Testament, resulting from this version and other causes; on the history, character, use and authority of the ancient versions and manuscripts of the old and new Testaments; on the canons of biblical criticism and on the authenticity of the several books of the sacred Code; on the Bible, more particularly on the history and character of our English version; and also critical Lectures on the various readings and difficult passages in the sacred writings.
>
> It shall be the duty of the Professors, by *private* instruction and advice, to aid the Students in the acquisition of a radical and adequate knowledge of the sacred scriptures in their original languages and of the old Testament in the Septuagint version; to direct their method of studying the Bible and all other writings. . . .[9]

Stuart was thus expected to cover the whole field: the languages of *both* Testaments, the exegesis of both, and the host of secondary subjects related to their critical study. In effect, this mandate became the outine of his teaching career at Andover. It was a significant requirement, and the manner in which he carried it out, the difficulties he overcame, and the successes he achieved constituted one of the most important chapters of Stuart's life.

The task was monumental. The first stone in the foundation of the monument was the reintroduction in America of graduate-level study of the

[9] Ibid., 235, 237.

biblical languages. That these had once been a subject of serious endeavor
at Harvard, Yale, and Princeton is well documented, as is also the fact of
the decline of such studies at those institutions, particularly during the later
decades of the eighteenth century. But such instruction as there had been
in biblical Greek and Hebrew was limited almost entirely to matters of
grammar.[10] Nor did the Great Awakening provide much positive impulse in
this regard, for it raised issues of doctrine, not biblical theology. Though it
is unfair to say that the American religious thinkers during and after the
revivals neglected the Bible, philological and exegetical studies were not
nearly as important to them as were the disciplines of systematic theology
and apologetics. Hence, the tendency was to pursue Greek and Hebrew
grammar deductively to support previously established doctrine. Deeper
probings into the theological meanings inherent within the texts or into
broader critical questions generally evoked little concern among New
England Calvinists—the very group which, by virtue of its educational
standards and institutions of higher learning, was best equipped in America
to pursue such investigation. The works of Jonathan Edwards, Samuel
Hopkins, Joseph Bellamy, and Nathaniel Emmons all testify to this approach to the Bible. The study of grammar alone could hardly compete
with the much more interesting and exciting work of speculative theology.
In short, though the eighteenth century produced brilliant systems of doctrine, it witnessed no similar accomplishments in biblical studies.

Nevertheless, by the beginning of the nineteenth century certain
realities were already discernible which would elevate biblical studies to a
primary status in American theological thought. In the first place, traditional Calvinism faced a serious challenge from Unitarian liberalism.
Orthodox formulations of such doctrines as the Trinity, original sin, the
atonement, and predestination all came under question. Further, the Unitarians themselves turned to the Bible to support their challenge,[11] and their
threat was intensified by the first rumblings of higher criticism from
Europe. Finally, speculative Calvinism had itself reached an impasse in
Hopkinsianism, that final logical resting point of some of the most typical
and stringent of Calvinist doctrines. Clearly, if orthodoxy were to survive,
some new creative impulse had to be discovered and channeled. It was this
combination of challenges, as much as anything else, that encouraged the
orthodox to a new and much more central study of the Bible.

In this revival, philology, interpretation, *and* grammar were each to
achieve a renewed theological relevance. The renewal anticipated much of

[10] Mary Latimer Gambrell, *Ministerial Training in Eighteenth Century New England*
(New York: Columbia University Press, 1937) 81.
[11] The writings of the English Unitarian John Taylor were introduced in America in the
1750s. His method of linguistic analysis of biblical texts to refute Calvinism found hearty support among the nascent liberal party in New England. See Conrad Wright, *The Beginnings
of Unitarianism in America* (Boston: Starr King Press, 1955) 77.

Moses Stuart's achievement as a mature scholar. Still, it should be remembered that, although Stuart was one of the chief contributors to the new interest in the Bible for its own sake, he was as much propelled by this configuration of external, apologetic concerns as he was by his more private interests and aptitudes.

Linguistic and Critical Tools Acquired

Stuart's first professional responsibility upon arrival at Andover was to acquire the additional linguistic tools necessary to perform the duties of his professorial chair. His deficiency in Hebrew was the most painful embarrassment. Late in the fall of 1809, even before he had officially accepted the call to Andover, Stuart wrote to Eliphalet Pearson and confessed to him with disarming frankness his misgivings about his "present fitness to discharge the functions of a professor." He would need immediate help. To this end he entertained the hope that Pearson would stay on at Andover at least during the winter and spring to give private instruction in Hebrew. "If I go to Andover, I must go there . . . as your pupil." Stuart was not just exercising deferential courtesy. On the face of it, the self-documentation of his weakness was startling. "My knowledge of Hebrew at present amounts to nothing. I have run over about 20 chapters in Genesis, and six or seven Psalms. I must pay attention strictly to it, for the space of 3 or 4 months, at least, and for years to come must study it more or less every week."[12] The request was apparently refused or at least not pursued, for Stuart was later to admit publicly that he never had "the aid of any teacher" in his learning of the Hebrew language.[13] Such aids as he did have in those first years of solitary study were what his colleague Leonard Woods described as the "very imperfect grammars" then available at Andover.[14]

Stuart also had to learn by himself the important cognate Semitic languages. He mastered Syriac, Chaldee (Aramaic), and Arabic in 1816 and 1817. The appropriation of these languages was obviously defensible and was expected, at least by Stuart and most of his Andover constituency. But the necessity of mastering German, a language hardly known among English-speaking American intellectuals, seems to have taken Stuart rather by surprise. Yet it must be said, and this without exaggeration, that German was the one language that most precisely and fundamentally determined Stuart's vocation as a modern scientific scholar. Stuart variously recorded the story of his discovery of the importance of German and the beginnings of his mastery of the language and its theological literature. The primary account is found in a series of private letters written from 1812 to 1814 to

[12] New Haven, 25 November 1809. Edwards A. Park Collection, Yale University.
[13] Moses Stuart, "Letter to the Editor on the Study of the German Language," *The Christian Review* 6 (September 1841) 448.
[14] Woods, *History of Andover*, 151.

Edward Everett, then pastor of the Brattle Street Church in Boston. Having assumed his prestigious pulpit before the age of twenty, Everett was already something of a prodigy among the liberals. In Everett, Stuart found a winsome and stimulating, albeit potentially embarrassing, comrade in the quest for new biblical learning.[15] Another account appeared in a letter to the editor of the *Christian Review*, published in September 1841. The *Review* article departs from the private correspondence in several important details, a fact that reveals either a surprising lapse of memory by Stuart or, more probably, his clear reluctance at this later date—when the lines of theological division between liberals and conservatives had long since hardened—to admit publicly his earlier scholarly kinship with Everett, an association sustained in part by their mutual excitement over the New German higher criticism, some of it already branded by orthodox partisans as notoriously radical. Moreover, it is clear from the Stuart–Everett letters that, contrary to what Stuart later would have his readers believe, he was propelled into the all-important mastery of the German language more by these German radicals than by their conservative colleagues.

Stuart had, however, felt earlier private stirrings of interest in the German language—curiosity over passages of German in Latin commentaries and Greek lexicons by the few German writers who could then be found in the fledgling Andover library, plus Stuart's "chance" personal acquisition of Luther's German New Testament and Noedin's German grammar and dictionary. All of these, Stuart said, "led me fully to resolve on an effort to become acquainted with the German language though I then knew as little about the treasures contained in the German as I did about those which are comprised in the Arabic or the Sanscrit."[16] His first sustained German reading was the Gospel of John, which he completed in a fortnight.[17] Then, in August 1812, he made his first serious (some might say fateful) acquaintance with the German higher critics. The place was Boston; the occasion was the spirited auction of the library of the late Joseph Stevens Buckminster (1784–1812), who had been the pastor of the Brattle Street Church of that city and was under appointment as first Dexter Lecturer in Biblical Criticism at Harvard at the time of his death. At the sale Stuart

---

[15] Edward Everett (1794–1865) was appointed Professor of Greek Literature at Harvard in 1815. That same year Harvard sent him to Göttingen where in 1817 he became the first American to receive a doctorate from a German university. He returned to Harvard where he remained as professor until 1824 when he was elected to the United States Congress. Henceforth his career was in politics and statecraft. For an account of Everett as biblical scholar and critic see Jerry Wayne Brown, *The Rise of Biblical Criticism in America, 1800–1870: The New England Scholars* (Middletown, CT: Wesleyan University Press, 1969) 33–44.

[16] Stuart, "Letter to the Editor," 448.

[17] Park, *Discourse*, 27.

purchased for himself and the Andover Library a number of important items. And prize books were there to be had, for Buckminster had collected some 2,300 works while in Europe in 1806 and 1807, many of which were on biblical subjects, and some of which he had introduced to America.[18]

The jewel for Stuart was Johann Gottfried Eichhorn's *Einleitung in das Alte Testament,* published in Jena in 1780–1783. We need to pause for a moment here, for with the procurement of this book Stuart was about to enter a new world. It is now generally conceded that Eichhorn's was the first truly comprehensive, modern introduction to Old Testament "higher" criticism. (The term itself was Eichhorn's creation.) It is impossible to overstress the importance of the work for Stuart's subsequent career as teacher and writer. Its pages were to excite him at almost every turn, and to open windows upon broad vistas of biblical learning totally new to his experience.

Eichhorn's *Einleitung* brought together in one coherent whole the methodologies as well as many of the factual conclusions of a century or more of critical labor. Here were outlined investigations that challenged the Mosaic authorship of most of the Pentateuch, posited the Elohistic and Yahwistic literary sources of Genesis, outlined the principles of Hebrew parallelism (which made it possible to distinguish poetry from prose and resulted in new understandings of the prophetic writings), stressed the aesthetic value of the Old Testament as the literature of a people of a particular spirit and life, and urged the unshackling of Old Testament study from predetermined dogmatic convictions.

Stuart described the sale some thirty years after the event. His words still convey something of the excitement of the occasion. For one thing, he soon found himself in a one-on-one competition with his friend Edward Everett.

> I remember, with lively and pleasant emotion, the contest between him and me at the sale for Eichhorn's *Introduction to the Old Testament.* . . . We bid upon the volumes (there were four) until we rose above six dollars a piece, (for a moderate octavo on coarse hemp paper); and finally I won the prize by bidding six dollars and a quarter for each volume. I have since purchased all four for as many dollars, yet the acquisition of that book has spread its influence over my whole subsequent life.[19]

But the *Einleitung*'s immediate significance for Stuart, and this as much by happenstance as anything else, was that it became the chief textbook in his self-mastery of modern scholarly German. The letters to Everett

---

[18] On Buckminster, see Brown, *Rise of Biblical Criticism,* 10–28; also, Milton Halsey Thomas, "Joseph Stevens Buckminster," *Dictionary of American Biography* (New York: Scribner, 1928–1944) 3:233–34.

[19] Stuart, "Letter to the Editor," 456–547.

coincided with the purchase. They indicate clearly how important Eichhorn soon became to Stuart's progress in learning the language.[20] He wrote
the following February (1813) that he was five or six weeks from finishing
the first volume but would then send it on. "It is indeed a difficult work to
read," he confessed:

> I thought that the first two efforts would cure me of German mania
> forever. It was like jumping from Corderius into Tacitus: and worse, for
> in such case you can obtain aid. But in Eichhorn sentences of a whole
> page—the most involved connections—the dubious endings of many
> words, and the multitude of particles, present very formidable obstacles.
> Resolution and perseverance conquered; and I can now read it with
> satisfaction—though I have not spent more than about an hour each day
> upon it.[21]

A month later he was still plodding, though it was getting easier. "I
seldom find a sentence in Eichhorn now, with respect to which I cannot
satisfy myself," he noted, except, that is, for those troublesome German
"particles. . . . In not a few places you have, for instance, the following
elegant commencement of a sentence; 'but still, however, notwithstanding
this,' etc. and a multitude of others equally *neat."* Still, "it is only on a few
occasions, that [Eichhorn] absolutely plunges you into a morass, whence
there is no escape."[22] And so throughout the spring. The busy summer term
reduced his German study to only two hours a week, but the mysteries were
finally dissipating. "I . . . find no difficulty, at present in that part of
Eichhorn, which I am reading, and which begins in some measure to grow
familiar, since I am accustomed to his style," he noted in July, and took
pleasure to confirm the judgment of a German Lutheran clergyman then
residing in New York City whom Stuart had visited on a recent vacation
and who had declared Eichhorn to be "a very polished writer."[23] It is clear
that by the end of 1813, less than a year and a half after he had begun studying German seriously, his mastery of the language was complete. The

[20] Eichhorn was not the only German author Stuart was reading at the time. The very
month of the Buckminster sale he began reading J. G. von Herder's *Briefe über das Studium
der Theologie.* He wrote to Everett, urging him to consider translating the work: "There is
a 'vivacity—a beauty—an enchanting something, a *je ne sais quoi,'* that will please you, I am
sure." The same letter mentions "the little store . . . of German books which I have," and
invites Everett to Andover to look them over. (Moses Stuart to Edward Everett, 12 August
1812. This and subsequently cited correspondence to Everett can be found in Everett Papers
at the Massachusetts Historical Society.) Still, Eichhorn's *Einleitung* was the most influential
German work he was to read in his first decade at Andover.

[21] Stuart to Everett, 13 February 1813.

[22] Stuart to Everett, 16 March 1813.

[23] Stuart to Everett, 9 July 1813. The friend was the Reverend H. Dreyer, who had studied
under Eichhorn at Göttingen before emigrating to America in 1811. Stuart purchased at this
time fourteen or fifteeen volumes which he supposed to be very valuable.

Einleitung was still Stuart's major language text, but now it was also serving to bring into focus matters of importance for biblical criticism in addition to the intricacies of the German language. In the fall of 1813, Stuart and Everett consulted about the possibility that Everett translate portions of the work, and the two corresponded about specific chapters and even paragraphs that might be most useful to their students were these pages to be published. But by now Stuart was wide awake to the delicate position the new learning had created for him with his Andover constituency, to say nothing of New England orthodoxy in general. He was enthusiastic in urging Everett to translate such safe sections as Eichhorn's essays on textual matters — the Masora and the Hebrew manuscripts — "Yes, by all means translate. What an admirable summary!" But the section in which Eichhorn raised questions about the extent to which the Old Testament authors can properly be called prophets had best be omitted, at least from any publication in which Stuart might be involved. Such "speculations of Eichhorn . . . would be obnoxious . . . they in no way [would] increase the value of his book, and . . . they would in many instances prevent the good he might do."[24]

Clearly, Stuart was learning more than German. He was gaining his first and, in some ways, his most profound and abiding exposure to a major frustration of his career, the knowledge that his professional competence was henceforth inexorably linked to the Germans. Some of them, like Eichhorn, were at once supremely able critics and dangerously threatening theologians, threatening certainly to one responsible to the Westminster Confession. In short, he could neither avoid them nor live altogether comfortably with them.[25]

[24] Stuart to Everett, 25 December 1813.

[25] Evidence from the letters to Everett, where book news was frequently exchanged, indicates something of the range of Stuart's early purchases. They included Johann David Michaelis's *Orientalische und exegetische Bibliothek;* Johann Christian Wilhelm Augusti and W. M. L. De Wette's German translation of the Bible; Ludwig F. O. Baumgarten-Crusius's *Schrift und Vernuft;* Johann F. Flatt's *Magazin für Dogmatik und Moral,* of which Stuart owned at this time only three volumes in the series, those immediately up to 1800; Siegmund J. Baugarten's *Erbauliche Erklärung der Psalmer;* Bellermann's *Archaeologie;* Gottlob Christian Storr's *Über den Geist des Christenthums* and his *De Modo interpretandi historico;* Johann S. Semler's *Abhandlung von der freien des Kanons;* and George F. Seiler's *Hermeneutik.* Of this list, the works of Semler and Seiler proved to be the most provocative, because they were related to the crucial problems of inspiration and interpretation. Stuart later noted that Seiler was given to him by "a friend in Boston who had studied theology in Europe" (presumably Everett is implied, though Everett did not even sail for Europe until 1815) and that "this opened to me the world of German sacred literature" ("Letter to the Editor," 557). It seems rather that Seiler came into Stuart's possession in 1814, fully a year and a half after he began reading Eichhorn, and that he obtained Seiler from some source other than Everett, to whom he mentions his discovery in a letter dated 14 May of that year. This discrepancy in attributing his early opening to German biblical studies to Seiler rather than to Eichhorn seems to have been a deliberate shifting of the facts on Stuart's part. By 1841 it was clearly

Written Aids for Teaching

Another difficulty for Stuart was finding enough books for his students for private and classroom study. This was a frustration much harder to resolve than that arising out of his own linguistic deficiencies. Regular persistent private study could and did accomplish the desired ends in the mastery of Hebrew and German. He could not, however, conjure up texts, lexicons, grammars, or commentaries in quantity for twenty or thirty students every year. In 1810 Stuart wrote to William Liffingwell, a former parishioner in New Haven, appealing for funds for the school. He extolled the character and ability of the students, some of whom had even "come to a solemn and deliberate resolution to devote their lives to *missionary* labors," perhaps with "Carey in Hindustan, or Van der Kemp in Africa," but, he continued:

> Our means of instructing them . . . are curtailed. . . . Our library suffers most. We have already gone further in buying books than we have any present means to meet. We are individually in debt as Professors about $300. Our library is straitened, books are high and such as we want rarely to be met with, at present, in this country.[26]

Among the most desperate needs was a "printed Harmony to facilitate the study of the Evangelists," and from 1810 to 1813 Stuart's annual reports to the seminary's Board of Visitors regularly pressed the point. Nothing of this sort was in print at home, and the disruptions in shipping occasioned by the War of 1812 made it impossible to purchase books directly from abroad, even if such could be found as would be suitable for American students. Stuart had no alternative but to publish his own harmony. The venture, completed in 1814, was a student work under the title *A Harmony of the Greek of the Gospels, with notes, by William Newcombe, D.D., Dublin, 1728; Reprinted from the text and select various readings of Griesbach, by the Junior class in the Theological Seminary at Andover, under the superintendence of Moses Stuart.* Nothing here was original except the doing of the book itself, a creative pedagogical exercise, to say the least, and one of immediate use to the compilers and to several subsequent generations of Andover students.[27]

There was also a need for copies of the Septuagint. In 1812 Stuart informed the Board of Visitors that, though the Andover Constitution required the students to pay particular attention to this ancient version, the number of copies in the library was insufficient.[28] This inconvenience was

---

more politic for him to claim, in public at least, his indebtedness to "that good old evangelical Seiler" than to the more radical Eichhorn.

[26] Moses Stuart to William Liffingwell, 13 July 1810. Manuscript at Yale University.

[27] A copy of the work, with manuscript marginalia by Amazi Benedict, an Andover student in 1815, is at Andover Newton.

[28] Papers of the Board of Visitors, 22 September 1812. Andover Newton Papers.

partially mitigated in 1827 when, once again, Stuart directed an educational exercise into a publishing venture. The result is self-explained in a similarly lengthy title, *Passages Cited from the Old Testament by the Writers of the New Testament, compared with the Original Hebrew and the Septuagint Version; arranged by the Junior class in the Theological Seminary, Andover, and Published at Their Request, under the Superintendence of M. Stuart.* The library also lacked dictionaries, lexicons, commentaries, and concordances. A "regular digest of Sacred Literature within a moderate compass," which could be used as a textbook for the students, was also needed. "Such a book," Stuart noted, "might serve as a substitute for Public Lectures, which time has not yet permitted me to prepare; and it would be easy to deliver a kind of extempore lecture, on the subject matter of every recitation. In this way, something like a complete course in Sacred Literature might be effected, before the Public Lectures are completed."[29]

Critical works, particularly those adequate to understand and meet the radical onslaughts from abroad, were also desired, and, though from time to time Stuart was able to make valuable purchases—as, for instance, at the sale of the Buckminster library in 1812—the passing of the years made it imperative to keep abreast of the European scholars. As late as 1826 Stuart wrote to the Board of Visitors complaining of the difficulties in this regard:

> We want adequate helps in our own vernacular language, and free from the sceptical neology of the continental writers. But to effect this, we must have more apparatus. Our library is yet so incompetent to purposes of this nature, that an investigator finds himself stopped at every turn, whenever he attempts to pursue to original sources multiplied questions of a critical and hermeneutical nature.
>
> It is in vain to expect that we can reach the European standard, until we are furnished with European means of doing it. It is truly mortifying to be obliged so often to abandon the investigation of questions, in my department, for want of means to pursue it farther. This is not an evil which the Visitors or Trustees have power to remedy; but it may be stated with propriety by the officers of our Seminary, as a reason why they do not reach a higher point in their investigations and lectures.[30]

The wants were not always caused by lack of funds. Many of the most necessary items were simply out of print or not available in quantity. This was true not only of Newcombe's *Harmony* but also of J. A. Ernesti's *Elements of Interpretation,* which was available only in its original Latin until Stuart translated and published it in 1822. Thereafter it was used regularly as a textbook in hermeneutics.[31]

[29] Ibid., 28 September 1814.
[30] Ibid., 27 September 1826.
[31] The full title was *Elements of Interpretation, translated from the Latin of J. A. Ernesti*

The assembling of materials for Hebrew studies, neglected as this discipline had been for decades in America, presented the greatest difficulty of all. Even Hebrew Bibles were hard to come by in the early years. Dated 7 September 1808, a letter from Leonard Woods to Jedediah Morse, a pastor in Charlestown, Massachusetts, urged Morse, then on a visit to New Haven, to buy up all the Hebrew Bibles and Septuagints he could find—"also Hebrew and Greek Lexicons. . . . We shall not be able to get enough."[32] Hopes were stirred at the news that Mills Day, Yale tutor and brother of Yale's president, Jeremiah Day, was engaged in composing an edition of the Hebrew Bible. Writing to Day in 1810, Stuart offered some suggestions in regard to format, but Day never even began to read the proof. His health was already failing, and he died in 1812 without completing the work.[33]

The situation with Hebrew grammars was even more desperate. The one American work available, that of John Smith, was merely an outline and obviously not suitable as an aid to intensive study.[34] Thus, in 1812, after barely mastering the language himself, Stuart prepared a Hebrew grammar of his own for the immediate use of that year's junior class. Day after day students copied the text from his written sheets, while Stuart labored over the business of publication, to which the chief obstacles were the absence in the Boston area of Hebrew type fonts, as well as a printer able to use them. It was decided to purchase the fonts—and, while they were at it, a press as well. Stuart himself solicited the funds. Since John Codman of Dorchester was the principal contributor, the press was named in his honor. The fonts were imported from abroad. With their arrival, Stuart assembled the press in his own house and proceeded not only to train a local printer but also to set half of the verb paradigms with his own hands.[35] It was not, however, a work of any lasting merit. Only 120 copies were printed, twenty of these to be sent to friends for correction and criticism.

---

and accompanied by notes; with an appendix containing extracts from Morus, Beck and Keil (Andover, MA: Flagg & Gould, 1822).

[32] Woods, History of Andover, 610.

[33] 15 October 1810, Yale University. For a description of the work Day planned to execute, see Proposals by Mills Day, New Haven, for Publishing by Subscription, an Edition of the Hebrew Bible from the Text of Van-der-Hooght. Prospectus (New Haven, CT, 1810).

[34] The title of Smith's book was A Hebrew Grammar, without the Points; Designed to Facilitate the Study of the Scriptures of the Old Testament; and Particularly Adapted to the Use of Those Who May Not Have Instructors (Boston: D. Carlisle, 1803). Smith (1752–1809) was a Dartmouth graduate who remained there as professor of languages until the end of his life. He had a genuine interest in promoting the study of oriental languages, but like Pearson at Harvard, taught at a time when language study was at its lowest ebb. See Sprague's Annals of the American Pulpit (New York, 1859–1869) 2: 90–99.

[35] Sarah Stuart Robbins, Old Andover Days (Boston, 1908) 21–22; see also Park, Discourse, 25. The full title of Stuart's grammar was A Hebrew Grammar With the Points; Designed as an Introduction to the Knowledge of the Inflections and Idiom of the Hebrew Tongue (Andover, MA: Flagg & Gould, 1813).

Eliphalet Pearson was one of the recipients. Stuart apologized in advance for the "errors and defects" that Pearson would find — "it has both" — and noted the tentative nature of the project. "I . . . have not ventured to put any into the Library," Stuart confessed, "my object being to get the aid of all the Hebrew Scholars in our land in bringing it to a state of more perfection, before I venture to offer it to the Trustees as a classical book."[36] Nevertheless, the 1813 grammar stands as a clear testimony to the amount of scholarship Stuart did manage to assimilate in a short period of time under difficult conditions.

Stuart made no pretense of originality. The chief sources he used were the *Sacred Philology* of Solomon Glass (ed. J. A. Dathe; Leipzig, 1623), the grammars of François Masclef (Paris, 1716) and John Parkhurst (London, 1762), and Charles Wilson's *Elements of Hebrew Grammar* (3d ed.; Edinburgh, 1802). Parkhurst, Wilson, and Masclef are of particular importance, for in the seventeenth- and eighteenth-century debate over the use of the Hebrew vowel point system, they had followed the textual work of Louis Cappel of Saumur (1585–1658), who, after a careful labor in which numerous manuscripts were compared, claimed the points to be a late addition to the original Hebrew text.[37] Having accepted this, the grammarians assumed that Hebrew could best be learned without the encumbrance of the later points.

Stuart followed suit, but not without a thorough examination of the relative loss and gain. On one level was the weight of theological argument: if the points were a later addition to the text, they did not share the same level of divine inspiration as the original material. The use of the points would entail an adulteration of the earlier inspired word, and this was clearly a loss that should be taken seriously. "It is not . . . a question of mere speculation," he told his students in a public lecture on the subject. "It is one, about which a minister of the gospel who explains the word of the life to others, should satisfy his conscience, as well as his understanding."[38] But the pragmatic question of whether or not the language was more

[36] Moses Stuart to Eliphalet Pearson, 12 December 1813. Pearson Papers, Yale University. Stuart also sent a copy to be shared by his Harvard friends Edward Everett and the Hancock Professor of Hebrew and Oriental Languages, Sidney Willard, both of whom he urged to make their "remarks without any reserve" (Moses Stuart to Edward Everett, 24 November 1813).

[37] Cappel's theory was formulated in his *Arcanum punctationes revelatum* published first in Basel in 1648. It was opposed by Johann Buxtorf the younger (1599–1664). Brian Walton (1600–1661), an Englishman, adopted the work of Cappel in the "Prolegomena" to his famous *Polyglot Bible*. Stuart was aware of the work of these men and refers to them in his own lectures on the vowel points. A subject of heated controversy at the time, the work of Cappel has long since been superseded.

[38] Moses Stuart, "Hebrew points — an examination of the *nature* of the *points* and *accents* as described by modern grammarians — *internal evidence* that they are not authentic," Lectures on Sacred Literature, Lecture 4. Andover Newton. Lecture 7 in the same series is dated 14 September 1812. Presumably Lecture 4 was delivered that same summer.

easily and firmly learned *with* the points, whatever their inspiration, was
also a question of conscience, or at least one requiring serious deliberation.
In a public lecture delivered in September 1812, Stuart noted, in favor of the
points, that they were "a kind of commentary or index to the meaning of
words, and [served] to render the language more euphonic and regular.[39]
Further, he was already in a position to observe that the trend in Europe
was toward the points and not away, all of which suggested that much was
left to be decided about the relative merits of either system. He wrote:

> Whether students can in fact become acquainted with the Hebrew
> sooner with the points or without them is a question that can be settled
> only by experience. In an institution like ours, it is of great consequence
> that the question should be settled and rightly settled. Should the means
> of doing this be furnished, it would be our duty to make such a trial as
> would satisfy all concerned what course in the future to be pursued.[40]

The trial was settled quickly, at least for Stuart. The unpointed grammar
had been out barely a month when Stuart wrote to Everett confessing his
capitulation:

> The more I study Hebrew, the more misgiving I have, about studying
> without the *points*. The best Hebrew scholars on the Continent all say,
> that sooner or later every man will repent it. I begin to believe it, and
> the more so, because almost all our philological helps, are constructed
> according to the arrangement of the points, and because, having begun
> to study Chaldee with the points, I know better how to estimate them.
> I have my doubts whether a person will not learn more Hebrew in one
> year with them, than without them; not withstanding all that Parkhurst,
> Houbigant and Masclef have said.[41]

That the unpointed grammar appeared at all is puzzling, especially
since the matter of protecting an unadulterated inspiration — the only possible remaining support for an unpointed grammar — seems to have been
forgotten. But the rationale again was practical. "My reason for publishing
a Grammar without points is, because we have no other help with them."[42]
There were simply no collateral pointed lexicons available in quantity for
students, and Stuart sensibly realized that a pointed grammar would be
next to useless in this vacuum. The unpointed grammar of 1813 represented,
then, less a stage of an experiment than a simple temporary expedient, and
it would be happily and entirely superseded eight years later in his *A
Hebrew Grammar with a Copious Syntax and Praxis*.[43] Nevertheless, the

---

[39] "Arguments for the points adduced and examined," Lecture 7, Lectures on Sacred Literature, 14 September 1812.

[40] Ibid.

[41] Moses Stuart to Edward Everett, 25 December 1813.

[42] Ibid.

[43] Stuart, *A Hebrew Grammar with a Copious Syntax and Praxis* (Andover, MA: Flagg &
Gould, 1821).

1813 unpointed grammar was the first American attempt to publish anything like a comprehensive exposition of the character and usage of the Hebrew language, and thus the book, though depreciated by its author and short-lived in its usefulness, constitutes something of a landmark in the history of American Hebrew studies.

As we conclude this account of Stuart's earliest days at Andover, we can only observe that these first years represent a triumph of intelligence, perseverance, and industry. Embarrassingly unprepared for his vocation, isolated from his scholarly peers by geography, language, and theological disposition, and lacking even the most elementary pedagogical resources with which to build and sustain a disciplined environment of learning for his students, Stuart nevertheless by sheer dedication and determination overcame these several obstacles. In a sense, the rest of our account here will be but a tracing of these lines of growth into his maturity as one of nineteenth-century America's most notable scholars and teachers.

II

THE TEACHER AT WORK

However great the pedagogical difficulties during Stuart's first decade at Andover, they did not deter him from his main purpose, which was "to lead [the students] to a correct interpretation of the Word of God," or, as he noted more simply, to lead them to a knowledge of "how to study the Bible."[1] He took to this task with enthusiasm. His teaching schedule was rigorous. Five days of the week he worked with the junior class in grammar and exegesis, in both Hebrew and Greek, this usually in the afternoons, for the weekday mornings were set aside for private study. The course of study that the junior class pursued varied only slightly throughout most of Stuart's years at Andover. In 1812, for instance, the students learned the elements of Hebrew grammar. Then they read in Hebrew twenty chapters of Genesis, sixty of the Psalms, and the first ten chapters of the book of Proverbs. They also read thirty-five chapters in Greek from the "Evangelists" and were assigned special readings to supplement public lectures on sacred literature. The middle and senior classes read exegetically from the Hebrew ten chapters of Proverbs, all of Malachi, and parts of Isaiah. In the New Testament, 1 and 2 Timothy were studied in Greek, these books having been chosen "because of the instruction with which they are fraught, respecting the ministerial character."[2] The public lectures in sacred literature were offered before the whole student body from time to time, but only infrequently at first, as the press of other matters prevented Stuart from accumulating a full series until a number of years had passed. The main work, then, was done in the regular class sessions through the recitation method. Even here, however, there was room for variation. In 1813 he assigned a written commentary to each pupil in the junior class, to be read in regular succession at the private class sessions. This he used in conjunction with the passages covered in the normal recitation course.[3] "No exercise in which they engage," he commented a year later, "appears to contribute more to their improvement."[4]

The method of teaching Hebrew was finally settled during the academic year 1816–1817, when Stuart began for the first time to teach with

---

[1] Papers of the Board of Visitors, 22 September 1812 and 22 September 1813.
[2] Ibid., 22 September 1812.
[3] Ibid., 22 September 1813.
[4] Ibid., 28 September 1814.

the vowel points. His report to the Board of Visitors is both an exultation and a confession. In spite of the "disadvantage of having neither pointed grammars or lexicons to aid them," he wrote:

> the class has read nearly one third more of Hebrew than any preceding class. I am persuaded that were they to pursue Hebrew study another year, they would at the end of it have acquired double what they could have learned without the use of the points. I have been misled on this subject by Parkhurst and Kennicott, and am very sorry for it, for I have not only lost much time myself but have been the occasion of much loss to others. . . . I am beyond all question in favor of the points.[5]

This section of the report concluded with the cheerful news that a "good supply of the best Hebrew Lexicons from Europe" was soon to arrive, which would make it possible for the next class to study the "original Jewish Scriptures under more favorable auspices than any class hitherto."[6]

Special readings, papers, and examinations were assigned at the will of the professors, but it was the custom of the seminary that during the commencement anniversaries the student body would stand before the assembled faculty, Board of Trustees, Board of Visitors, and public, to be examined on the discipline with which it had been primarily concerned during the two terms.[7] Accounts of the examinations with lists of the questions and the titles of the papers submitted sometimes appeared in the religious periodicals. The *Panoplist*, for instance, reported on the exercises for 1818. It noted that the junior class was first examined on Hebrew grammar and that fourteen essays were delivered on various subjects:

1. Essay on the present state of Hebrew Literature in this country, and the advantages to be expected from the cultivation of it. By E. Hollister.

[5] Ibid., 25 September 1817.

[6] Ibid. It is likely, too, though not conclusive, that Stuart already had in hand his own copy of the recently published and already acclaimed pointed grammar of Heinrich F. W. Gesenius (1786–1842), and that this work, one which was to become the model for Stuart's own later grammars, was also a factor in his change at this time. Gesenius, professor at the University of Halle, was the most influential Hebraist of the nineteenth century and one of the great pioneers in Hebrew philology. The *Hebräische Grammatik* (Halle: Renger, 1813) passed through numerous German and foreign editions and is still widely respected. Stuart may also have had a copy of Gesenius's equally important Hebrew dictionary, the *Hebräisches Handwörterbuch über die Schriften des Alten Testaments mit Einschluss der geographischen Namen und der chaldäischen Wörter beym Daniel und Ezra* (Leipzig: F. C. W. Vogel, 1812). See R. Kraetzschmar, "Gesenius, (Heinrich Friedrich) Wilhelm," *The New Schaff–Herzog Encyclopedia of Religious Knowledge* (Grand Rapids, MI: Baker, 1958) 4:477–78.

[7] At times the crowds were so large that many people stood through the whole exercises, and some could not gain entrance to the chapel at all. Often the sheriff and constable were called to help preserve order. See Henry K. Rowe, *History of Andover Theological Seminary* (Newton, MA, 1933) 60.

5. By what kind of evidence is the genuineness of the New Testament supported. By J. N. Loomis.
7. Exegesis of Colossians ii, 16, 17. By J. Boardman.
8. What are the dangers to which the critical study of the Scriptures exposes a Christian, and how are they to be avoided? By W. Williams.
9. Essay on the importance of the Septuagint version to the critical interpreter of the New Testament. By E. Edmond.
12. On what evidence does the fact rest, that all the present books of the Old Testament belonged to the Canon of the Jews in the time of our Savior? By A. Cummings.
14. Is there any difference between the study of the Hebrew and Greek Testaments, and the study of sacred exegesis; and what is it? By J. Brown.[8]

Such a list provides a record of what Stuart expected from his pupils; but even more, it reveals the unusually wide range of his teaching. Unfortunately, the accounts do not record the manner in which these presentations were received, but considering the novelty of advanced biblical study, as well as the timeliness of some of the questions, the audience must have found them of commanding interest.

As the years passed, Stuart felt increasingly burdened by the demands of his subject. He wrote to the Board of Visitors and the Board of Trustees in 1817 to complain, not without reason, that the department in which he worked was of "unbounded extent" and demanded "far more severe labour and fatiguing study than any other department prescribed by the Constitution of the Seminary." Finally, in 1821 he secured partial relief when the first student assistant was annually appointed to hear the Hebrew and Greek grammar recitations of the juniors. Although he always spoke with appreciation about these men—at least two of whom, Edward H. Robinson (assistant in 1823–24 and 1828) and Calvin E. Stowe (assistant in 1829), went on to achieve eminence in the field (Robinson as a professor at Union Theological Seminary in New York, Stowe as Stuart's successor at Andover) —the problem was never resolved to his satisfaction. On the other hand, he pressed constantly, albeit unsuccessfully, for curriculum revision whereby at least students who showed the aptitude could devote two years to their biblical studies rather than the customary one. Further training, he insisted, was essential for the health of the church. Only those thoroughly equipped as biblical scholars could ward off the attacks on the "latitudinarians and sceptics."[9] Three years later, the extra year still not granted (indeed, it never was), he addressed the Board of Visitors in pessimistic tones:

[8] "Exercises at the Annual Examination of the Theological Seminary in Andover, September 23, 1818," *The Panoplist* 14 (September 1818) 420–21.
[9] Papers of the Board of Visitors, 22 September 1824.

I have only to add that having put my hand to the plough, I am not
disposed to look back. If my department cannot be made more of, it had
better be merged. For a "little learning here is a dangerous thing." It
makes men conceited but not any the wiser. If a student does not go far
enough to reap his harvest, it is lost times to clear away the wood and
brush and stones, to plow and harrow, and sow the seed, and then leave
the field unhedged and suffer the whole to be devoured for want of
interest and care.[10]

The inadequate collegiate background of many students added to the
teaching burden. Stuart wrote in 1813 that the class was "exceedingly defective with respect to grammatical analysis. Some have been wrongly taught
and are obliged to unlearn some things and subdue habits which will ever
be fatal to good scholarship." "Forty weeks," he added, "is a very limited
period to learn two new languages."[11] The situation was exacerbated by the
fact that Andover had no formal Greek or Hebrew entrance requirement.
It could be assumed that the college graduate would know Greek, though
even this was not always assured; but nothing could be assumed regarding
Hebrew. In 1824 Stuart urged that a knowledge of Hebrew be made an
entrance requirement and suggested that it would encourage the study of
Hebrew in the colleges.[12] This was done in 1827 in the revised Laws of the
Seminary,[13] though ten years later, for reasons not stated, the seminary
dropped the requirement.[14] But even the rising standards did not decrease
the burden on Stuart, for the advanced level of the students required added
labor from him to "carry them over ground" that he had not "frequently
trodden before."[15]

Whatever the external handicaps, an abundance of evidence confirms
Stuart's exceptional abilities as a teacher. He combined in his classroom
presence a paradoxical mixture of exuberance, reverence, rashness, and care
toward his material and a freedom and strictness toward his pupils. Of the
many tributes from his students, none was more revealing of Stuart's traits
as a teacher, or more lovingly stated, than that of Francis Wayland, who
later became a respected political economist and the president of Brown
University. As a young Baptist, Wayland sat under Stuart in the years 1816
and 1817. His testimony needs to be quoted at some length:

[10] Ibid., 24 September 1827.
[11] Ibid., 22 September 1813.
[12] Ibid., 22 September 1824.
[13] Woods, *History of Andover*, 286.
[14] Ibid., p. 318. Stuart contributed several articles to the *Quarterly Journal of the American Education Society* in favor of more and better study of Hebrew and Greek in colleges.
These were: "Letter on the Study of the Classics" 1 (July 1828) 75–98; "Study of the Hebrew"
2 (April 1829) 193–204; and "Sacred and Classical Studies" 3 (February 1831) 161–66.
[15] Papers of the Board of Visitors, September 1830.

If I do not err, Stuart was one of the most remarkable teachers of his age. His acquaintance with his subject in the class-room was comprehensive and minute. There was no sacrifice in his power which he did not rejoice to make, if by it he could promote the progress of his pupils. It seemed as if all he asked of us was, that we should aid him in his efforts to confer upon us the greatest amount of benefit. He allowed and encouraged the largest freedom of inquiry in the recitation-room, and was never impatient of any questioning, if the object of it was either to elicit truth or to detect error. The spirit which animated his class was that of a company of well-educated men, earnestly engaged in ascertaining the meaning of the word of God, under the guidance of one who had made every sentence and every word in the original languages the object of special and successful study. This alone would have been sufficient to place Moses Stuart in the first class of instructors. But to this he added a power of arousing enthusiasm such as I have never elsewhere seen. The burning earnestness of his own spirit kindled to a flame everything that came in contact with it. We saw the exultation which brightened his eye and irradiated his whole countenance, if he had discovered some new use of *vav conversive* which threw light upon a phrase of the Old Testament or if, by some law of the Greek article, a saying of Jesus could be rendered more definite and precise; and we all shared in his joy. We caught his spirit, and felt that life was valuable for little else than to explain to men the teachings of the well-beloved Son of God. If any one of us had barely possessed the means sufficient to buy a coat, or to buy a lexicon, I do not believe that he would for a moment have hesitated. The old coat would have been called upon for another year's service, and the student would have glorified over his Schleusner, as one that findeth great spoil. It seemed as though in his class-room we became acquainted with all the learned and good of the past and the present; we entered into and we shared their labors; we were co-workers with them and with our teacher, who was the medium of intercourse between us and them. We hung upon his lips in the lecture-room; we coveted his sayings in his walks or at the fireside; and any one of us was rich for a week, who could report his *obiter dicta*, ever replete with wit, learning, and generous, soul-stirring enthusiasm.

With all this love of inquiry, his discipline in the recitation-room was strict and exacting. He expected every man to be like himself, *totus in illis*, and his expectation was rarely disappointed. His reverence for the word of God was deep and all pervading. I remember but one instance, under his teaching, of any trifling with the word of God. The offender, who was odd, opinionated, and constitutionally wanting in reverence, had read an essay which seemed intended to create a laugh. The rebuke which he received was as such that we all quailed in our seats. I fancy that many years elapsed before such an experiment was attempted again.[16]

Others, too, testified to Stuart's unbounded enthusiasm and his extraordinary power at kindling this same trait in his students. John Todd, a student from 1823 to 1825, described Stuart as a "war-horse, . . . rushing upon the pikes of the enemy, . . . now rearing and plunging like a colt

[16] Francis and H. L. Wayland, *A Memoir of the Life and Labors of Francis Wayland, D.D., L.L.D.* (New York: Sheldon, 1867) 68–69.

newly harnessed. . . . He carries an enthusiasm that would open a mine of
quicksilver in the most barren mountain. He has a sort of magnetic power,
never wanting, by which the whole seminary is lighted up into his region
of thought and study."[17] Calvin E. Stowe was more subdued, but he too
remarked that Stuart's enthusiasm was "wonderfully contagious," and he
described the lecture room as Stuart's "paradise . . . , the circle of admiring
pupils his good angels."[18] Leonard Bacon, also one of Stuart's distinguished
successors, though in this instance at the Center Church pulpit, noted that
Stuart approached his daily recitations as a "joyous exercise — *labor ipse
voluptas*" and that this "delighted earnestness transfused itself" into all of
the students.[19] Even in his old age humor sparkled in the classroom. An
anonymous student described him as "a unique old man . . . jocose, and
facetious, getting off some queer or witty remark almost every day, enough to
make us roar."[20] Often such humor was used to good effect against theological
enemies. This same student wrote: "he has no small quantity of sly, severe
satire in his composition, and it is rare sport to see him bring it to bear, as he
often does upon neologists, sceptics, and the whole posse of heretics." Nor
could he tolerate laziness or stupidity. He was particularly impatient when he
had been ill. "When the dyspepsia or influenza has been at work with him —
look out. If things don't go to his liking he will run us up as though we were
schoolboys on the first form." On the other hand, nothing gave him more
pleasure than the prospect of a large or brilliant entering class. Mrs. Cornelius
noted that if it promised to have an unusual number of top scholars he was
"almost in ecstasies." His conversations about them were charged with anima-
tion. He could not sit still, and, pacing back and forth, he would speak of his
high hopes for one or another of the students. And in numerous instances in
the collection of his annual reports to the Board of Visitors he praised the
accomplishments of this or that class under his instruction. Special marks of
perseverance, such as the continued efforts of a young man whose poor
eyesight made him dependent upon his classmates for much of his reading,
received his enthusiastic praise.[21] To those who were slow but at least were
trying, he offered encouragement and hope. "Don't be discouraged young
men," he would say, "don't get mired in the Slough of Despond."[22]

Though always demanding the best from his pupils, Stuart was not

[17] John Todd, *The Story of His Life, Told Mainly by Himself*, ed. John E. Todd (New York:
Harper, 1876) 99.

[18] Sprague, *Annals*, 2:479.

[19] Bacon, "Moses Stuart," 50.

[20] Mrs. H. C. Cornelius, "A Chapter of Reminiscences: Moses Stuart," *New Englander* 32
(July 1873) 557. Mrs. Cornelius's personal observation is worth noting: it seemed, to those like
herself who were not privileged to sit in Stuart's classroom, that his influence over his students
was "magical" (555).

[21] Ibid., 557.

[22] Quoted in Rowe, *History of Andover*, 55.

overbearing. Leonard Bacon made special note of the freedom of discussion Stuart allowed and even encouraged in his classes. Bacon wrote that although he and his classmates had the "profoundest reverence" for Stuart as a teacher, this was in no way "inconsistent with the utmost freedom in the statement of objections to any of his views and in drawing out from him the solution of our doubts." "It was a new pleasure," he continued, "to find ourselves on such a footing of friendship and unembarrassed intercourse with one whom we so delighted to honor."[23]

The social distance between professor and student was also bridged by Stuart's friendly demeanor, and by occasional informal contacts. Students frequently visited at the Stuart home—particularly when the daughters of the family grew into young womanhood—and often Stuart would counsel his students about their problems or visit them when ill. Occasionally professor and students worked together at some task of manual labor. Wayland recorded that while he was a student the whole junior class—at Stuart's invitation—helped the professor get in his hay.[24]

The professor at Andover was expected to enter into other activities of the seminary: attending the morning chapel services each day, taking his turn in preaching at the regular Sunday services of the seminary church, reading and correcting senior sermons, preaching in nearby towns when called upon, delivering in due succession addresses at the weekly meetings of the "Wednesday Evening Conference" on pastoral ministry, and advising or attending one or more of the several student literary, spiritual, or handcraft societies.[25]

Stuart's schedule was taxing, and only rarely did he set aside any

---

[23] Bacon, "Moses Stuart," 50.

[24] Francis and H. L. Wayland, *Memoir*, 66. Wayland's account of a conversation with Stuart on this occasion provides a humorous glimpse of Stuart as a New England farmer: "The crop was a sorry one, and as I was raking near him, I intimated to him something of the kind. I shall never forget his reply. 'Ba!! was there ever climate and soil like this! Manure the land as much as you will, it all leaks through this gravel, and very soon not a trace of it can be seen. If you plant early, everything is liable to be cut off by the late frosts of spring. If you plant late, your crop is destroyed by early frosts of autumn. If you escape these, the burning sun of summer scorches your crop, and it perishes by heat and drought. If none of these evils overtake you, clouds of insects eat up your crop, and what the caterpillar leaves, the canker-worm devours.' Spoken in his deliberate and solemn utterance, I could compare it to nothing but the maledictions of one of the old prophets. I trust that both climate and soil of this hill of Zion have improved since I last raked hay here in Professor Stuart's meadow."

[25] Of these Andover had a number: the Lockhart Society for the Improvement of Sacred Music, the Porter Rhetorical Society, the Bartlet Athanaeum (literary), the Mechanical Association (woodworking and other hobbies), and the Society of Inquiry for Foreign Missions. To these can be added various other meetings that were generally attended by the professors whenever possible, for example, the Monthly Concert of Prayer for Foreign Missions, and the Jews' Meeting, the latter of which was sponsored by Mrs. Porter for the purpose of prayer for the conversion of the Jews and held weekly at her home. See Rowe, *History of Andover*, 35, 40–47; and Robbins, *Old Andover Days*, 73–88.

extended period for relaxation. Once a year during the summer term he allowed himself a full day of recreation when he invited his class on an outing to Prospect Hill, which lay within hiking distance of the school. On this day, noted his daughter, the "professor" was laid aside, and the students "with whom he talked in his inimitable way" became his boon companions.[26]

Stuart was not without his faults as a teacher. One of these was his sometimes incautious haste in stating a proposition or arriving at a conclusion. He taught with enthusiasm, but often at the expense of caution. John Todd noted that he could "never feel that Stuart's *ipse dixit* was safe to follow without reexamination. . . . If with this everlasting go-forward of his he was well balanced with judgment, he would be a giant; . . . but he is like our five-hundred-year comet, bright, fiery, dazzling, but so eccentric in its orbit and so rapid in its course that you have difficulty in calculating its progress."[27] Stowe said the same thing in different but equally colorful words. In comparing Stuart with James Murdock, Andover's first church historian, Stowe remarked that whereas the latter "would put, piece by piece into the hands of his students, the finished coin all nicely stamped and milled and burnished, . . . Stuart would be tossing at their heads great nuggets of the unwrought metal with the earth and slag still adhering to them."[28] Probably most of the suspicion that the students entertained against their professor was the natural result of their inability to keep up with his quick mind. He readily incorporated the new learning in biblical criticism, a field that many of the students were previously conditioned to approach with the utmost conservatism if not outright rejection. Many of the vain or superficially pious students were chilled by Stuart's scientific study of the scriptures, and for this he was not to blame. But inasmuch as his students often found it difficult to keep up with him, he certainly was at fault. In the light of all this, it is interesting to observe that from the rather large body of evidence covering the content of what Stuart actually taught, he was, if anything, extremely cautious; yet he *was* fond of quoting the radical opinions. No wonder that students were sometimes shocked, not withstanding his usually clear disavowal of these speculations as his own. Too, as Wayland stated, Stuart's "impromptu opinions were frequently erroneous. But when he gave himself time, and really did justice to himself, few men were, in fact, more reliable."[29]

[26] Robbins, *Old Andover Days*, 130–31.

[27] Todd, *Story of His Life*, 99.

[28] *A Memorial of the Semi-Centennial Celebration of the Founding of the Theological Seminary at Andover*, prepared by J. L. Taylor (Andover, MA: Warren F. Draper, 1859) 221. In regard to the character of thought of the two men, Stowe remarked that "Professor Stuart's hold of a subject was like the hug of a bear, rolling and crushing in its grasp; while Dr. Murdock's was more like the pounce of a hawk, with beak and talon piercing and severing and comminuting" (Ibid., 219).

[29] Francis and Wayland, *Memoir*, 67.

Closely associated with this tendency toward rashness was the streak of dogmatism he often manifested, particularly as his fame as a critic and scholar grew. But Woods, his closest colleague, noted that he was always open to new investigation and willing "to change his opinions, and equally ready to acknowledge the change."[30]

Another fault was his tendency to be abrupt in his judgments of students, particularly "those who did not enter at once with an ardor kindled to his own in the studies of the junior year."[31] Mrs. H. C. Cornelius noted that he was sometimes forgetful that the students were awed by him and that he tended to be thoughtless of the feelings of the shy and diffident.

Such were Stuart's human frailties, but these must be expected from anyone. In a way, they seemed only to strengthen the picture of his personality. The sum of it was more than any teacher could ask—a host of students turned friends, many of whom themselves rose to positions of distinction and honor and who looked back upon their experience in his presence as uniquely formative of lifelong patterns of conduct and thought.

But perhaps the most abiding testimony to his accomplishments as a teacher was that paid to him by former students in far-off mission posts who translated the Bible from the original Greek and Hebrew into a variety of tongues, translations that painstakingly followed principles of philology and grammatical-historical scholarship first learned in the plain classroom of Andover under Stuart's tutelage. Some of these translations live prominently to this day as the standard biblical texts in their languages. The list resonates with the romance of "the great century" of Christian missionary expansion: Adoniram Judson in Burmese, Gordon Hall and Samuel Newell in Marathi, Miron Winslow and Levi Spaulding in Tamul, Asa Thurston and Hiram Bingham in Hawaiian, William Goodell in Armeno-Turkish, Daniel Temple and Jonas King in modern Greek, Cyrus Byington, Cyrus Kingsbury, and Alfred Wright in Choctaw, Samuel Worcester in Cherokee, Elias Riggs and Harrison Dwight in Armenian, Elijah Bridgman in Chinese, William Schauffler in Hebrew-Spanish, John T. Jones in Siamese, Justin Perkins in modern Syriac, Sherman Hall in Ojibwa, Aldin Grout in Zulu, James Bryant in Grebo, and William Walker in Mpongwe. All labored under his inspiration.[32] As William Adams noted in a fervent but justifiable eulogy:

> Something bordering upon the romantic is there, that while he, in solitary toil, was gathering from all the dialects of the East whatever could

[30] Woods, *History of Andover*, 154.

[31] Cornelius, "Chapter of Reminiscences," 556.

[32] William A. Adams, *A Discourse on the Life and Services of Professor Moses Stuart; Delivered in the City of New York: Sabbath Evening, January 25, 1852* (New York: J. F. Trow, 1852) 59–60. This by no means completes the list of missionaries who studied under Stuart. One hundred twenty-eight were graduated from Andover during his tenure. See *Andover Theological Seminary, General Catalogue, 1808–1908*, (Boston: Thomas Todd Printer, 1909) 512–13.

elucidate the inspired Scriptures, his reward was to come when men trained by his wisdom, and inspired with his enthusiasm, carried his name and influence back to the Acropolis at Athens, to the isles of the Aegean, the valley of the Nile, to Jerusalem and Damascus, the Tigris and Euphrates, to Ararat and Mesopotamia, and to the remoter lands beyond the Ganges.[33]

The influence went to humble places too, but no less directly. One of his students, Cyrus Byington of the class of 1819, a missionary to the Choctaws in Indian Territory, recalled how Stuart urged him to read some Hebrew every day, and how that advice had an almost legal force with him for many years. "In my log cabin in the woods, often have I dreamed of being back at Andover, till in my dream I have wept." Remembering a visit with Stuart in the summer of 1851, only six months before Stuart's death, Byington continued:

> I met him once more, when he was taking his morning walk. His greeting was specially kind. And there I parted with the man whose influence over me had been the most marked and decisive all my life. And there, in my memory, with his staff in his hand, and his kind looks on a Choctaw missionary, he lives, and will live in my memory till I go where I hope to meet him in the presence of our Saviour in heaven.[34]

In a real sense Byington, and some fifteen hundred others who studied under Stuart, were a chosen company, scholars whose minds were opened to the Bible in new and faith-shaping ways, men who were freed by him from their rigid orthodoxies and led by his skill into a life-giving critical study of the word of God.

[33] Adams, *Discourse,* 60. Leonard Bacon's tribute should also be added: "It is perhaps, the highest illustration of [Stuart's] usefulness that, in so many languages, the Bible will be given by his pupils to so many tribes and nations, not in the form of hasty translations from a translation, but in the form of translations made directly *from* the inspired original, with all the aids afforded by the most advanced investigations" ("Moses Stuart," 42–55).

[34] Quoted in Adams, *Discourse,* 47–48.

III

THE OLD TESTAMENT CRITIC

In its detailed stipulation of the duties of the Professor of Sacred Literature, the Andover Constitution required that the incumbent not only teach grammar and exegesis but also deliver public lectures on biblical literature and criticism. These were given before the assembled student body and interested public at regular intervals throughout the school year. Stuart's series was part of a broader course that he shared with the professors of theology and preaching, both of whom were under a similar constitutional mandate to investigate in a public forum materials more extensive than those normally covered in daily student recitations.

Though Stuart was responsible for teaching both of the testaments, the extant lectures are solely related to Old Testament matters.[1] The reasons for the one-sided emphasis are not entirely known, but the fact that Stuart's entering students were almost totally deficient in Hebrew meant that in this subject, valuable time, which in the Greek recitation classes he could allot to discussions of critical issues, had to be spent mastering the language. The public lectures thus became the only occasions during which Old Testament critical matters could be aired.[2] But perhaps more important is that until 1820, at least, European New Testament studies had not advanced sufficiently to

[1] Stuart listed fifty-five lectures in his "Expression of my desire as to the disposal of my manuscripts" (Andover Newton Papers, 1837). Of these, only Lecture 48 is missing. One other is dropped from the numbered sequence but appears to have been combined later with another, that is, Lecture 41 with Lecture 40, both on Daniel. The collection grew only gradually, for, as Stuart often complained in his reports to the Board of Visitors, lack of time prevented him from accomplishing more. An average of seven or eight appeared annually. By 1814 he noted that he had thirty "in hand," though never were all of the lectures delivered in one year. In 1815, for instance, he delivered nineteen lectures, ten of which were repeats. Notations appear on a number concerning the date or dates on which they were read. In no case is the earliest date later than 1822, and even here the notation is "read again:—summer of 1822" (Lecture 47) or "Read bis. July 1822" (Lecture 49). It seems safe to assume then that few, if any, of the lectures were composed subsequently. Though without giving any specific dates, Stuart remarked that they were written during the *early* period" of his labors, and he strongly urged that they not be published for that reason. (See Andover Newton Papers, 1837, and the note on the title page of Lecture 1. See also Stuart's reports to the Board of Visitors, Papers of the Board of Visitors, 1812–1820, *passim.*)

[2] The few public lectures on New Testament subjects that Stuart did offer, mostly after 1822, were not kept in manuscript since they were incorporated into later published articles and commentaries.

have produced the level of discussion that had already engaged Old Testament scholars. This advance would come in due course, and Stuart's attention to New Testament criticism would be directed accordingly; but until then his career as a critical biblical scholar would be devoted almost exclusively to the Old Testament.

The first lectures — on the name "Hebrew," the confusion of tongues, the origin of the letters, and the vowel points — were all delivered before 1813. Since they draw almost exclusively on standard seventeenth- and eighteenth-century English and Latin sources, they may be considered as a unit separate from the lectures that followed. The chief authorities were the *Philology Hebraeus* by Johannes Leusden (1624–1699); the "Prolegomena" to the *Polyglot Bible* by Brian Walton (1600–1661); the "Prolegomena" to the *Pentateuch* by Jean Le Clerc (1657–1736); the *Observationes Sacra* by Campegius Vitringa (1659–1722); the supplement by C. Taylor to *Dictionary of the Holy Bible, Historical Critical, Geographical, and Etymological* by Augustin Calmet (1672–1757); *The State of the Printed Text of the Old Testament* by Benjamin Kennicott (1718–1783); and the *De arte grammatic* by Isaac Vossius (1618–1689). As a text for the students, Stuart recommended *The Institutes of Biblical Criticism* by Gilbert Gerard (1760–1815), a work that he felt to be less than satisfactory, but this judgment, he admitted, was more from the arrangement of the parts than from the content.[3]

Stuart was aware, through the Pentateuchal examinations of Le Clerc and Vitringa, of the theory of the composite nature of the book of Genesis. Le Clerc and Vitringa had followed the earlier and more famous investigations of the French priest Richard Simon, whose *Histoire Critique du Vieux Testament* was published in 1678. But most of the authors Stuart consulted at this early stage in his career, and certainly Gerard, the latest on the list, were otherwise not interested in the critical questions even then exciting European biblical scholars. They were old works, reflecting the interest of seventeenth- and eighteenth-century writers in problems of text and language, and showed little of the higher critical concerns. Thus, Stuart's first lectures did little more than present accepted conclusions, namely, that Hebrew was the earliest known tongue,[4] that it had survived the dispersion at Babel, the historicity of which he did not question, and that it had remained in a comparatively pure state up to the time of the Babylonian captivity.[5] He likewise asserted the antiquity of the Hebrew characters, the Samaritan forms appearing to be the most ancient.[6] His conclusion from the lectures on the Hebrew points we have already observed. Though Stuart's scholarly contemporaries abroad were by this time caught up in

---

[3] Stuart, *Lectures on Sacred Literature*, No. 1.
[4] Ibid., "Prolegomena," 1, 3.
[5] Ibid., Lecture 2.
[6] Ibid., Lecture 3.

other matters, the authors upon which he relied covered useful material as far as they went and thus provided him with important knowledge in matters of lower criticism, much of which would remain standard during his lifetime.

Through 1812, then, Stuart could be said only to have caught up with the most obvious and accepted discoveries in a field already beginning to produce new, and, to conservative Andover, disconcerting theories and facts. But after 1812 and his exposure to the German critics, particularly Eichhorn, Stuart had an entirely different perspective, which stimulated him to investigate new topics. But for Eichhorn, the higher critical approach involved not only a desire for the truth but also an apologetic interest — that of explaining "the Bible, according to the ideas and methods of thought of the ancient world," and defending it "against the ridicule of its enemies."[7] The *Einleitung* honestly reflected these concerns, despite its occasional naturalistic tendencies or rash conclusions. Thus, the work had a direct appeal to a scholar such as Stuart, who, though he was careful to point out his spiritual kinship with such orthodox traditionalists in Germany as George F. Seiler, whose conservative *Hermeneutik* was soon to come into his hands, and though he differed from Eichhorn on basic critical questions, could still admit to an attractive solidness in Eichhorn, the apologist.

In short, it was from Eichhorn that Stuart learned the method of "critical defense." From the beginning of his work, Stuart was a theological conservative, much more so than Eichhorn. Yet his discovery of Eichhorn prevented him from falling back on an anachronistic defense of his beliefs. He learned early that higher criticism judiciously applied could be as useful to defend as to destroy, and though this truth does not shine through in everything Stuart did and said at Andover, it stood out in crucial issues in later years, especially when he became a participant in the debates on the Trinity which swept New England.

Stuart transmitted his new critical knowledge to his students almost immediately in a second series of lectures on such themes as the formation of the Old Testament canon; the dates, authors, and circumstances of the several books; and his appraisal of the various texts of the Old Testament along with their critical helps. He delivered the new lectures in 1813 as an introduction to problems of the Old Testament canon. Lecture 8, on the publication and preservation of the sacred books of the Hebrews, noted the probable destruction and loss of certain sacred books but held that enough remained in the present Old Testment "for the instruction and guidance of all men." The question of whether or not synagogues existed before the Babylonian exile Stuart decided in the negative and argued, therefore, that the present Old Testament canon stems from the library of the second

---

[7] Carl Bertheau, "Eichhorn, Johann Gottfried," *Schaff-Herzog Encyclopedia* 4:97.

temple at the time of Ezra. He also discussed the various names for the
scriptures and concluded with Chrysostom's introduction of the word
"Bible" into common usage.

Lecture 10 discussed the order and genuineness of the Old Testament
books, and here Stuart[9] marshalled a variety of arguments to prove that the
writings could not be the products of imposters. As for the term applicable
to the biblical writers, Stuart held out for "prophet" against the opinion of
Eichhorn, who, having studied the history of religion, limited the true
prophets to those who were products of a more advanced religious age.
Unlike those of an earlier religious stage who claimed to see divine import in
natural events, the true prophets, suggested Eichhorn, came from a more
sophisticated period. As a result, they lived under the influence of the divine
in the highest sense. Eichhorn's view was of singular importance for Stuart,
because if followed to its logical conclusion it undermined the genuineness
of the books believed to date from the earliest periods. How, for instance,
could Eichhorn account for Moses?

> How came the legislator of the Jews to burst forth from all the gross
> absurdities of Egyptian polytheism, like the sun in his strength from the
> bosom of gloomy mists and cheerless clouds? Is this the slow, cautious,
> gradual progress of the children of nature toward the most exalted acqui-
> sitions of spiritual knowledge? No, it is contradictory to the common
> sense of nature! It imperiously demands,—it demonstrates the presence
> and special aid of the Divinity. Let Eichhorn or any other critic account
> for these phenomena independently of this if he can. The supposition of
> such exalted improvement without aid—without the lapse of "thousands
> of ages"—and without supernatural assistance—is against the theory of
> Eichhorn himself—against the universal experience of all nations, and a
> mystery more difficult of explanation than the common supposition, that
> the Hebrew writers were *divinely inspired*.[8]

But more important was the responsibility of Stuart the conservative to
oppose with every measure of intellectual strength at his command any
opinion harmful to the genuine, miraculous character of the scriptures.

Lectures 11 to 14 dealt with working definitions of the terms *apocryphal* and *canonical*, and three of these lectures surveyed ancient Jewish,
New Testament, and patristic testimonies regarding the Old Testament
canon. Of importance was Stuart's definition of *canonical* as designating
"those books to which Christ and his apostles referred when they gave
religious instruction." Not all of the Old Testament books were quoted in
the New Testament, and six (Ezra, Ecclesiastes, Canticles, Obadiah,
Nahum, and Zephaniah) were not even referred to. But even these Stuart
included in the threefold division of the "law, prophets and psalms" mentioned in Luke 24:44.[9] Hence, all of the Old Testament books shared the

[8] Andover Newton Papers, Lecture 10.
[9] Ibid.

divine sanction given by Christ and the apostles, a fact of supreme importance in Stuart's subsequent considerations of the genuineness of each book.

At the end of Lecture 14, Stuart inserted two provocative comments.
First, he acknowledged his qualified indebtedness to Eichhorn and admitted that "although his theological views are such, as, in my apprehen-
sion, ought to be regarded with horror, yet where the mere literary history
of the Old Testament is concerned, I have not perused any writer of equal
ability."[10] Second, he issued a clear manifesto, a ringing summary of the
critical task at hand:

> On the whole, an ample investigation of the genuineness and canonical
> credit of the Old Testament can hardly fail of providing a good effect
> upon the open and ingenious mind. These subjects are involved in great
> darkness, in the minds of most men. Very few books give us any valuable
> information respecting them, and these few are seldom read. If the in-
> vestigations in which we have been engaged serve to convince you that
> the Bible does not shrink from the examination of critical inquirers; that
> the result of such examination fairly conducted will always be favorable
> to the word of God; and that the genuineness and canonical credit of the
> Old Testament rest on better grounds than you had even imagined; in
> a word, if your rational faith in the sacred scriptures is strengthened, and
> you feel with more weight your obligations to obey a book, which bears
> the incontestable stamp of heaven upon it, then will the time and labour
> which we have expended upon this subject, not be lost. God grant that
> the happy result of all our labours may be the better to understand, the
> more firmly to believe, and the more faithfully to obey the divine
> precepts.[11]

Here for the first time a self-consciousness about the "investigation of the
scriptures" can be clearly discerned—a spirit not evinced in the earliest
lectures—as if Stuart were just now aware of his apologetic role. Henceforth
his twofold course was clear, to defend the scriptures against the "super-
critics" like Eichhorn and yet to claim the worth of Eichhorn's critical meth-
odology against the potentially troublesome New England conservatives.

Lecture 15 began the discussion of the specific books in the Old Testament canon, and the first consideration was the authorship of the Pentateuch, particularly the book of Genesis. With Eichhorn, Stuart readily
accepted the theory of the Elohim–Yahweh (Jehovah) sources and presented
to his hearers the scriptural references necessary to trace the two accounts
on their own. Again like Eichhorn, Stuart believed that such a discovery by
no means precluded the assumption that Moses was the compiler:

> How shall we account for this [the Elohim–Jehovah distinction] without
> the supposition of two original written records, blended by Moses?—How
> comes it to pass, that the whole book of Genesis (with the exception of
> about three chapters, which have peculiarities that distinguish them

[10] Ibid., Lecture 14.
[11] Ibid.

from all the others) can easily be divided between the records with
Elohim and Jehovah, and which one of these appellations is exclusively
confined to each record? Are the rest of the Mosaic writings thus sepa-
rable? Have they these peculiarities? Let every reader examine, and he
will be satisfied.[12]

Stuart was aware, however, of what this acknowledgment of the two Genesis sources might imply. Lest his own orthodoxy be questioned, he appealed
to the orthodox Campegius Vitringa, who, as a lesser figure in the history
of modern criticism, had held to the Mosaic authorship and posited a multiple source theory, though had not hit upon the later Elohim–Jehovah
distinction of Astruc.[13] Stuart struggled over the issue:

> The mind of a pious man is, no doubt startled at first, by a suggestion
> of this nature, for it creates some apprehension in him, that the credit of
> the book of Genesis may be diminished. And then, this sentiment has
> been principally defended by those who are by no means remarkable for
> their reverence for the sacred scriptures. It should, however, be noted,
> that it is but very lately, this subject has been thoroughly discussed.
> Eichhorn is the first, who has presented the world with such a discussion.
> How far his labours have met with success among the serious divines of
> Germany, I know not. I observe, that Baumgarten–Crusius however,
> rejects his opinions on this subject, although the reasons he has given for
> rejections, will apply only to a small part of the critical labours of Eich-
> horn, & not to his general principles. The great Vitringa, whose knowl-
> edge of sacred criticism, whose orthodoxy & piety no one can justly call
> in question, was decidedly of the opinion, that the book of Genesis is
> compiled from different records, previously extant. Instead of shaking the
> credit of the Book, he thinks this supposition will enhance it. . . .
> Certainly nothing forbids the supposition, that the records which
> Moses made use of were inspired. . . .—I confess I cannot see any thing
> impossible, nor even improbable in it. And then, the supposition, that
> Moses made use of different records in compiling the book of Genesis,
> surely relieves us from a multitude of difficulties with which we must be
> pressed, if we deny this.
> I see nothing contrary to piety in the suppositions of Vitringa; and
> the evidence from critical examination of Genesis appears so strong in its
> favour, that I confess myself inclined to adopt it. At the same time, as this
> conclusion is made out only by the aid of criticism, should any historical
> testimony to the contrary be added which is credible, the supposition
> must be abandoned.[14]

However qualified and tentative, higher criticism had arrived at Andover.
The spirit embodied here would inform Stuart for the remainder of his long
career.

[12] Ibid., Lecture 18.
[13] Charles A. Briggs, *The Higher Criticism of the Hexateuch* (New York: Scribner, 1893)
44.
[14] Andover Newton Papers, Lecture 18.

He covered the rest of the books of the Pentateuch briefly and left Mosaic authorship unquestioned except for the last chapter of Deuteronomy, which Stuart assigned to Joshua in concord with accepted tradition. He then interrupted the series on the books of the canon to deliver four lectures on the history of the Hebrew manuscripts. These too were based on Eichhorn. The lectures covered factual knowledge about textual discoveries, the history of text criticism, laws for the copying of synagogue rolls, difficulties in determining the age of manuscripts, and other miscellaneous information. One point of interest was Stuart's acceptance of the preexilic dating of the Samaritan Pentateuch. Had it appeared later, he observed, it would have contained the remainder of the canon put together at the time of Ezra.

Lecture 23, on the book of Joshua, resumed the discussion of the Old Testament books. Stuart was inconclusive about the authorship and date of Joshua, but he rejected Joshua as the writer and indicated that the book must have been written at different times by different people, though it had been put together certainly by the time of Ezra. The genuineness of the book was attested by its geographical accuracy and the fact that its place in the canon had never been disputed.

As for the book of Judges, Stuart held it to consist of two divisions, one early, the other dating perhaps from the reign of Hezekiah in Judah. The book had to be genuine, for it contained material detrimental to Jewish glory. The question of its authority as divinely inspired Stuart preferred to leave in the hands of the department of theology. He objected strenuously to Eichhorn's explaining away the miraculous events. "If everything miraculous is to be expurged from the Bible by the ruthless hand of modern incredulity; then men ought not to dissemble. They ought to be ingenious, and say at once that the Bible has no more real authenticity than the Veda or the Koran."[15]

Stuart dated the book of Ruth well after the reign of David because of the "Chaldaisms" in the text and the similarities in diction to Samuel and Kings. That the book was genuine he proved by its "effortless" and "sincere" writing, and by the fact that no attempt had been made to conceal its lateness. (Here and elsewhere, "genuineness" to Stuart meant that the book is a true account of actual persons and happenings). The design of the author was to set forth the genealogy of David. The fact that four generations were made to fill the space of four hundred years need not bring the genuineness into question, he said, for genealogies were commonly abbreviated in the East.[16]

That the books of Samuel shared common authorship, possibly with the book of Ruth as well, seemed clear from stylistic similarities. Internal

[15] Ibid., Lecture 24.
[16] Ibid.

evidence indicated that the author used sources written close to the time of the actual happenings. The Chronicler used the same sources, though neither he nor the author of Samuel borrowed directly from one another.[17] And Stuart reached much the same conclusions about the book of Kings, though he agreed with Eichhorn that the final editor was probably the writer who compiled Samuel.[18]

The main question of Chronicles was that of the genuineness of the genealogies in book 1. Stuart was impatient with scholars who refused to admit the obvious errors in the section — the omissions and later additions — but he was equally impatient with those who blamed the errors upon the original authors. "Are the sacred writers to be taxed with the faults of transcribers? Is the want of arrangement of perspicuity any solid objection on our part to the credit of these genealogies?" Lists of numbers and names were always subject to error in transcribing. The honest critic will admit this while affirming the integrity of the whole:

> It does not become the friends of truth to assert that no difficulties exist in these matters, as they now stand in our Bibles. But it does become them to show, how these difficulties may exist, independently of the original authors, and that they constitute no imperilment of their credibility. We must show our readiness and our ability to meet the objector to the sacred scriptures, on grounds which are capable of fair examination, and which are common to all ancient writings. Such ground being admitted, we have no reason to fear the result.[19]

In discussing the other sections of Chronicles, Stuart observed the author's interest in the temple and compared it with Kings, where such an interest is lacking, and suggested a late date. The style and orthography bore this out and pointed to Ezra as the author — a highly probable theory, thought Stuart, especially since no argument prevailed against it.[20]

Ezra was the compiler of the book that bears his name, though he was the author only of the last four chapters. Stuart recognized the problem of identifying Artaxerxes but offered no solution. Again he upheld the genuineness and noted with approbation that Eichhorn had remained firm against counter-opinions from other German critics.[21] The sections in Nehemiah that used the first person Stuart accepted as genuine, whereas the author of the middle section remained unidentified. Though subsequent genealogical additions suggested a later writing, Stuart dated it in the reign of Artaxerxes. The book was so different in style and expression from the other

---

[17] Ibid., Lecture 25.
[18] Ibid.
[19] Ibid., Lecture 27.
[20] Ibid. The lecture is dated August 1814.
[21] Ibid., Lecture 28.

books of the Bible that its genuineness could not be questioned.[22]

A whole lecture examined the book of Esther, which presented a number of weighty critical problems. Though Stuart was aware that some critics "now believe it to be a mere rabbinical fiction," he found internal evidence that the whole and certainly the "first part" of the book was a genuine account of actual happenings set down by Mordecai. The problem of dating was more difficult, hinging on the identity of Ahasuerus, whom Stuart, following Eichhorn, identified with Xerxes. The improbabilities in the book could be explained without too much difficulty. Ahasuerus's half-year feast with the nobles was not necessarily inconsistent with the maintenance of order in the provinces, for it could well have been only a succession of banquets in preparation for the Grecian war. Ahasuerus's insolent message to his queen, which, in asking her to appear before strangers, violated the customs of his country, could be explained by the fact the he and his seven counselors were probably drunk.[23] That Mordecai knew Esther to be a Jew even though she was said to have kept this a secret indicates that she was not always closemouthed about her race.

In Job, too, historicity was the pressing critical problem. Like Eichhorn, Stuart accepted the historicity of the story and of the collateral accounts of Job in the Near East. But whereas Eichhorn believed that all the Job stories were embellished, Stuart held that the biblical account, if not the others, accurately presented historical facts. To suggest that the biblical story was even partly fictitious would be to accuse the author of "extravagance, bad taste, and feeble powers." As for such problems as the author's incredible transmission of the long speeches, or his account of God's conference with the angels—two points Eichhorn used to argue that much of the book could not be accurate history—Stuart reasoned that the speeches could have been transmitted orally, as was often done in the Near East, and that the heavenly conference might well have been communicated like a prophet's vision, a representation of a "prophetical personification." The place and scene of the poem is Uz, which, following Eichhorn, Stuart placed in Petraea or Edom. He described the work as "a didactic dialogue in poetic numbers," not a dream. He agreed with Bishop Lowth and with Eichhorn about the beauty of the poem, but believed that it revealed a God of nature, not a God of supernatural power and transcendence. Hence he preferred Isaiah as a more spiritually edifying work, if a choice were to be made.[24] Stuart followed Eichhorn in regard to the author and date of the book. The author, though unknown, was probably born and educated in Arabia. Since there was no reference to Mosaic law or institutions, the book originated in the time of the patriarchs. The prologue and epilogue dated from the same time as the body.

[22] Ibid.
[23] Ibid., Lecture 29.
[24] Ibid., Lecture 30. "Read 1816, 1819."

Stuart recognized at once the composite character of Psalms and the
difficulties in determining authorship and date of individual pieces. Eichhorn was again the authority. Stuart noted that the psalms came from
various ages in the history of the Hebrews, though only the ninetieth dated
before David. Under David the psalms reached their perfection, and he
undoubtedly wrote a number, though not all that traditionalists assigned
to him. Some of the pilgrim psalms probably dated from the reign of
Hezekiah, when the annual temple feast was restored, and here Stuart used
Eichhorn's own terminology and called them the songs of "going up." Others
dated from the age of apostasy; still others from the captivity. There is no
evidence that any were composed later, and thus the psalter was closed with
the making of the canon at the time of Ezra. To explain the division of the
psalms and the order of the present collection, Stuart cited Eichhorn's
opinion that the Jewish division of five parts suggested a composite from
several earlier collections.[25]

Lecture 33 dealt with the book of Proverbs. Stuart ascribed a good
part of the book to Solomon; certainly the first part (according to the
superscription) and portions of the second and third sections either came
from his own hand or were compiled by him. A fourth division mentions
Agur, a sage in Solomon's court (after Eichhorn), and the fifth section
Stuart ascribed to Lemuel, king of Massa, whom he did not further identify. He briefly discussed parallelism as a characteristic of poetic form.[26]

Stuart was unsettled over Ecclesiastes. Though tradition would ascribe
it to Solomon, he not only noted the late postexilic words and idioms but
also observed that, contrary to the customary practice of Solomon, the writer
uses *Elohim* instead of *Jehovah*. It was surprising that Eichhorn missed this
point, observed Stuart, though Eichhorn too would deny Solomon's
authorship. Still, Stuart was reluctant to defy tradition, and "he would not
be understood positively to advance a different opinion." Stuart was also
disturbed by the philosophical outlook of the book, but he praised the spirit
of trust in the conclusion. A later note, probably inserted into the lecture
in 1819, indicates that Stuart's earlier doubts about the historical and theological issues had only become stronger:

> An introduction to this book, and a comment upon it which would give
> satisfaction to the pious and intelligent Christian, who believes in the
> divine authority of the sacred scripture are yet a desideratum, in the
> province of Sacred Literature. I wait with anxiety for the time when
> these shall appear. Till then, or until I have some better light than I now
> possess, I must profess my ignorance of the real economy of the book, and
> of the best method of solving its difficulties, or accounting for its style.
> I once thought that I had found a result which was tenable, but the more

[25] Ibid., Lecture 32.
[26] Ibid., Lecture 33.

I examine the more I doubt the sufficiency of any theory hitherto advanced, to explain or remove its difficulties.[27]

In the lecture on Canticles, Stuart was more assured, but even here he found much uncertain. A stylistic comparison with the first part of Proverbs convinced him that the author could not have been Solomon. But he dated the work from the period of Solomon and suggested that it was written by a contemporary. This was in contrast to Eichhorn, who, from the book's mention of Tirzah, a town prominent only at the time of Jeroboam, placed the book in a later era. Stuart noted that the style suggested a "happier, more peaceful time," but beyond this "nothing *certain* can be determined." Stuart did tend to deny any mystical or allegorical interpretation and noted that those who would declare the work unworthy of scripture without such an interpretation were arguing on a *petitio principii.* "Why," he asked, "should the most interesting of all affections merely human be deemed unworthy of an exhibition in the sacred volume?"[28]

Lecture 36 constituted an introduction to the prophetic literature. Stuart treated such subjects as the origin of the prophetic office, the definition of the term *prophet* (here Stuart included "anyone who is the subject of *special divine* influence"), modes of revelation to the prophets, and a description of the prophetic office. About the last topic he took issue with Eichhorn, whom he criticized earlier for his developmental views of the prophetic role. Especially dangerous, Stuart held, was the "modern" view that ignored divine inspiration and described the prophets merely as "wise, patriotic and observing men." It was a matter of regret to Stuart "that exalted talents and consummate literary acquisitions should be devoted to undermining the faith, and marring the hope of the meek and pious followers of the Redeemer."[29]

The unity of the book of Isaiah was already under discussion by Stuart's time, mainly through J. B. Koppe's notes in his translation of Bishop Lowth's *Isaiah*.[30] Here Koppe presented the theory that the prophetic book contained a number of different writings. This view, transmitted by Eichhorn, Stuart rejected. To question the integrity of the fifteenth and sixteenth chapters or to credit the last twenty-six chapters to another "Isaiah"

---

[27] Ibid., Lecture 34. "Read December 1815, 1819." It was not until late in his life that Stuart believed he had reached a solution concerning this work. This he published in *Critical History and Defense of the Old Testament Canon* (Andover, MA: Allen, Morrill, & Wardwell, 1845), and more extensively in *A Commentary on Ecclesiastes* (New York: G. P. Putnam, 1851).

[28] Ibid., Lecture 35.

[29] Ibid., Lecture 36.

[30] Robert Lowth, *Jesaias neu übersetzt nebst einer Einleitung und kritischen philologischen und erläuternden Anmerkungen,* vol. 4 (Leipzig: Weidmanns Erben und Reich, 1779–1781). Koppe (1750–1791) was a sometime professor of theology at Göttingen and preacher at the court of Hanover.

was to deny inspiration. Nor was Stuart convinced by Eichhorn's word study, which attempted to show that the remaining chapters used words and idioms from the postexilic period. Stuart remained unmoved by Eichhorn's theory that someone had placed this section by accident on the end of some early Isaiah scroll.[31]

In Jeremiah the chief issue was not its unity but its disorder. Stuart believed this to have been the result of the mixing up of smaller rolls when the larger, complete copy was drawn up. He noted the differences between the Greek and Hebrew copies and followed Eichhorn in reasoning that the discrepancies possibly arose from there being two editions, a shorter one for contemporary use, a longer one for posterity. The Greeks copied from the former. The question of the authorship of the last chapter Stuart answered briefly and noted only that it was part of Jeremiah's book. Lamentations he accepted without question as an authentic work of the prophet.[32]

Stuart became aware through Eichhorn of G. L. Oeder's attack upon the integrity of the book of Ezekiel.[33] He devoted his lecture on Ezekiel largely to pointing out the peculiarities in the work, including prophetic visions and the "Chaldaisms" and "Syriacisms" in style. The integrity of the work and the authorship by Ezekiel, however, he did not question, in contrast to Oeder, whose opinions Eichhorn conveyed. Stuart recognized the difficulties hindering a proper understanding of the book, and he pleaded for an abandonment of literalism in favor of a more figurative approach, which would yield the meaning of the difficult passages.[34]

In contrast to Eichhorn, who rejected the historicity of the book of Daniel, Stuart believed that Daniel was an actual person living through the events described in the first six chapters and that he was the author of the prophecies. Much of Stuart's lecture provided an elaborate defense of this view. In contrast to his plea for figurative interpretation in Ezekiel, Stuart argued here for a literal reading. His chief concern, however, was to establish the genuineness of the work, and for him a theory such as Eichhorn's led the reader to regard the book as "incredible or fabulous."[35]

The lectures on the minor prophets, with the exception of that on Jonah, presented few problems for Stuart, so he quickly discussed author, date, and circumstance in summary statements.[36] The book of Hosea he

---

[31] Andover Newton Papers, Lecture 37.

[32] Ibid., Lecture 38.

[33] Oeder's work was written in 1756 and entitled *Freye Untersuchung über einige Bücher des alten Testaments* (Halle: G. J. L. Vogel, 1771).

[34] Andover Newton Papers, Lecture 39.

[35] Ibid., Lecture 40.

[36] The lecture on Hosea (Lecture 42) is dated 1820, and it is probable, though not definite, that the remainder of the series as it now stands dates from this later period. However, since most of these still rely on Eichhorn as the major secondary source, they maintain an inherent unity with the lectures preceding.

dated after the death of Jeroboam and presented it as an authentic por-
trayal written at different periods in Hosea's life. He believed it to be the
prophetic book least appropriate "to the Gospel state of the Christian" and
quoted Bishop Horsely to the effect that it revealed few details about
redemption, limited as it was on the subjects of incarnation and atonement.[37] With Eichhorn he agreed that it was original in style. On the question whether the "peculiar symbols" for Hosea's marital difficulties were
real or figurative, Stuart accepted a figurative interpretation, believing that
the chronology of events — at least ten years to have three children — could
not have been historical.[38]

The books of Joel, Amos, and Obadiah were treated in one lecture.
With Eichhorn, he considered Joel to be one of the oldest prophecies
("before the Assyrian threat") in the canon. At the same time it was one of
the most artistic — "scarcely a more perfect piece of composition in the
whole Bible." The book of Amos he characterized as one composition, "rich,
imaginative and pictorial," though a "monument to what God has done
rather than . . . a present guide to duty." He dated Obadiah from the commencement of the Babylonian captivity and noted that Jeremiah copied
from the work.[39]

The book of Jonah, however, opened a host of critical problems,
mainly occasioned by the "insult and skepticism" of those who rejected the
historicity of the account. Here again Eichhorn was the antagonist. "As
usual," Stuart observed, he has "mustered all the hosts of opposition to the
book . . . , marshalled their ranks and burnished their armour." Stuart took
issue on several points. To the objection that no whale was large enough to
swallow a man, Stuart noted that the text reads "large *fish*," possibly a
shark. To the objection that even if swallowed no man could remain alive
in the stomach of a fish for three days, Stuart offered several arguments. In
the first place, the Bible *said* he was alive. Second, he was not digested.
Third, though it could easily have been a miracle, there had been cases
where people "who retain the uterine conformative of the vital organs" had
remained submerged in the water twenty-four hours and still were revived.
Jonah could have been in a little over twenty-four hours and still have
fulfilled the three days. Fourth, and what is most important, the divine
stamp of authenticity appeared in Jesus' typological reference to the three
days. Stuart pointed out that Eichhorn himself could account for the events
only by resorting to the miraculous. In most places, Eichhorn tried to throw
out miracles. Here he tried to magnify them. Stuart denied Eichhorn's

[37] Samuel Horsely [1733–1806], *Biblical Criticism on . . . the Old Testament* (London:
Longman, Brown, Green, 1820). Stuart felt this to be "one of the most respectable efforts at
exegesis which the English have lately produced" (Andover Newton Papers, Lecture 42).
[38] Ibid., Lecture 42.
[39] Ibid.

theory that the book was an allegory, though he admitted that points in the book needed further explanation, including the purpose of the story as a whole, the later idioms in the writing, and the character and personality of Jonah.[40]

Lecture 45 treated the books of Micah, Nahum, and Habakkuk. On the first two, Stuart appealed to internal evidence of date, circumstance, and author, and he discussed no critical questions and made only an occasional comment on the literary beauty of a passage. The book of Habakkuk posed questions, however, about the identification of the "Chaldeans." Eichhorn's solution was to follow J. D. Michaelis (1717–1791), who in his *Geographia Hebraea* (1769–1790) had identified them as a wandering horde from the Gordian mountains. Since these tribes presumably did not come into power until the Babylonian captivity, Eichhorn dated the book sometime from this period, too late a date for Stuart, who held that the word "Chaldeans" was a common biblical synonym for Babylonians. The motivation for Stuart's argument was the desire not only to correct history but also to assert his presuppositions about the prophetic role—presuppositions that he believed to have been denied in the arguments of Eichhorn and Michaelis:

> The assertion that Chaldea no where occurs in the earlier writings of the Hebrews has been already sufficiently answered, by producing proofs of the contrary, from Job, & from the book of Genesis. The assertion, that no prophet, who mentions the Chaldees, as enemies of the Jews, could have lived before the time of Jehoiakim, when the Chaldees attacked Judea, is grounded entirely on the assumption, that no prophet did predict any events, or was divinely inspired to foretell future events: a supposition of rather too serious a nature to be received as a *gratis dictum*, & one which can only be established, by disproving the inspiration of our Saviour & the apostles.[41]

The final lecture in the series on the canon considered the last of the minor prophets—Zephaniah, Haggai, Zechariah, and Malachi. Again, internal evidence provided the substance of most of Stuart's comments, and they need not be repeated. A discussion of the visions and symbols in Zechariah, however, is of interest. Stuart insisted that in the elaborate expositions of some commentators "the strength of imagination has been the measure by which the prophets' meaning has been tried." This he claimed was the result of making too much of the visions themselves. The vision should not be taken as the literal representation of actual scenes that passed before the eyes of the prophet, but rather as prophetic ideas, "clothed" in a visionary "garb." He noted, however, that this supposition could not always be proved, and either view, used with care, "may be

[40] Ibid., Lecture 44.
[41] Ibid., Lecture 45.

adopted *salva fide, et salva ecclesia* because in explaining the import of a vision you will investigate by the same principles and come to the same conclusion."[42]

The last lectures in the series dealt with "those critical helps, which may aid us in investigating what is the true text and real sense of the Hebrew Scriptures."[43] These were mainly descriptive presentations covering information on such topics as the original appearance of the Hebrew scriptures; the Masoras; the Septuagint; Aquila; Symmachus; Theodotion; the Fifth, Sixth, and Seventh Versions; the Targums; the Vulgate; citations in Philo, Josephus, the Rabbis; and, finally, the editions of the Hebrew Bible. The *State of the Printed Text of the Old Testament* by Benjamin Kennicott (1660–1728) and the *Variae lectiones Vet. Test.* of Giovanni D. de Rossi (1742–1831), as well as Eichhorn's *Einleitung*, served as sources. Adding a few critical comments on currently available Hebrew Bibles, Stuart noted that he preferred "as a critical edition, Jahn's recently printed at Vienna as the only one worth purchasing."[44]

A few important characteristics of these lectures can be observed and summarized. On the whole they exhibited a strong and consistent faith in the worthwhileness of critical investigation, despite Stuart's conservative positions. Thus, while he accepted and defended the Mosaic authorship of the Pentateuch, the unity of the book of Isaiah, and the historicity of Esther, Job, Daniel, and Jonah, he avoided a literalistic view, especially where he felt the text to be at fault, as in the genealogical tables in Chronicles, or where he observed extreme prophetic imagery, as in Ezekiel or Zechariah. In some instances, however, he was willing to accept newer critical opinions as justified or worthy of serious attention, as for example the multiple source theory in the composition of Genesis, Eichhorn's classification and dating of the Psalms, and his treatment of Jeremiah. Even the most radical of the contemporary opinions he objectively presented, though not without detailed rebuttal when he felt it necessary. Stuart was reluctant to form definite conclusions on minor issues when evidence seemed lacking, but on the all-important questions of genuineness and inspiration he did not waver.

Taken as a whole, the lectures represent a nondevelopmental approach to Old Testament revelation, a point illustrated in Stuart's view of the prophetic office as qualitatively constant and entirely independent of the so-called religious development of the Hebrew nation. Hence, Stuart seemed quite willing to deal with the writings in their canonical, rather than chronological, sequence. The figure of Christ was central, not the history

---

[42] Ibid., Lecture 46.

[43] Ibid., Lectures 47–55.

[44] Johannes Jahn (1750–1816) was a Roman Catholic biblical scholar and professor at the University of Vienna. The Hebrew Bible was published in Vienna in 1806.

of God's revelation to God's people. The authenticity of the Old Testament canon was for the most part determined by Christ, and that alone established it as a Christian book. Furthermore, its content underlined and enhanced the Christian revelation, not so much because of its story of the religious history that ends in the coming of Christ, but because the covenant, the law, and the prophetic proclamations serve both as a testimony to the later fulfillment and as sources of doctrine relative to this event. The Old Testament was not, however, construed as proclaiming Christ on every page. The centrality of Christ was implicit in the work as a whole, but Stuart was already too much of a critic to belabor the point by relying on mystical and allegorical interpretation.

This Christocentric view and his preoccupation with genuineness led Stuart to minimize or ignore the inherent greatness of his material. The idyllic story of romance and toleration in Ruth was overshadowed by the genealogy of David. The missionary moral of the book of Jonah was lost in the discussion of its authenticity. The theme of the book of Job was obscured in a similar pursuit. One of the most distracting omissions was the failure to grasp the theme of love and reconciliation in the book of Hosea or to find in it any Christian significance. The role of the major prophets in pointing up the meaning of the sweep of Hebrew history Stuart also minimized or ignored.

Still, although one must allow for all the biases and omissions that modern scholarship must inevitably detect, the lectures remain a landmark in the history of American theological education. For whether or not Stuart accepted or rejected the new learning, the students at Andover were among the first in America to be made aware of the new currents already flowing inexorably into the stream of traditional biblical studies; and having been made aware, they were not only equipped as apologists for the old orthodoxy that Andover strived to represent but also, in some cases, prepared to advance eventually beyond their teacher into the progressive orthodoxy of the later nineteenth century.

IV

THE GRAMMATICAL-HISTORICAL APPROACH

The Andover Constitution required that the Professor of Sacred Literature teach not only the biblical languages, exegesis, and canon but also the theoretical principles of interpretation. Stuart accepted this mandate with enthusiasm, for he rightly discerned the central role that hermeneutics had held in the history of biblical studies and was anxious to set his own vocation as a biblical scholar within both a traditional and contemporary interpretive framework. A full course of classroom lectures on hermeneutics, several published essays, and a translation of an important foreign work indicate that Stuart's labors in the subject went far beyond simple compliance with the constitutional requirement.

Stuart's interest in hermeneutics developed early in his teaching career. We have already noted his acquisition of the orthodox George F. Seiler's *Hermeneutik*.[1] Within the decade from 1810 to 1820, Stuart had become acquainted with writers from the middle as well as the extremes of German hermeneutical opinion. The most acceptable for him was the moderate Johann August Ernesti (1707–1781), philologist and theologian at Leipzig, whose great *Institutio interpretes Novi Testamenti*, first published in 1761, was by 1818 required reading (in Latin) for all of Stuart's students.[2] But his pietistic and dogmatic New England religious background inclined

---

[1] See above, 11–12, note 25.

[2] Moses Stuart, Report to the Board of Visitors, Andover Newton Papers, September 1818. Stuart himself translated Ernesti under the title *Elements of Interpretation Translated from the Latin of J. A. Ernesti, and Accompanied by Notes and an Appendix Containing Extracts from Mories, Beck and Keil* (Andover, MA: Flagg & Gould, 1822). Other authors cited in his Lectures on Hermeneutics are J. S. Semler (without referring to a specific work) and George L. Bauer, *Hermeneutica Sacra* (Leipzig, 1797) among the rationalists; J. A. Turretin, *Sacrae Scripturae . . .*, G. J. Planck, *Einleitung in die theologischen Wissenschaften* (Leipzig, 1794–1795), and Christopher Wollius, *Examen regularum Hermeneutica ab August Calmeto civita Christianae commendatarum* (Leipzig, 1733) among the orthodox. Together with the *Institutio* of Ernesti, Stuart's classes were also reading the *Essay on the Historical Sense of the New Testament* by G. C. Storr in an English translation by J. W. Gibbs (Boston: Wells & Lilly, 1817). Another hint regarding Stuart's sources is his negative mention in his *Letters to the Rev. William E. Channing, Containing Remarks on His Sermon Recently Preached and Published At Baltimore* (Andover, MA: Flagg & Gould, 1819) of the extreme rationalists C. F. Ammon (1766–1850) and Johann Thiess (1762–1810). Channing, incidentally, agreed with Stuart's assessment.

45

Stuart to look with scorn upon rationalistic interpretations from abroad. Still, and of paramount significance to an understanding of his career, he accepted without question the grammatical-historical method, provided that the only presupposition on which it proceeded was open acceptance of the primacy of biblical authority. This is not to say that Stuart's interpretative work was "objective" in the sense advocated by later nineteenth-century interpreters. No one who taught at orthodox Andover and repeated the Andover Creed at five-year intervals could labor in isolation from dogmatic considerations; no one who had led a successful revival in New Haven could minimize the influence of the Spirit. On the other hand, no one who had been schooled in the intricacies of Puritan logic could escape the demands of reason. Each of these factors influenced Stuart's exegetical researches and must be kept in mind in a review of his hermeneutical principles.

Stuart delivered his first public lectures on the subject in 1822. From time to time throughout the remainder of his career he expounded in published articles certain points in the lectures, though with no fundamental departure from their content. The outline of the lectures, then, together with the expansions (which will be introduced topically rather than chronologically), present a fairly uniform description of his thought in the discipline.

Underlying all and revealed at many points was Stuart's concept of biblical authority. Though nowhere did he present in a systematic fashion his complete view on the subject, he accepted as normative the statements of the Andover Creed, which affirmed a belief in "the one living and true God" and proclaimed "that the word of God, contained in the scriptures of the Old and New Testaments is the perfect rule of faith and practice."[3] At the outset of the hermeneutical lectures, then, Stuart clearly affirmed this statement from the creed as the fundamental consideration in all that was to follow.[4]

---

[3] Woods, *History of Andover*, 248.

[4] Andover Newton Papers, Lecture 1. Stuart's colleague, the theologian Leonard Woods, handled the formal treatment of the doctrine of biblical authority as stipulated in the division of labor set forth in the Andover Constitution. Woods accepted and defended the doctrine of plenary inspiration, noting such matters as miracles and the testimonies of the "sacred writers" as proofs for his argument. In regard to the older concept of *verbal* inspiration, however, he noted that "according to the best philologists, [the] leading signification [of verbal] is, *'spoken; expressed to the ear in words; not written.'* But no one supposes, that when God inspired the sacred writers, he generally spoke to them in audible words.... His influence was *inward.*" (*Works* [Andover, MA: J. D. Flagg, 1849] 1:98.) Yet later in the same work, Woods makes the point clear that the writings are still God's *word:* "for ... God so influenced the sacred writers, that they wrote just *what* he intended, and in the *manner* he intended; ... and what they wrote is as truly *his* word, as though he had written it with his own hand on tables of stone, without any human instrumentality" (162). In regard to authority, he noted, in comparing scriptural revelation to reason, "we have ... only one question;

The norm thus established, Stuart next considered the relationship of sacred to secular hermeneutics. He agreed that the Bible is difficult to interpret because of its lofty subject material, obscurity of language, variety of styles, difference in revelation between the Old and New Testaments, and numerous contradictions; but almost in the same breath he insisted that the Bible is subject to the identical principles of interpretation as other books or, for that matter, language in general. Hence, from the outset we note his acceptance of a cardinal principle of the grammatical-historical school: The Bible was written in human language which was meant to be understood. It would otherwise be no revelation—unless it were insisted that the interpreter must "rely on inspiration alone to come to the sense of the biblical writers." "Everything which pertains to the externals of the Sacred Scripture is human in its manner. . . . The Bible was written by human pens, in letters of human alphabets, on parchment prepared by hands of men [and] with such ink as is employed for other writings." Still, Stuart hastened to add: "Though the *manner* was human, the *matter* is of divine authority."[5]

Stuart steered a careful course between interpretations either coldly rationalistic or irresponsibly enthusiastic. The crux of the issue lay in his positive view of divine inspiration. But Stuart did not develop his ideas on inspiration any more than he did those on the wider topic of authority. His hints in the lectures about revelation, expanded in other writings, show that he rejected literal verbal inspiration, in keeping with his grammatical-historical emphasis on the human. He could not believe that the "sacred writers" were "mere instruments in the hands of the Spirit of God, as a musical instrument is in the hands of him who plays upon it." To suggest such a belief would amount to a denial that the "writers were . . . the authors, in the usual sense of that word," of what they themselves had written.[6]

At the same time, and this must be noted with considerable emphasis, Stuart held firmly to the doctrine of plenary inspiration. But he did not deny that the writers were possessed of "their own consciousness [and] voluntary rational agency."[7] They were moved directly, though never in the sense of mere automatons, by a special "*divine* influence, . . . *which guarded them*

---

and this is, what the God of truth says. . . . The simple fact, *that God declares it*, is the highest possible evidence of its truth" (187). That Stuart agreed, in spite of minor variations, will be seen in the course of this chapter.

[5] Andover Newton Papers, Lecture 2. Stuart declared the identical point in an article entitled "Are the Same Principles of Interpretation to Be Applied to the Scriptures as to Other Books?" *American Biblical Repository* 2 (January 1832) 129.

[6] Stuart, "Remarks on Hahn's Definition of Interpretation and some Topics connected with it," *American Biblical Repository* 1 (January 1831) 143.

[7] Ibid.

against error or mistake when they composed the sacred books."[8]

Thus, for Stuart, the scriptures were authoritative and inspired, while yet amenable to interpretation with rational rules of exegesis, as one would interpret any human literary achievement. In fact, his understanding of inspiration enhanced the reasonable aspect of the Bible. Stuart noted that *because* "the Bible contains a revelation from God, designed for the use of all men . . . we have entire security" that the authors always used their language "in the most rational manner. [Therefore] we may argue from the nature of the case presented, that the rules of exegesis will apply to the Bible preeminently above all other books."[9] Because the Bible is divine revelation, its language is the same as that of any other book. But not all of the hermeneutical principles that apply to the Bible apply also to other writings. Every writer has unique characteristics, especially the inspired writers of the Bible.[10]

Next, Stuart examined objections and competing systems, beginning with the problem of subjectivism and the work of the Holy Spirit in the mind of the interpreter. Does the presence of the Holy Spirit suspend the rational processes? Stuart did not deny that the internal teaching of the Holy Spirit was necessary to apprehend the more profound revelations of the Bible. "The humble Christian . . . by entering into the spirit of those who wrote the Scriptures, and acquiring feelings similar to those which they possess . . . obtains one of the highest qualifications to understand their writings." But this does not eliminate the simple truth that all persons by natural ability are able to "understand every rule of doctrine and practice contained in the Bible. If they do not see the light, it is "because they shut their eyes, and will not see it." Even the unregenerate, with no experience of the gospel, can know something about it. "I have never tasted of the banana," noted Stuart, "but I know enough from the description of others concerning it to make it appear a very desirable fruit." By the same token, "the sinner knows enough concerning religion, to conclude, that it gives happiness which the world can neither give nor take away."[11] In a summary paragraph he stated his conclusion:

> That illumination and guidance are promised to humble inquirers after heavenly wisdom, is a most delightful truth, by no means to be obscured or surrendered. But that the Bible contains such revelation from God, as may be understood in every thing not strictly experimental, by all men, who use in a proper manner their reason and understanding, is equally plain. To abandon this truth, would be to palliate the guilt of men who reject the Sacred Scriptures; to detract from the sufficiency of the Bible;

[8] Stuart, *Hints on the Interpretation of Prophecy* (Andover, MA: Allen, Morrill, & Wardwell, 1842) 15.

[9] Andover Newton Papers, Lectures on Hermeneutics, No. 2.

[10] Ibid.

[11] Ibid.

and to render inspiration as necessary to every individual, in order that he might understand the Sacred Scriptures, as it was to those who wrote them. Of what use is a written revelation to the world, which is unintelligible without new miracles, in every case where it is understood: And where is the guilt of those, who do not see, what cannot be seen, without a miraculous interposition on the part of heaven?[12]

Stuart next considered various dogmatic systems of interpretation. Catholic sacerdotalism he quickly rejected because he affirmed the private "right and obligation" of all persons to interpret the scriptures for themselves. As for Protestants, Stuart denied no one the right to identify with party or creed, but he insisted that laws of exegesis based on reason are more important than those based on superimposed rule or *"analogy of faith"*:

A man, who is to bind my faith or any body of men who are to regulate it, must produce either the authority of inspiration, or of reason and argument to do it. My rights to interpret the Bible can never be surrendered to any man; to *command* me, he must have a commission from heaven; to *lead* me, he must shew me the path of reason and argument.[13]

Symbols of faith freely believed are useful, however, for they give coherence and unity to the scriptures as a whole. "If I find doctrines clearly revealed in one part of the Scriptures, or rather, perhaps, in the writings of any particular author, and in another part of the same author's writings, I find something which may seem to be discrepant, but is obscure; then I interpret an *obscure* place, by the aid of one that is *clear*."[14] With all scripture accepted as revelation, this rule extends to the whole Bible.

Here Stuart moved directly into the related problems of biblical unity and inerrancy. Again he struggled to maintain the delicate balance between the authority of the Bible as the fully inspired word of God and the authority of reason to interpret this revelation. He noted at once that the "analogy of faith" cannot dominate the laws of philology and seek to make contradictory passages say the same thing. Yet this posed the fundamental question: Are there really such passages in the Bible? "I answer without hesitation, so far as I understand them, there does not appear to be any. Defective views of one part of the Scriptures may make another part appear contradictory; but the more extensive any person's knowledge of the Bible

[12] Ibid. See also Stuart, "Principles of Interpretation," 135, 136. Here Stuart expands the point, noting that *"religious feeling"* is as necessary to an understanding of "the meaning of the sacred writers," as is "poetic feeling" to an understanding of Milton, or a "mathematical feeling" to a comprehension of La Place. However, "a great part of the Bible is addressed to rational, moral beings as such. All men belong to this class; and because this is so, they are capable of understanding the sacred writers, at least so far as they are designed originally to be understood by all, and so far as the great purposes of warning and instruction are concerned."
[13] Ibid.
[14] Ibid.

is, the more he will see of the real harmony of all its separate parts."[15]

The context in which he raised the question, however, suggests that Stuart approached the problem with less assurance than his answer indicates; and it is important to note that he was not wholly above suspicion. Though Stuart and Leonard Woods agreed on most fundamentals, Woods felt that Stuart was occasionally loose in his statements on plenary inspiration, and Woods remarked in his *History of Andover* that Stuart "freely expressed his opinions on the subject in his lecture room, and hinted at them in some of his publications."[16] Such "hints" were not easy to discern, though Stuart's stress on the "human," for instance, in his articles on hermeneutics, supported the stronger evidence that, according to Woods, emanated from the classroom. But however much Stuart may have strayed earlier, by the end of his life his orthodoxy no longer stood in doubt. In his *Critical History and Defense of the Old Testament Canon,* one of his last major works, he argued that despite minor errors and discrepancies in the ancient texts that have survived, "it does not follow that the Bible in its origin, is not a divine book. ... Some things of comparatively small moment have been disturbed," he continued, "or by mistake in transcribers or redactors subjected to error; [but] not one doctrine is changed by all this; not one duty affected, not even the relation of any one historic event has been so disturbed, that the moral impression which it was designed to make is in any important degree subverted.[17] He went on to observe that though upwards of 800,000 readings had been detected in the Hebrew manuscripts already examined, the great mass of such errors amount to nothing more than the difference in spelling "a multitude of English words" — such as *"honour* or *honor."*[18] Thus Stuart readily held for the plenary inspiration of the autographs of the scriptures. But this by no means demanded verbal infallibility as a corollary. In fact, he set the two concepts clearly apart. Verbal infallibility is an "antiquated view of the subject that *'humanum est errare.'"* Still, plenary inspiration holds. Such errors as do appear in the Bible are of no serious import against "the claims ... of the Scriptures ... as the stable ground of our belief, and confidence and obedience."[19]

[15] Ibid.
[16] Woods, *History of Andover,* 153.
[17] Stuart, *Critical History and Defense,* 191.
[18] Ibid., 192.
[19] Ibid., 192–94. Much of the strength of Stuart's emphasis in this issue depended upon the side toward which his remarks were being directed at any particular time. This is illustrated in his last published article, in which some of the German "neologists" are taken to task for their views on inspiration. *"Our all is at stake in the Bible,"* he noted. "As surely as its *inspiration* is set aside, and our people are taught that enlightened views demand them to give it up, so surely is there an end to all evangelical religion among the mass; and all the authoritative power of the Bible will cease thence forth to be recognized." Though he would not deny the personal piety of such men as Neander and Tholuck, he considered their acknowledgment of "errors of fact, of science, ... and of discrepancy and contradiction among the various

Having thus treated dogmatic forms of interpretation, Stuart turned next to a discussion of "mystical and spiritual" methods. Though he refused to call into question the piety of the church fathers, or even of later writers who delved into allegory, numerology, and mysticism, he nevertheless believed such readings of the Bible to be faulty and therefore injurious to truth. "It is never proper to use unlawful means in promoting a good cause," he wrote, "and if the temporary interests of piety can be served by mystical exegesis; the ultimate injury to the cause of truth (if mystical exegesis be not well grounded) must be greater than will be compensated, by all the good which it may have accomplished."[20] Again, a crucial truth stands behind the definition of "revelation": unless the writer is "designedly composing enigmas ... [he] intends to be understood by his readers."[21] No rule of interpretation is possible unless this principle be admitted.

This for Stuart was most true in the interpretation of prophecy, which, of all his hermeneutical interests, received his greatest attention. Stuart's main point, that biblical prophecy does not contain mystical or double meanings, was simple. Those who believe that it does and cite their evidence from the *post facto* clarification that the fulfillment of predictions sometimes brings argue from incorrect presuppositions. "The mistake ... lies in this; that they argue from a better understanding of the *subject* of the prophecy, to the prediction itself; and from a more *lively* impression of the energy of the prophetic words, to a *different meaning* of them. This, however, can never establish a double sense, in the words themselves."[22] To believe otherwise is to argue in a circle.

In a later article, Stuart countered the view of Ernst W. Hengstenberg, who argued for a double sense in prophecy on the basis of a presumed visitation of the spirit upon the prophets. In genuine prophecy, said Hengstenberg, the human soul goes out of the prophet and the Spirit of God comes in as its replacement. It is possible, Hengstenberg argued, that the

---

writers of the scriptures" to be dangerous to many of their readers and to "the undiscriminating multitude of men. . . . The ground once abandoned, which Paul has taken, that all SCRIPTURE IS GIVEN BY INSPIRATION OF GOD, everyman of common attainments will feel at liberty to say whatever his own subjective feelings may dictate; to say, 'this is unimportant, that is a contradictory one; this is in opposition to science, and that to reason; this may be pruned, and that lopped off while the tree may still remain as good as ever. . . . What now has become of the book of God, true, authoritative, decisive of all duty, and all matters of faith? Gone, absolutely gone, irretrievably gone, as to the mass of men who are not philosophizers in casuistry and in the things of religion" ("Hebrew Criticisms: Ps. 22:7," *Bibliotheca Sacra* 9 [January 1852] 66–69). Woods claimed this statement to be a recantation of Stuart's earlier views, but there is little different here, other than the degree of emphasis, from what he had been saying all along. See Woods, *History of Andover*, 153–54.

[20] Lectures on Hermeneutics, Lecture 4.
[21] Ibid.
[22] Ibid.

prophets could not themselves have understood what the Spirit of God was really saying through them. Such an idea Stuart categorically rejected. The human soul is not in exile. It is the very image of God. There is no "fitter residence" for God's Spirit. Citing Bishop Lowth, he observed "that inspiration may be regarded not as suppressing, or extinguishing for a time the faculties of the human mind, but of purifying, and strengthening, and elevating them above what they would otherwise reach." "Can anything," Stuart queried, "be more rational than this?"[23]

In all, Stuart's main proposition in each of his discussions of prophecy, from Lecture 4 of his hermeneutics series in 1822 through his *Hints on the Interpretation of Prophecy* in 1842, reaffirmed his second lecture. Revelation, by definition, whether prophecy or not, must be intelligible in its single, literal sense, both to the writer and to the interpreter.

This principle of the single sense Stuart applied without undue elaboration to allegory and typology. Allegory must be understood merely as figurative language and nothing more. As for types, the interpreter must always distinguish between the ceremonies, transactions, and "things" of an event, and the words describing them. Such a type as the sacrifice of the paschal lamb is an emblem designed to teach the Jews "the necessity and virtue" of the atonement. It is therefore in its action valid and useful. But the language describing the event "is never a type; never can be. Only persons and things can be types. The language then of the Old Testament which describes *things* that are typical, has no double sense, and is not to be interpreted in a manner different from that of any other part of the Bible."[24]

Having developed his hermeneutical principles, Stuart turned to the laws of grammatical-historical exegesis. The grammatical-historical method, he noted, "demands that everything belonging to grammar, rhetoric and history ... be considered in giving an interpretation to any passage." Thus it "comprehends all, which strictly speaking, is a matter of scientifical, philological research."[25] For meaningful interpretation, he

---

[23] Stuart, "On the Alleged Obscurity of Prophecy," *American Biblical Repository* 2 (April 1832) 221–22, 227–28. Stuart also refuted Hengstenberg's contention that just as the prophets were often obscure about the nature of events that they predicted, so they were regarding the time in which the events would occur. Stuart noted that most of the prophecies were not intended to speak in this manner. "God revealed *facts* to his people, but often he did not reveal the time or manner of these facts. What he did reveal, was plain and intelligible; what he did not reveal, was of course not to be understood; but then how could or why should it be?" (Ibid., 237–38). Hengstenberg's views appeared in *American Biblical Repository* 2 (January 1832) 138–73, in an article entitled "On the Nature of Prophecy," which was translated by James F. Warner from *Christologie des Alten Testaments* (Berlin: L. Oehmigke, 1829).

[24] Lectures on Hermeneutics, Lecture 4.

[25] Ibid., Lecture 6. The manuscript collection of lectures in hermeneutics contains no Lecture 5. It would seem, however, that since there appears to be no break in continuity from

would add the dimension of subjective experience. So conceived as a method, and having as its object the discovery and true representation of the sense of any written and spoken language, hermeneutics was amenable to scientific organization by specific rules.

Here Stuart appropriated the grammatical principles of Ernesti, together with what he felt to be the best of Semler's historical approach, and synthesized them. Stuart outlined the grammatical considerations, which could be framed in one general rule: the interpreter must "interpret the language of any writer, agreeably to the *usus loquendi,* or customary sense of words, in the language, in which he writes."[26] Such a rule demands that each writing be interpreted with regard to the age and nation of the writer and to the writer's style and sense. Specifically, it requires two careful pursuits: (1) the search for the meaning of *words* — through attention to etymology, context, scope of the discourse, parallel passages, tactic parallelism, kindred dialects, versions, lexicons, and grammars; and (2) a search for the meaning of *things* — through attention to "whatever belongs to the circle of Hebrew archeology; which comprises civil History, Geography, Chronology, natural History, agriculture, cult and manufactures, Religion, Literature, philosophy, and manners and customs both religious and civil."[27] In short, all that would apply toward establishing the *literal* sense of any writing applies to the Bible.

For historical investigation Stuart proposed two rules. The first demanded a knowledge of the audience to which the writings were first addressed. The interpreter must *"interpret a writer agreeably to the spirit of his works, in reference to the views, opinions, and circumstances of those, for whom his work was originally designed."* The rule was important for interpreting the New Testament, a work which is best "understood in the light of the surrounding Jewish community." The second rule demanded a knowledge of the author. *"We must regard the whole character and circumstance of an author, in explaining his compositions.* His lineage, education, condition, occupation, manners, opinions, in a word, his whole character, contributes to give coloring to his writings and to influence his style." This was the rule Stuart believed to be most often slighted by his contemporaries. He wearied at the multitude of scholars who tried to make the biblical writers speak in modern language and thought. Citing an example close to home (undoubtedly the Unitarian controversy was in his mind), he noted the incongruity of trying to make John express himself in the "metaphysics and philosophy of the present day . . . as though he really had in his eye, the disputes on these subjects by which our times are agitated."

Lecture 4 to Lecture 6, Stuart either revised the series, adding 5 to 4 or 6, or simply misnumbered at this point.

[26] Ibid.

[27] Ibid., Lecture 7.

On the other hand, the attempts to explain John, "a humble fisherman educated on the shores of the lake Gennesareth as if he were deeply versed in
the Platonic philosophy, the writings of Philo, and the mysteries of Gnosti-
cism . . . are equally preposterous . . . and yet, how many books are filled
with expositions of this writer, built upon such a basis!"[28]

Equally disturbing was the attempt to accept or reject the authority
of the biblical writers on the basis of modern science. Given the nature and
tone of the ensuing nineteenth-century conflicts between science and religion, Stuart's argument is of significance:

> Divine Revelation was not designed to teach geography or physics, or
> astronomy, or chemistry; nor did it any more control the popular *notions*
> of the Jews about ghosts, and the regions of the dead, than it has done
> ours. What if the sacred writers had spoken in language borrowed from
> Ebeling, on geography; Newton, on physics and astronomy; Berthollet,
> on Chemistry; or many writers of our times, on the subject of ghosts and
> apparitions? First, who of their age would have understood them? Next,
> what had they to do, with teaching geography, or physics. . . . When
> men learn, that a revelation from God respects religion, not the sciences,
> then they will be content to ascribe to every writer the opinions of his
> times which do not pertain to the subject of religion and to interpret him
> in a manner that accords with this. . . . Let every writer be placed in his
> own age, and if possible, transfer yourself back there, with him. View
> him in writing the Sacred Scriptures as teaching religion, not science and
> then you are disembarrassed, in a moment, of a thousand perplexities.
> The sacred writers refer to subjects of science, just as all other writers do,
> agreeably to the views of their days. What can be more unreasonable,
> than to demand, that because a writer is inspired to teach religion,
> therefore he is inspired to have a perfect knowledge of all the arts and
> sciences? The difficulties attending such a supposition are insuperable.
> And after all, what matters it to me, whether David understood the
> Newtonian Philosophy; or John the metaphysics of Locke, or Kant? If
> David or John have undertaken to give instruction on the subjects, this
> is one thing; but if they have not, but have merely touched them in the
> popular way (as we speak at the present moment of the sun's rising and
> setting), then that is another.
> These considerations may lead us readily to ascribe to every sacred
> writer, views on such subjects consonant with his character and his age—
> and to reject the monstrous exegesis which explains him as though he
> spoke but yesterday and with all our feelings and prejudices. What can
> make greater difficulties in interpretation than this; and what can be
> more unreasonable and unjust![29]

Here Stuart struck a new note in modern hermeneutics. It was a theme he
would reiterate effectively in his discussions of Genesis and geology.

With this he had completed his hermeneutical system. Such principles,
taught at Andover and exemplified in Stuart's exegetical and theological

---

[28] Ibid., Lecture 6.
[29] Ibid.

writings, raised orthodox biblical criticism in America to a new and stimulating level. Stuart never questioned the propriety of the claim that historical criticism and biblical authority should march hand in hand. It was
fundamental to his work that they were united. Yet Stuart's system of interpretation stood in tension with his heritage. Though he never denied the
dogmas of New England theology, his hermeneutical principles supported
an interpretation which not only transcended but, in the eyes of many,
undermined that theology's most stringent symbol, Andover's own creed.

Stuart's work was, however, never a conscious negation. It pointed to
a theological reconstruction based on the Bible as the master, not the slave,
of the interpreter. Certain perceptive contemporaries could see the trend
better than Stuart himself, and in this movement they rejoiced. The method
of instruction that Stuart had imparted, noted Leonard Bacon, would lead
to a new theology— "fundamentally scriptural, and therefore free of a
catholic spirit."[30] The time was not quite ripe for the realization of Bacon's
vision, for the extremes of the rationalist grammatical-historical critics had
yet to run a long and sometimes bizarre course. But Bacon was at least
partially correct. Stuart had laid the scientific, yet evangelical, foundations
of the biblical theology upon which others would later build.

[30] Bacon, "Moses Stuart," 54.

V

THE THEOLOGICAL CONTROVERSIALIST

Unitarianism

Moses Stuart's biblical researches, buttressed by the conviction that the Bible would yield authentic testimony to Christian truth, could not be contained by his limited, though not inconsequential, duties as a philologist and commentator. As his fame as an exegete increased, so did the importance of his exegetical studies to theological and social issues. The Unitarian controversy, the great crisis that had already led to the founding of Andover Seminary, was the first to engage the scholar's attention.

While still a pastor in New Haven, Stuart had exhibited some interest in the controversy which was then creating theological parties in and around Boston. Though removed from the scene of the skirmish, he was in correspondence with his orthodox friend Jedidiah Morse, pastor in Charlestown, Massachusetts, and he identified himself with Morse's party and did what could be done from Connecticut.

He was eager to find articles for Morse's partisan journal, *The Panoplist,* and went so far as to submit a "piece" of his own, no longer extant.[1] His move to Andover early in 1810 placed him both geographically and ideologically close to the center of the struggle, but even here the heavy burden of teaching during the first years prevented his active involvement in the affair. Not until late in the decade was he finally drawn into the public controversy, but when he was, with the publication in 1819 of his *Letters to the Rev. Wm. E. Channing,* he moved to the center of the conflict, where he was recognized as one of a handful of orthodoxy's most able defenders.[2]

The occasion was William Ellery Channing's public admission and defense of Unitarianism. Channing's instrument was his famous *Sermon Delivered at the Ordination of Rev. Jared Sparks,* delivered and published in Baltimore in 1819. Though relatively brief considering its importance, the sermon marked the culmination of more than a half-century of increasingly pointed criticisms of Calvinist doctrines raised by a succession of

---

[1] See correspondence from Stuart to Morse, 11 May, 3 June, 16 June, and 25 June 1809, Morse family papers, Yale University.

[2] Stuart, *Letters to the Rev. Wm. E. Channing, Containing Remarks on His Sermon Recently Preached and Published at Baltimore* (Andover, MA: Flagg & Gould, 1819).

influential preachers, most of whom were Harvard graduates living in and around Boston. Joining in the trend, Channing not only accepted the pejorative appellation of "Unitarian" but also openly outlined its major tenets and claimed for them both rational justification and scriptural support. Unnerving to the Calvinist traditionalists whom Channing opposed was his insistence on the primacy of reason and of the scriptures reasonably interpreted, over against biblical literalism and Calvinist creedalism, including the creed of Andover. On this ground Channing proposed to organize the liberal position. The result was the first significant outline of American liberal theology. The immediate effect was to raise the controversy to a new level, for in this public revelation of their principles, the liberals provoked the Calvinists to a first-rate response. The orthodox looked to Andover, now established as the seat of Calvinist learning. Dividing the task between them, both Moses Stuart and Leonard Woods responded.

Channing's work was organized in two sections, principles of scriptural interpretation and doctrines of God and Christ. Channing noted his high regard for the scriptures "as the record of God's successive revelation of his will by Jesus Christ. Whatever doctrines seem to us to be clearly taught in the Scriptures, we receive without reserve or exception."[3] But his next sentence introduced a qualification. "Clearly taught" meant comprehensible by ordinary reason. Human reason is necessary to catch the "infinite connexions and dependencies" in revelation, to interpret the figurative language, "to compare, to infer, to look beyond the letter to the spirit," and to discover new truth. Reason is a valid authority and should not be depreciated and cast aside in favor of a credulous acceptance of contradiction and error. If reason be depraved, and if the Bible contains contradictory and obscure "truths" beyond the grasp of reason, "then Christianity, and even natural theology must be abandoned; for the very existence and veracity of God, and the divine original of Christianity, are conclusions of reason and must stand or fall with it."[4] Moreover, it is God's own plan as a skillful pedagogue that we understand the revelation God has given to us.[5]

Channing next discussed the doctrines derived from the scriptures, the first being that of the unity or oneness of God. Scripture both affirms this truth and denies traditional trinitarian assertions:

> The proposition, *that there is one God*, seems to us exceedingly plain. We understand by it, that there is one being, one mind, one person, one intelligent agent, and one only, to whom undeprived and infinite perfection and dominion belong. . . . We find no intimation, that this language

[3] William Ellery Channing, *A Sermon Delivered at the Ordination of the Rev. Jared Sparks* (Baltimore, MD: J. Robinson, 1819) 4.
[4] Ibid., 10.
[5] Ibid., 12–13.

was to be taken in an unusual sense, or that God's unity was a quite different thing from the oneness of other intelligent beings. . . . We are astonished that any man can read the New Testament, and avoid the conviction that the Father alone is God. Always Father and Son are distinguished. We challenge our opponents to adduce one passage in the New Testament, where the word God means three persons, where it is not limited to one person, and where, unless turned from its usual sense by the connexion, it does not mean the Father.[6]

Likewise, Channing declared for the singular unity of Christ. "We believe that Jesus is one mind, one soul, one being, as truly as we are, and equally distinct from the one God."[7]

To denominate him one person, one being, and yet to suppose him made up of two minds, infinitely different from each other, is to abuse and confound language, and to throw darkness over all our conceptions of intelligent natures. . . . The doctrine, that one and the same person should have two consciousnesses, two wills, two souls infinitely different from each other, this we think an enormous tax on human credulity.[8]

As in his discussion of God's unity, Channing referred the problem to the New Testament. It was a clear challenge. "We ask our brethren to point to some plain, direct passage, where Christ is said to be composed of two minds infinitely different, yet constituting one person. We find none." There are indeed texts which ascribe to Jesus divine properties, but we need not suppose two minds to accept these. This is to try to "find our way out of a labyrinth by a clue, which conducts us into mazes infinitely more inextricable."[9]

On the other hand, the passages that speak of Jesus as the Son of God, or as being sent from God, give abundant evidence for the doctrine of unity. If we examine these passages, Channing continued, "we shall see that they not only speak of him as another being, but seem to labour to express his inferiority."[10] To be sure, Jesus had received God's power, but this did not make him *very* God. Passages that refer to Christ as God Channing explained as analogous to other texts referring to humans as gods. Nowhere does Channing state more clearly the primacy of reason:

These latter passages we do not hesitate to modify, and restrain, and turn from the most obvious sense, because this sense is opposed to the known properties of the beings to whom they relate; and we maintain, that we adhere to the same principle, and use no greater latitude in explaining,

[6] Ibid., 13–14, 15.
[7] Ibid., 15.
[8] Ibid., 20.
[9] Ibid., 21.
[10] Ibid., 22–23.

as we do, the passages which are thought to support the Godhead of Christ.[11]

He discussed two more doctrines, the "moral perfection of God" and Christian virtue. Leonard Woods agreed to reply to Channing's arguments, leaving Stuart to concentrate his attention on the biblical issues.[12]

Before the year 1819 was out, Stuart's *Letters to the Rev. Wm. E. Channing* appeared. His rebuttal began with a lengthy quote from Channing, which professed agreement in principle with the rules of interpretation Channing had outlined, but urged modifications at two points. The first was Channing's subordination of the Old Testament to the New Testament. Stuart wished that the value of the Old Testament "had been described in somewhat different terms," for in spite of the clearer revelation in the New Testament, we are not absolved from our obligations to the Old. Nor should the great devotional sections of this work be set aside or diminished.[13]

More important, however, was Stuart's criticism of the status Channing had assigned to reason in interpretation. Stuart would not reject reason entirely. It is to our reason, he noted, "that the arguments which prove the divine origin of Christianity are addressed; and it is by reason that we prove or admit this origin, on general historical grounds." Reason "develops and sanctions" the laws of interpretation. Nevertheless, Stuart believed Channing to have overstated the case. Once one had admitted that the scriptures had divine authority as the word of God, "the sole office of reason in respect to them is to act as the *interpreter* of Revelation, and not in any case as a legislator."[14] Despite the initial appearance of agreement, then, Stuart and Channing differed profoundly—more, in fact, than Stuart seemed able to understand, even with this admission.

Granting the divine authority of the Bible, which Stuart understood Channing still to admit, and allowing for the secondary rules of interpretation that we have discussed, Stuart held that the abiding exegetical question was "What does the Bible say?" rather than "Is what the Bible says reasonable?" Thus, although Stuart's views on the Trinity and Christology were important, he never engaged Channing on the all-important hermeneutical issues from which the conflicting doctrinal expositions developed.

Stuart proceeded to Channing's position on the Trinity, including its definition and identification. He began by noting that Channing had been unfair in his description of the traditional trinitarian position. "I cannot

[11] Ibid., 24.
[12] Leonard Woods, *Letters to Unitarians* (Andover, MA: Flagg & Gould, 1820; included in *Works* [Andover. MA: J. D. Flagg, 1850] 4:1–121).
[13] Stuart, *Letters to the Rev. Wm. E. Channing*, 7–9.
[14] Ibid., 11.

help feeling that you have made neither an impartial nor a correct statement of what we are accustomed to teach and defend,"[15] he complained,
and he urged Channing to grant the Trinitarians the same liberty as the
Unitarians in the use of terms. The Trinitarians are concerned with subjects
that must be discussed in *"figurative* language," and they ought not be
denied the same freedom "which all men take on difficult subjects, for the
accurate description of which language is not framed, perhaps is not in its
nature adequate."[16] The orthodox do affirm the numerical unity of God.
But at the same time they claim that "the Son (and also the Holy Spirit)
does in some respect, *truly* and *really,* not merely nominally or logically,
differ from the Father."[17]

Stuart's problem now was to meet Channing's objection that the *real*
existence of the Son and Spirit is inconsistent with the *numerical* unity in
the Godhead. To justify this seeming contradiction, Stuart, like Trinitarians
since at least the third century, turned to a discussion of the word "person"
and urged upon the Unitarians the traditional Nicene and Chalcedonian
interpretations of the term as denoting a real distinction in the Godhead,
without describing "independent, conscious beings, possessing *separate* and
equal essences, and *perfections":*

> We speak of *persons* in the Godhead, to express that which in some
> respect or other corresponds to *persons* as applied to men, i.e. some
> *distinction; not* that we attach to it the meaning of three beings, with a
> *separate* consciousness, will, omnipotence, omniscience etc. Where then
> is our inconsistency in this, or the absurdity of our language; provided
> there is a real foundation in the Scriptures, on which we may rest the *fact*
> of a distinction, that we believe to exist?[18]

The reference to the scriptures shows how important Stuart's hermeneutical orientation was for the issue. He made no apologies for his conservative biblicistic position, and nowhere did he state it more directly:

> *I receive the* FACT *that* [a distinction] *exists, simply because I believe
> that the Scriptures reveal the* FACT. And if the Scriptures do reveal the
> fact, that there are three *persons* in the Godhead, (in the sense ex-
> plained;) . . . then it is, like every other fact revealed, to be received
> simply on the credit of divine revelation.[19]

---

[15] Ibid., 15.

[16] Ibid., 17–18. That Channing's interpretation of New England trinitarianism was partially correct must be admitted. As Frank Hugh Foster points out, "almost all of the phrases
to which Channing objects are to be found in [Nathaniel] Emmons, as well as in many a lesser
light of orthodoxy" (*A Genetic History of the New England Theology* [Chicago: University
of Chicago Press, 1907] 290). However, the extremes of Emmons and the "lesser lights" were
not representative.

[17] Stuart, *Letters to the Rev. Wm. E. Channing,* 19.

[18] Ibid., 22–23.

[19] Ibid., 24.

The results of Stuart's argument thus far were twofold. First, his reliance on the divine authority of scripture removed the discussion from the realm of purely speculative thinking, especially when he discussed the unity of Christ; and, second, his theory of language, especially as applied to the word "person," tended to blur rather than sharpen the distinctions being defended. It was, as Frank Hugh Foster noted, "a form of statement in which there could be nothing to quarrel about because it was so low and indistinct."[20]

Stuart was not altogether unaware that his argument had left the doctrine of the Trinity without precise form, and he offered some negative statements in clarification.

> In regard to this distinction, [in the Trinity] we say, *It is not a mere distinction of attributes, of relation to us, of modes of action, or of relation between attributes and substance or essence*, so far as they are known to us. We believe the Scriptures justify us in these *negations*. But *here* we leave the subject. We undertake, (at least the Trinitarians of our country with whom I am acquainted undertake) *not* at all to describe *affirmatively* the distinction in the Godhead. When you will give me an affirmative description of *underived* existence, I may safely engage to furnish you with one of *person* in the Trinity. You do not reject the belief of self existence, merely because you cannot *affirmatively* define it; neither do we of a distinction in the Godhead, because we cannot *affirmatively* define it.[21]

No one, he correctly pointed out, has ever been able to form an adequate affirmative definition of the distinctions—the fact of their existence, yes, but their nature, no. Indeed, the Unitarians are just as presumptive in their attempts to define the *unity* of God as Trinitarians are the distinctions:

> Familiar as the assertion is, in your conversation and in your Sermons, that God is ONE, can you give me any other definition of this *oneness*, except a negative one? Is it possible to show, what constitutes the *internal nature* of the divine essence, or attributes; or how they are related to each other; or what internal distinctions exist? Of all this, Revelation says not one word; certainly the book of nature gives no instruction concerning it. The assertion then that God is one, can never be fairly understood as meaning any thing more, than that he is *numerically one;* i.e. it simply denies polytheism, and never can reach beyond this[22]

One further argument of the Unitarians remained to be considered in this section. They had asked quite simply: "How can three be one and one three?" Once more the answer rests solely on biblical authority:

> *We do not maintain that the Godhead is three in the same respects that it is one, but the reverse.* . . . Suppose I should affirm that two subjects,

[20] Foster, *A Genetic History*, 292–93.
[21] Stuart, *Letters to the Rev. Wm. E. Channing*, 25–26.
[22] Ibid., 38–39.

> A and B, are numerically identical in regard to what may be called X,
> but diverse, or distinct, in regard to something else called Y; is there any
> absurdity, or contradiction in this affirmation? ... *We do not maintain*
> *that the Godhead is three in the same respects that it is one, but the*
> *reverse.* In regard to X, we maintain its numerical unity; in regard to Y,
> we maintain a three-fold distinction; I repeat it, *we maintain simply the*
> *fact that there is such a distinction, on Scripture authority.* We do not
> profess to understand in what it consists.[23]

After dealing with the problem of the unity and distinctions in the Godhead, Stuart tackled Channing's challenge concerning the proper understanding of the personhood of Christ. Again, for Stuart, the biblical evidence is clear and absolute: *"The New Testament gives to Christ the appellation of God; and in such a manner that, according to the fair rules of interpretation, only the SUPREME GOD can be meant."*[24] He cited passage after passage to support this declaration, made note of textual variants when these threatened to alter correct readings, and offered a careful and ample defense of his position. The section is divided into three parts: texts in which Christ is called God;[25] those "which attribute to Christ equality with God, or that power and dignity or honor which belong to God";[26] and texts that "assert or imply, that particular divine attributes or works" — omniscience, omnipotence, etc. — "belong to him."[27]

In like manner, he discussed the scriptural proofs of the humanity of Christ, noting ironically that in Channing's sermon he "was not able to find an intimation that Christ was truly and properly a man," adding that "if the evidence be not overwhelming ... I cannot conceive it possible, that any point in theology or morals is capable of being established." Stuart would have no room for the "Docetae," "Gnostics," or "Arians."[28] Once more the New Testament provided the basic witness.

The concluding words of Stuart's work addressed the hermeneutical issue. Channing's rationalism, dangerous as it might be, may yet be tempered by the checks of his "former education and belief" and may yet safeguard him "against the bolder conclusions of some of your brethren, who have not been placed under instruction such as you enjoyed in early life." The thought of these less constrained folk vexed Stuart:

> You have more serious views of the importance of religion, than many,
> perhaps most of those who speculate with you. Consistency too, will

[23] Ibid., 40–41.

[24] Ibid., 57.

[25] I.e., John 1:1, 10; Heb 1:10–12; Col 1:15–17; Rom 9:5; John 5:20; *Letters to the Rev. Wm. E. Channing*, 57–93.

[26] I.e., Phil 2:5–8; John 5:19; 17:10; 15:17, 21–23; *Letters to the Rev. Wm. E. Channing*, 93–102.

[27] I.e., Matt 11:27; 1 Cor 4:4–5; Rev 2:23; Phil 3:21; John 1:1; 5:23; 17:5; Heb 1:6; *Letters to the Rev. Wm. E. Channing*, 103–18.

[28] Ibid., 132.

afford strong inducement not to give up the divine authority of the Scriptures. Yet many of your younger brethren have no inconsistency to fear, by adopting such views.... They will throw off the restraints which the old ideas of the inspiration and infallibility of the Scriptures impose upon them, and receive them simply on the ground, on which they place any other writings of a moral and religious nature.[29]

Thus, in his closing pages Stuart introduced the "argument from tendency," subsequently used by both sides in the Unitarian controversy, which shifted attention from the Unitarian formulations toward the presumed results of accepting such principles. In a sense, this was a diversionary tactic, but Stuart did not mean it so. If the tenets of Unitarianism, however rational and beautiful, led Christians to cast aside the authority of the word of God, the result demonstrated their inadequacy. Though Stuart accused no one in America of going so far, the evidence from abroad was cause for anxiety. He noted that in Germany "such rules of exegesis have been ... introduced, as make the Scripture speak *nolens volens* whatever any party may desire."[30] To prove his point, he had but to trace the history of German critical studies from Semler through G. W. Meyer.[31] To be sure, the Unitarians "do not at present avow or defend" such views, but neither did the Germans until "their numbers increased" and they became "fearless of consequences." When "their antagonists urged the laws of exegesis upon them, they abandoned the ground of defending the divine authenticity of the Bible at once."[32] The argument was two-edged, for Stuart was speaking not only to the Unitarians but also to members of his own party who viewed his use of the German "neologists" with alarm, and on occasion had suspected him of heresy because of what they considered his dangerous preoccupation with German critical studies. "It was whispered," Stuart recorded later,

> that I had not only secretly gone over to the Germans, but was leading the Seminary over with me, and bringing up, or at least encouraging, our young men to the study of deistical Rationalism; and, besides this, it was also whispered about, in a very significant way, that it was all the other professors could do to keep the Seminary from going over into Unitarianism.[33]

The affair was distressing to Stuart, for he had found much to admire in the Germans. The accusation that he had become Unitarian, based on guilt by association (inasmuch as Cambridge and Boston Unitarians were also reading the Germans) was particularly goading. The chance to bring up

[29] Ibid., 160–61.

[30] Stuart, *Letters to the Rev. Wm. E. Channing,* 161.

[31] Ibid., 162–66. Together with these two, Stuart notes the results of Eichhorn, C. F. Ammon, Johann Theiss, and G. L. Bauer, all of the naturalistic school.

[32] Ibid., 168.

[33] Stuart, "Letter to the Editor," 455.

the Germans in this context afforded him an opportunity both to deny, once and for all, the German extremes, and to affirm the positive values accrued from exposure to their writings. Stuart lost no time in calling the attention of suspicious colleagues to the latter point. Upon being congratulated by Ebeneezer Porter on the success of the *Letters to the Rev. Wm. E. Channing,* Stuart reminded his friend, who was aware of the criticism of Stuart, that the work never could have been written had he neglected to pursue his German studies.[34]

Insofar as the *Letters to the Rev. Wm. E. Channing* originated as a front line defense of orthodoxy, it was a decided success. It carried the day in volume of sales alone. The first edition sold out in a week, the second in almost as short a time; three editions appeared in the first year.[35] But more important, Stuart's exegetical arguments seemed sound and persuasive to the orthodox, who believed that Stuart had preserved the doctrines of the Trinity and the person of Christ for evangelical faith. Still, though the *faith* was preserved, evangelical *theology* was weakened, particularly the doctrine of the Trinity. As Foster observed, Stuart's minimal formulation of the Trinity caused it to lose "its place as the great fundamental doctrine of the system." Its apologetic value for defending doctrines of the eternity of God, creation, and the Christian consciousness of sin and redemption and "its constructive part in the erection of Christian theology, incarnation, atonement, and the rest" were gradually forgotten.[36] Stuart's theology was in no sense heretical. He affirmed all that needed to be affirmed, but he could not explain, nor did he apply. He was not creative.

Response to the *Letters to the Rev. Wm. E. Channing* divided along party lines, though little was done to advance the arguments from either side. Stuart contributed two further pieces, more to clarify the positions of his own party than to debate further with the Unitarians or to modify earlier points. One was a short article in the *Christian Spectator,*[37] the other a long pamphlet, *Letters on the Eternal Generation of the Son of God, addressed to Samuel Miller, D.D.* (Andover, MA: Flagg & Gould, 1822). His most interesting contribution was his later translation with notes of

---

[34] Ibid., 457. The suspicions were not entirely put to rest at this time. Woods noted that in 1825 the Board of Trustees appointed a committee to investigate the use of German works in teaching at Andover. The concern here was not that the study be abandoned, but that the professors remind their students to approach those books with "a degree of cautious interest" and that frequent mention be made to the students of the "reverance, meekness, simplicity, and implicit submission which should attend all their inquiries at the Divine Oracle, of the utter incompetence of human reason, as a religious guide, and of the danger of listening to the suggestions of infidel philosophy" (*History of Andover,* 177). It was a warning, not a chastisement, and the committee was careful to point out that it was "far from intimating a suspicion of any defect in past time."

[35] Moses Stuart, "Letter to the Editor," 457.

[36] Foster, *A Genetic History,* 300–301.

[37] Stuart, "Review Reviewed," *Christian Spectator* 6 (August 1821) 425–35.

Friedrich Schleiermacher's "Über den Gegensatz zwischen der sabelliani-
schen und der athanasianischen Vorstellung von der Trinität."[38] A modified
Sabellianism represented to Schleiermacher the only tenable formulation
of the trinitarian problem, and Stuart agreed, adding only that the reality
of the trinitarian distinctions lay in something deeper and more fundamental than the "hypostatic developments" described by Schleiermacher.
"From *eternity* existed that distinction in the Godhead which was developed in the economy of redemption."[39] Hence he could not give up the
eternal distinctions, even though the distinctions themselves could not be
properly defined. All reasonable clarification, he admitted, was impossible:

> Here then is TRINITY: and Trinity in its essential nature, from eternity
> to eternity. If you ask how this modification or property or distinction
> can be described, as it originally existed in the Godhead, my answer is,
> that we have no data by which we can make out a description. The fact
> of some distinction in the divine nature, which laid the foundation for
> the manifestations of the Trinity in the economy of redemption, we may
> and should fully admit. But to describe this seems not to be given to
> created intelligences who are of yesterday.[40]

Thus, from the *Letters to the Rev. Wm. E. Channing* through the discussion of Schleiermacher, Stuart's position remained unchanged.

It is difficult to measure the effect that his views on the Trinity had on
later American theology. But when one considers his own statement, plus
the fact that he introduced Schleiermacher's even more minimal position —
one that found American expression in the system of Horace Bushnell — it
can be safely said that Stuart's work contributed to the decline of the
importance of the doctrine in nineteenth-century New England theology.[41]
Indeed, his biblical defense won the victory, but the conquest left the
theological land too empty for any quick upbuilding of an imaginative
trinitarian Christian theology.

Genesis and Geology

In January 1829, when Stuart published at Andover the first edition
of his *Hebrew Chrestomathy*, a selection of annotated passages from the
Hebrew Bible designed as exercise materials for students of the language,
he inserted about halfway through the book, immediately following the
grammatical notes on Gen 2:1–3, a brief essay protesting the serious misuse

---

[38] Stuart's translation, "On the Discrepancy between the Sabellian and Athanasian
Method of Representing the Doctrine of the Trinity," appeared in *American Biblical Repository* 5 (April 1835) 265–335 and *Quarterly Observer* 6 (July 1835) 1–116.

[39] Stuart, "Discrepancy," 95 (italics mine).

[40] Ibid., 96.

[41] Throughout most of the nineteenth century the doctrine of the Trinity occupied what
Claude Welch has termed a "second rank" status. See Welch, *In This Name* (New York:
Scribner, 1952), for an excellent account of this decline.

of this and related Genesis passages by "recent critics and geologists!"[42] Herewith the American phase of the long, sometimes obscure, and usually heated controversy between biblical literalists and geologists may be said to have begun.

The geologist Stuart had most in mind was his longtime Yale friend, Benjamin Silliman (1779–1864). When Silliman returned in 1806 from a year of study in Scotland, where he prepared for his career as Professor of Chemistry and Natural History at his alma mater, he arrived as an invigorated but unsettled scholar. His inquiring mind was searching to accommodate the popular theories advanced to explain the origin of the earth and the creation of its physical features. Among these views was Vulcanism, which held the primary geological force to be the volcanic fusion of siliceous and bituminous materials—a long and gradual process involving natural forces still at work within a time span clearly longer than the six days in the Genesis account. Another important theory was Neptunism, which held that all rock formations resulted from either chemical or mechanical precipitation of minerals held in suspension in an aqueous solution that one time covered all the earth and resulted in stratifications occurring in well-defined, relatively brief, completed epochs. The Neptunist theories proved remarkably adaptable to the Genesis account of creation, if liberties were taken with the biblical text.

Whatever the scientific truth of these theories, Silliman wrestled with their theological implications. He was a practicing evangelical Christian. Like Stuart, he had been converted in Timothy Dwight's Yale revival. He was not only sympathetic to the scriptural account, but he also believed the Genesis story to be the inspired and infallible word of God. He had then the task of pursuing some accommodation with the geological theories, and with the Genesis account as well. He chose to accept the best of all the possibilities. He agreed with the Vulcanists on the formation of igneous rocks, and with the Neptunists on the successive stages of stratification.[43] Such a synthesis would cover both the volcanic data, which Silliman the scientist could not deny, and the Genesis account, which Silliman the believer could not abandon. He affirmed "that the geological formations are in accordance with the Mosaic account of the creation,"[44] but he would set aside the usual literal sense of the Mosaic chronology. It was clear to Silliman that the time required for the events before the creation of humankind exceeded the six "days" of the Genesis account. Thus, he was ready to

[42] A Hebrew Chrestomathy Designed As the First Volume of a Course of Hebrew Study (Andover, MA: Flagg & Gould, 1829) 115.
[43] George Park Fisher, The Life of Benjamin Silliman (Philadelphia: Scribner, 1866) 170–71.
[44] Benjamin Silliman, "The Consistency of Geology with Sacred History," in Robert Bakewell, An Introduction to Geology, 2d U.S. edition from the 4th British edition, ed. by B. Silliman (New Haven, CT: H. Howe, 1833) 461.

embrace the view of Georges Cuvier, a pioneer comparative anatomist and theorist for still another party of geologists, the Catastrophists, who urged that "day" must be interpreted to mean an indefinite period of time necessary for the completion of a geological epoch, not a mere twenty-four hours.[45] Professor Robert Jameson, Silliman's teacher at Edinburgh, lectured on the theme,[46] and whether or not he learned it from Jameson, the young American came home converted. Geology and Genesis seemed now entirely compatible.

Stuart became aware early of Silliman's position. This we know from Silliman's mentioning that Stuart wrote him in 1824 and took him to task for his theory. [47] The correspondence is not extant. Not until 1829, with the publication of the *Hebrew Chrestomathy*, did Stuart reveal how strongly he opposed Silliman's accommodation. Stuart's curious method of inaugurating the public debate through the *Chrestomathy* was forced, but he made his point, if only to the limited audience of Hebrew experts: geologists have no right to bend the Genesis text to suit their peculiar scientific views. To be sure, he said, "the *costume* of the Genesis narration is altogether *anthropopathic*, i.e. accommodated to the feelings, views, and methods of expression, existing in the time of Moses." The Hebrews described natural phenomena according to their "optical" appearance—the sun "rising and setting," for example. But there was no illusion in this, no design to mislead. The issue for Stuart was one of basic hermeneutics: "The Bible was not designed to teach the Hebrews astronomy or geology."[48] Everything proceeds from this caution. No matter what the opinion of the geologists, the text must be received in its simple literal meaning. As for the particular passage in question:

> I believe the account in Gen. 1., to be an account of *matters of fact*, or real verities; not a mere philosophical or poetical speculation . . . ; and that the record is authentic, and entitled to our full credit. . . . Common

[45] Fisher, *Benjamin Silliman*, 2:134. The Catastrophists believed that early geological history was marked by a succession of widespread cataclysmic events involving the dislocation and upheaval of great land masses and the sudden flood and retreat of the seas. After the Noachian deluge the cataclysms ceased and only gradual geological phenomena have been in operation since. (See Charles Gillespie, *Genesis and Geology: A Study in the Relations of Scientific Thought, Natural Theology and Social Opinion in Great Britain, 1790–1850* [Cambridge, MA: Harvard University Press, 1951] 98–102.) Though Silliman believed in the early existence of localized cataclysms, he did not hold that these involved the sudden lifting or sinking of whole continents. He did, however, believe in the Noachian deluge. (*Outline of the Course of Geological Lectures Given in Yale College* [New Haven, CT: H. Howe, 1829] 35, 58, 60 n., et passim). See also Silliman's "The Consistency of Geology," in Bakewell, *Introduction*, 439–62.

[46] Ibid., 439.

[47] Fisher, *Benjamin Silliman*, 2:115.

[48] *Hebrew Chrestomathy*, 117.

tradition, from Noah downwards, propagated the original true account, with some additions, among heathen nations. How could it be otherwise?[49]

Let the geologists object, but let them first come to terms with each other. "They will deserve more serious consideration, when any two responsible authors among them ever come to agree with each other, and when the earth shall have been penetrated and examined, a little more than an eight thousandth part of its diameter; for this has not yet been done."[50]

As for chronology, he questioned first the theory of *"gradual formations"* that lay behind Silliman's interpretation of the six Genesis days. "One might ask how it can be proved, that all substances must have been formed in an incipient state merely? Were only acorns made at first instead of oaks? And was man an *infant*, when first from the hands of his creator?" But far more serious to Stuart was the philological license such an interpretation revealed. Moses said "day," and this was exactly what he meant; and "if Moses . . . contradicts geology, then be it so; but to violate the laws of exegesis in order to accommodate a geological theory . . . is not acting in accordance with the precepts of Scriptural Hermeneutics."[51]

Stuart was not all negative, however. He noted with obvious approval that "the latest and highest efforts of geologists, are turning toward the confirmation of the Scripture account of the deluge" and that some are even accepting the sacred account of the days of creation in "its common and obvious meaning." It is clear that he did not feel that geology and the scriptures must of necessity part company. He longed for the "cheering day" when "all the lights of science will serve to render more intense, and more widely to diffuse, the light of revelation."[52] As long as the one enhanced the other, Stuart fully approved of the relationship.

Seven years passed before Stuart published again on the subject. The immediate occasion was a response to a series of three articles appearing in the *American Biblical Repository* in 1835 and entitled "The Connection Between Geology and the Mosaic History of the Creation."[53] The author, Edward Hitchcock (1793–1864), who was a Congregational clergyman and professor of chemistry at Amherst, was a former pupil of Silliman, second only to him in American geological circles, and with him a firm believer in the positive relationship between Genesis and what Hitchcock liked to call "the religion of geology."[54]

[49] Ibid., 116.
[50] Ibid., 118.
[51] Ibid.
[52] Ibid., 119.
[53] Edward Hitchcock, "The Connection Between Geology and the Mosaic History of Creation," *American Biblical Repository* 5 (January and April 1835) 113–138, 439–511 and 6 (October 1835) 261–332.
[54] See, for example, Hitchcock, "Connection," *American Biblical Repository* 5 (April 1835)

The heart of the article concerned the "alleged" discrepancies in chronology. Hitchcock found untenable anything that denied either the essentials of Mosaic chronology or the findings of modern geology. As for the Bible, "the terms employed are to be understood in their literal and common acceptation," but as a whole they form an account that is "pictorial and figurative," true, but not literally and exactly true. As for geology, creation began as described in Gen 1:1, "In the beginning God created the heavens and the earth"; but between this and the first "day" lie unknown periods of geological development that the Bible passes over in silence. In other words, the world was practically completed before the Genesis days began, but when they did begin (according to Hitchcock, "less than 6,000 years ago"), they followed in regular succession as six normal days, when the world was filled up "for its present inhabitants with their creation."[55]

The key to this blending of science and religion was biblical philology, more particularly, the proper translation of the Hebrew particle *wāw* that stands at the beginning of Gen 1:2 (omitted in the RSV), customarily translated *and*, and the words *tōhû wā-bōhû* in that same verse, commonly translated "without form and void." For Hitchcock, *wāw* "discharges all the functions of the conjunctions," and hence the passage can be read, "In the beginning God created the heavens and the earth. Afterward the earth was desolate. . . ." *Tōhû wā-bōhû* would be more accurately translated "waste and desert" or "empty and vacuous, i.e., uncultured and unfurnished." The chaos then "was not an absolute and real one but only a comparative one. . . . All the elementary principles of matter already existed and were at work."[56] Hitchcock rested all of this on what he felt to be unimpeachable authority, the philological investigations of two noted German scholars, J. G. Rosenmüller (1736–1815), and Johann David Michaelis (1719–1791), who seemed to give the argument an air of academic respectability.

Hitchcock acknowledged the objections to his theory but claimed these could be met with little difficulty. He reported Silliman's complaint that his theory did not "assign particular events to each of the successive periods called days" and answered "that there may have been several repetitions of certain demiurgic processes since the earth began to exist." He observed that other critics pointed out that the creation of light is not described in Genesis until the first day. If this were true, they asked, how could the now fossilized ancient plant and animal life have come about? Verse three merely described the "recreation of light," Hitchcock replied. The creation of the heavenly bodies he treated similarly. The Genesis account assigned them to the fourth day, but according to Hitchcock they

138 and his *The Religion of Geology and Its Connected Sciences* (Boston: Phillips, Sampson, 1851).

[55] Hitchcock, "Connection," *American Biblical Repository* 6 (October 1835) 288, 314.

[56] Ibid., 315, 318, 314.

were actually created with the "heavens" at the beginning. Later, "these bodies had their offices and stations assigned them." Still others might argue that the explanatory words given with the fourth commandment invalidate the opinion that a long period preceded the demiurgic days, "for in *six days* the Lord made heaven and earth" (Exod 20:11). But it is a common principle of hermeneutics, said Hitchcock, that in the case of two similar statements made by the same writer, the briefer must be interpreted by the longer—in this case, Exod 20:11 by Gen 1:1ff.[57]

The following year, 1836, Moses Stuart reentered the controversy with his strongest defense of literal interpretation, a long and careful essay entitled "A Critical Examination of Some Passages In Gen. 1 with Remarks on Difficulties That Attend Some of the Present Modes of Geological Reasoning."[58] Although he was broadly concerned with the relationship between Genesis and geology, his essay replied point by point to what he felt to be the dangerous and unfounded theory of Hitchcock.

Once more Stuart laid down the principle that the meaning of the words in Genesis cannot be determined by theories of modern science. But more irksome to him was the fact that the geologists were now purporting to speak with authority on philology, a subject in which they were plainly incompetent. What is their equipment to determine the meaning of Moses' language? he asked. They have every right to disagree with the *sentiment* of Moses' words, if this is their inclination, "but to show that the sentiment of the author is not what philology has educed from his words, is a different thing from examining rocks or assaying ores."[59]

Fundamental to Stuart's argument was his rejection of Hitchcock's reading of the particle *wāw*. He scorned Hitchcock's German authorities not because they were German but because they were inaccurate and out of date. No "recent" philologist of good standing would ever admit that *wāw* could here be translated *afterwards*. Though Michaelis had given thirty-seven "different significations" for the word, this was hardly a telling argument. "Anyone who knows fully the fashion of Michaelis' philology will wonder that he stopped short of twice that number." If "afterwards" meant only that what occurred in the second verse followed the creation related in the first verse, Stuart would permit the translation, but to construe this to imply a long passage of time was impossible. *Wāw* indicated "simply the sign of connection between the first and second verse." To suggest any other construction "would be no small departure from the plain and obvious principles of Hebrew grammar and lexicography."[60] Thus the

[57] Ibid., 323, 324, 325, 327.

[58] Stuart, "A Critical Examination of Some Passages in Gen. 1; with Remarks on Difficulties That Attend Some of the Present Modes of Geological Reasoning," *American Biblical Repository* 7 (January 1836) 46–106.

[59] Ibid., 55.

[60] Ibid., 61, 62.

simple philological construction of verse 2 would not allow for the long
period of ages that Hitchcock believed to have passed before the beginning
of the first day.

Nor was Stuart more kindly disposed toward *tōhû wā-bōhû* as "waste
and desert" rather than "without form and void." Aramaic and Arabic roots
as well as an array of Hebrew usages argued against the view. The display
of philological erudition was dazzling, but we need only note Stuart's
conclusion:

> If now there are any words in the Hebrew language which are capable
> of expressing a state completely waste and void, desolate as to any pro-
> duction, ornament, fruit, buildings, inhabitants, organized or animated
> beings, etc., the words *tōhū vābōhū* [*sic*] are the very ones. It was im-
> possible that Moses should have described more strongly the chaotic and
> desolate state that followed original creation. . . .[61]

Once again, the simple and direct meaning forms the standard. Words cannot be construed to mean what they do not, theory or no theory.

This was enough to demolish Hitchcock's "renovation" theory that the
present earth rested upon the foundations of an earlier creation. But Stuart
had still another philological weapon. What of the length of Hitchcock's
first day? Hitchcock, too, believed that "day" should be taken in its literal
sense, but Stuart felt that Hitchcock had waited too long to apply the principle. "What is the meaning of the declaration, that *the evening and the
morning* were the first day?" The only way the obvious sense of the passage
could be taken was "that the writer compared the alternate periods of light
and darkness which made up the first day of the creation with the same
periods which made up a day when he wrote." The first day began with the
night or evening, just as the Jewish Sabbath begins today. Of the record of
that first evening nothing exists. Certainly it did not *follow* the light season
of the first day. "Here then," Stuart added, with obvious sarcasm, "are the
myriads of ages in which weeds 80 feet in length, lizards longer than
whales—*monstra ingentia, horrenda,* I might add (if it did not spoil the
poetry) *quibus lumina adempta,* flourished and pampered in their inglori-
ous sloth! A night of *twelve hours* for all this!" And why did God need a rest
after the "refitting and readorning" of the six days, whereas apparently God
needed no rest after that earlier, more difficult creation, "the most sublime
of all the Maker's doings? I cannot force my mind to admit the thought;
because of its evident incongruity."[62]

Stuart closed with a page or two of criticism of other geological
theories, the Vulcanists and Neptunists in particular, and could not refrain
from pausing to ridicule the contradictions among the geologists themselves. He hoped they would not complain. Had they not already presumed

[61] Ibid., 63.
[62] Ibid., 73, 74, 75.

upon his science? He would let them go with this admonition: "The digging of rocks and the digging of Hebrew roots are not as yet precisely the same operation."[63] Yet he would bid them "God speed!" All he would ask was that geology:

> would not lay down positions before she is ready to demonstrate them; that she would not call upon us to believe, this year, deductions from certain supposed facts, which next year's examination will entirely over- throw; that she would be more moderate in her course, and not go so far at a leap; that she would be more patient in making out her final conclu- sions, and wait until the strata of all the continents are examined . . . ; and finally, that she would not force upon Moses *nolens volens* the Hebrew text, the conclusions which she thinks herself entitled to draw from her own speculations. When she takes these new positions, I shall be one of the number who will most heartily applaud her efforts and rejoice in her success.[64]

Stuart's essay provoked replies from James L. Kingsley of Yale and from Hitchcock himself,[65] in which both men developed more or less the same argument. Stuart, they maintained, had himself applied post-Mosaic scientific findings to his interpretation and thus had violated his own canon of criticism. If Stuart made an exception to his own rule regarding the separation of the scientific and philological spheres, the geologists felt free to do likewise. As Kingsley put it, "everything is granted which we need, or can ask."[66] He thought Stuart was particularly vulnerable in his discus- sion of the firmament (Gen 1:7). Stuart had maintained that, though Moses undoubtedly believed the firmament to be solid and extended, "the welkin or apparent arch of the heavens, or the clouds over our heads with the atmosphere, is meant."[67] But this was admitting an interpretation that could not be determined from Moses' usage, Kingsley asserted. Stuart was therefore guilty of precisely that which he condemned. Similarly, Hitch- cock singled out Stuart's interpretation of the word "light" to mean both light and heat. "It would be pertinent to inquire of Stuart," Hitchcock asked, "whether an individual well acquainted with the Hebrew language, but ignorant of the discoveries of modern science, would suspect that Moses meant in that place, any thing but simple light? . . . The moment Stuart forgets the geological spectre, that had been conjured up before his imagi- nation, he thinks of nothing but to find out the meaning of the passage

[63] Ibid., 103.

[64] Ibid., 106.

[65] James L. Kingsley, "Remarks on a 'Critical Examination of Some Passages in Gen. 1; with Remarks on Difficulties That Attend Some of the Present Modes of Geological Reason- ing. By M. Stuart, Prof. Sacred Lit. Theol. Sem. Andover,'" *The American Journal of Science* 30 (January 1836) 114–30; and Edward Hitchcock, "Remarks on Prof. Stuart's Examination of Gen. 1., in Reference to Geology," *The American Biblical Repository* 7 (April 1836) 448–87.

[66] Kingsley, "Remarks on a 'Critical Examination,'" 115.

[67] Stuart, "A Critical Examination," 50.

before him, and seizes upon aid wherever he can find it."[68]

Inasmuch as both Hitchcock and Kingsley were correct in pointing out Stuart's discrepancy in interpretation, they came out the clear winners of the last round. But more than this, Stuart's position was bound to be unpopular. Scientists, most clergymen, and laity all applauded the union of the Bible with geology. Stuart's literalism denied the "religion of geology," and without this accommodation either the findings of scientific investigation or the belief in biblical inspiration would have to go. Silliman, Hitchcock, and Kingsley were never able to make this choice. The nineteenth-century discussion between science and religion had not come far enough for these men, as devoted to their religion as they were to their science, to regard Stuart's position as anything less than a threat to both fields. Hitchcock's refusal to accept the dilemma Stuart had created was a typical reaction. The Bible and science must be united. "*We shall never give up the Bible*," he exclaimed. "We love science also. . . . And we cannot but view with pain any efforts, from whatever quarter they may come, to put asunder what God has united."[69]

Through it all Stuart's was a lone voice. No one rose to defend him in print, and he himself published no answers to his critics, who went their ways and chose to ignore him.[70] Yet for all of its seeming negativeness, his was still a positive witness. As Conrad Wright has observed, when "Stuart, the conservative literalist" insisted that the philologists, not the scientists, be the final judge of what the ancient writings really mean, he "was closer to the truth than the advanced thinkers of the time."[71] Though weakened by literalism and obscured by inconsistency, the hermeneutical position that Stuart was struggling to affirm remained basically sound. In the end, though neither Stuart nor his detractors could have anticipated this, his view rather than theirs led most directly to an understanding of the positive roles of both science and religion in their diverse, but not mutually exclusive, attempts to explain the origin of the universe.

[68] Hitchcock, "Remarks on Prof. Stuart's Examination," 457.

[69] Ibid., 486.

[70] Edward Hitchcock's most complete statement was *The Religion of Geology*. Stuart is mentioned twice, but in matters remote from the main argument. Otherwise he is completely passed over.

[71] Conrad Wright, "The Religion of Geology," *The New England Quarterly* 14 (June 1941) 344.

VI

HEBREW AND GREEK PHILOLOGY

Though Stuart's public debut as a biblical philologist came in 1813 with his first Hebrew grammar, it was eight years later that he published his first important philological study. Beginning with the publication of his Hebrew grammar in 1821, however, he was almost constantly at work on the grammar and usage of both Hebrew and Greek. In all, some twenty-five articles and books on philological subjects — grammars, translations, reviews, and monographs — appeared under his name; and these works alone, apart from his other productions, call attention to his significance as the pioneer in modern biblical studies in America.

Hebrew Studies

The Hebrew grammar of 1813 was the product of a tyro in the language; by 1817, when Stuart had accepted the vowel points, the grammar became obsolete. Meanwhile, European Hebrew philology had made rapid strides, in large measure through the work of Heinrich Gesenius. His first edition of *Hebräische Grammatik* (1813) was probably in Stuart's hands by 1817, and his augmented second edition of 1817 reached Stuart shortly thereafter. Gesenius' erudition and exacting method, coupled with a balanced judgment that transcended minor controversial issues, made his works among the most valued to appear in Hebrew studies.[1] Stuart seldom doubted the prodigious scholarship of Gesenius and became one of his devoted disciples. It was Stuart's aim to present to his country the best linguistic scholarship available. To this end, he openly incorporated Gesenius' philological discoveries into his own Hebrew grammars.[2]

---

[1] This is illustrated, at least in part, by the remarkable number of editions, numerous foreign translations, and borrowings through which his grammar passed — some twenty-seven editions in German alone, plus translations in English, French, Danish, Polish, Hungarian and other languages. See R. Kraetzschmar, "Gesenius, (Heinrich Friedrich) Wilhelm," *Schaff-Herzog Encyclopedia* 4:478. The success of the *Hebräische Handwörterbuch* (1813), which in its later editions and translations (e.g., *The Hebrew and English Lexicon of the Old Testament* by Brown, Driver, and Briggs [Boston: Houghton Mifflin, 1906], still a highly respected lexicon) testifies to Gesenius' importance in the history of Hebrew studies.

[2] Stuart never questioned the propriety of this confidence. He deplored Gesenius's rationalistic slighting of the doctrine of inspiration, noting that "it is . . . [a] matter of deepest regret, that Gesenius should spend all his life in the pursuit of such all-important knowledge, and

In his report to the Board of Visitors for 1820, Stuart noted that a new Hebrew grammar was in progress and that some of the public lectures composed for that year would become part of it.[3] The volume appeared in 1821 under the title *A Hebrew Grammar with a Copious Syntax and Praxis*.[4] Here at last was a full-length, carefully organized, scholarly, up-to-date manual of the Hebrew language for Americans; and inasmuch as its superiority could be largely attributed to borrowings from Gesenius, Stuart acknowledged his source in glowing terms: "The most important work which has ever appeared on this subject, is the Larger Hebrew Grammar of Gesenius, Professor of Theology at Halle. . . . The publication of it has made a new era in this department; and it leaves but little to expect from further improvement, except in some of the details which minute observation may correct, and some arrangements of matter which may be rendered more conspicuous." Since he realized "the wants of the Seminary, with which the Compiler is connected," plus his own desire "that the Hebrew Students, in general, of his native country might enjoy an opportunity of access to what has been lately accomplished," it seemed reasonable to offer the discoveries of Gesenius to the American public. Stuart flattered himself that "nothing very important will be found wanting; as the substance of Gesenius' great work is incorporated in it."[5]

Though admitting his indebtedness, Stuart said forthrightly that he did "not profess to be a mere translator of Gesenius, whose Grammar is too large for common use,"[6] but preferred rather to lean on Gesenius's general plan, making minor changes and deletions wherever it seemed necessary. Some sections, however, he augmented in hopes that the grammar would be more useful to students, in keeping with Stuart's pedagogical purpose. Hence, he expanded the noun and verb paradigms, to the delight of the

---

yet place that knowledge virtually in the same scale of *authority* which the knowledge of Plato, or of Cicero holds. . . . How it would heighten the pleasure of his labours," Stuart added, "if he regarded every step he takes in any direction, as taken upon *holy* ground! I cannot help feeling that the difference between his belief and true Christian faith is . . . *fundamental*—yea, nothing less than a question of final and eternal life or death." Yet as a "philologist" Stuart had to admit that he knew "not his like in Hebrew." In 1821, the same year that Stuart's larger Hebrew grammar was published, he noted that Gesenius is "probably the best Hebrew scholar in Europe. He is the author of the best Dissertation on the Samaritan Pentateuch; of the best Hebrew Lexicon and Grammar; and of the best critical History of the Hebrew language, which have yet appeared" ("Hebrew Lexicography," *American Biblical Repository* 8 [October 1836] 484–85; see also *Dissertations on the Importance and Best Method of Studying the Original Languages of the Bible, by Jahn and Others, Translated from the Originals, and Accompanied with Notes, by M. Stuart* (Andover, MA: Flagg & Gould, 1821) vi.

  [3] Papers of the Board of Visitors, 27 September 1820. The task, he added characteristically, "has borne harder upon me than I have been well able to support and has injured my health."
  [4] Andover, MA: Flagg & Gould, 1821.
  [5] Stuart, *Hebrew Grammar* (1st ed.) iv.
  [6] Ibid., iv–v.

reviewers;[7] he gave the accents more detailed treatment; he brought together in one section the rules regarding tone syllables, previously scattered throughout Gesenius' work; and he enlarged the tables of suffixed pronouns. In all, the work comprised five main units: an introduction dealing with the origin and history of the Hebrew language (incorporated from Stuart's public lectures); orthography; forms and inflections; syntax; and a praxis or selection of exercises from the book of Genesis. The mechanical features alone made it a publication of some significance. It contained 386 pages, and the Hebrew was clearly printed in large readable type with a format that was at once attractive and simply arranged. The response of the public was gratifying, and within two years the entire edition was exhausted.

Such reception warranted a second edition in 1823. Stuart wrote in the preface that it was no mere reprint of the previous work, but that "every important part of the grammar has undergone an investigation *de novo*," and that many of the changes "great and small" are drawn "from no other source than the author's own experience and investigation."[8] His dependence on Gesenius, though not forgotten, was nevertheless qualified. He modified and simplified the sections on the vowels and vowel changes, changed the classifications of the verbs and conjugations, and altered the rules and order of declining nouns, but he maintained the form and outline of the first edition. He lengthened the work by considerable expansion of the praxis. Stuart recognized that some wished the first edition had been shorter and hoped that "the author" would publish an abridged edition. This, however, he believed to be impossible. He had studied Hebrew enough, he noted,

> to know that a mere synopsis of Hebrew grammar must of course be a mere smattering of it, and leave at least as many difficulties unexplained as it explains. No synopsis can enable any one to read even the first chapter of Genesis, and account for all the forms of words which there occur. It is beyond question that every student, who is to obtain even a tolerable knowledge of the language, must have a grammar that embraces the whole body of the anomalous forms.[9]

On the other hand, the beginning student need not study the whole of the

[7] See "Review of Stuart's Hebrew Grammar," *North American Review* 13 (October 1821) 477. This review, however, complained that Stuart's system of vowel classification as adapted from Gesenius was too complicated and that the work was much too large for beginners. On the other hand it was admitted that the combination of "ample grammatical commentaries" with "what is primarily important . . . will in the end, save the trouble and expense of multiplying books of a similar kind. . . . We will not, therefore, find fault with what may seem to be redundant" (476).

[8] Moses Stuart, *A Hebrew Grammar with a Praxis on Select Portions of Genesis and the Psalms* (2d ed.; Andover, MA: Flagg & Gould, 1823) v.

[9] Ibid.

work at one survey. "Nothing can be more tedious than the abstract study of a grammar, without applying it to use," Stuart observed. Hence, he selected from the body of the grammar a primary course in hopes that the student could be "led, step by step, to a survey of the whole grammatical ground, through the medium of direct study of the language itself; so that the tedium of abstract grammar lessons may be in a great measure avoided."[10]

With the third edition in 1828, Stuart yielded to the requests of "several teachers in the department of Hebrew" for a more compact work and again made a number of revisions, notably in the section on syntax, which he felt was now more complete and better arranged.[11] He made few real abridgments, however, and the only important deletions were the survey of the history of the Hebrew language and the praxis. Stuart was aware that some would prefer to teach from a "*skeleton* grammar," but he had become more firm in his opposition to a simplification of the language. "Whoever uses a skeleton grammar merely," he noted, "must either remain ignorant of more than one-half of the grammatical phenomena of a language, or he must consume his time in filling up, by means of his teacher or of other Grammars, the skeleton which he uses." The loss of time, the perplexity, and the discouragement would be "difficult to foresee," he concluded.[12] Stuart might submit to demands for compactness but never to the temptation of incompleteness.

He supplemented the deleted praxis with a separate book of exercises, which he announced in the preface to the 1828 grammar and published the following year under the title *A Hebrew Chrestomathy, Designed as the First Volume of a Course of Hebrew Study*.[13] His aim was to present selections from the Old Testament in a graded scheme, which would be augmented by extensive notes and references to the relevant passages in his grammar—in order that the student could learn the language from the written text without the aid of an instructor, if need be.[14] It was, in short,

---

[10] Ibid., v–vi.

[11] He noted his renewed attempt to make the subject of the Hebrew vowels and their changes—"the great stumbling block of teachers and learners"—more "*intelligible*"; but he found it impossible to make them "*less complex*, unless the nature of the vowels themselves be changed. . . . If the grammarian follows the nature of the language itself which he labours to explain, and builds on *facts*, he is not answerable for it, that there is complexness in his work" (*A Grammar of the Hebrew Language* [3d ed.; Andover, MA: Flagg & Gould, 1828] vii).

[12] Ibid.

[13] Andover, MA: Flagg & Gould, 1829.

[14] Stuart felt that his *Hebrew Chrestomathy* would also be useful for students with instructors, that it could conduct a student through his initial course in Hebrew "in a way more accurate, thorough, and complete, in respect to his initiatory studies, than is the power of most instructors in this language to do, as they are at present qualified in our country" (Papers of the Board of Visitors, 23 September 1828).

an experiment in self-education, the teacher speaking through the notations, which sometimes accompanied every word in a passage. "That which
is done *viva voce* in the lecture room," he noted, "it is my aim to exhibit here
to the eye of our students on printed pages."[15]

The *Chrestomathy* also served the Andover entrance requirements,
which in 1827 contained a new provision that entering students have some
acquaintance with elementary Hebrew.[16] With the *Hebrew Grammar* of
1828 and the abridged version of Gesenius' *Handwörterbuch*, published in
an 1828 English translation by J. W. Gibbs,[17] a chrestomathy would provide
the Hebrew student with a complete course of study. Even without the aid
of a teacher, the reasonably intelligent student could expect to meet
Andover's entrance requirements. Always interested in getting the best
materials to the public at the least cost, Stuart assured the Board of Visitors
that the three books "will not cost together more than the Hebrew Lexicon
has hitherto cost, so that no student can be embarrassed in his preparation
by *expense;* and none need fail in it for want of a teacher. The Chrestomathy
will be his teacher throughout."[18] Hence, in 1832 the terms of admission to
the seminary required not only a knowledge of the Hebrew grammar but
also "the Hebrew Chrestomathy of Professor Stuart, so far as the extracts
from Genesis and Exodus extend."[19]

Practical matters of cost and entrance requirements were not upper-
most in Stuart's mind. More important was the philosophy of teaching
contained in the *Hebrew Chrestomathy*. Stuart wanted to involve students
in learning by plunging them immediately into the language. Graded
materials and minute explanations must be provided, but the students
should both discover and solve the problems on their own initiative. Stuart
made clear his views in the preface to the *Chrestomathy,* where he compared European educational procedures to his own. He noted the difficulty
of learning Hebrew when the student never recites but merely attends
lectures and tries to master classroom notes:

[15] *Hebrew Chrestomathy* (1st ed.) iv.
[16] Above, p. 22.
[17] Josiah W. Gibbs (1790–1861) graduated from Yale in 1809 and became a student under
Stuart at Andover in 1815. He assisted in the publication of Stuart's *Hebrew Grammar* of
1821, in the meantime working on his own translation of the larger edition of Gesenius'
Handwörterbuch (1815 ed.), which was finally published unter the title *A Hebrew and
English Lexicon of the Old Testament Including the Biblical Chaldee* (Andover, MA: Flagg
& Gould, 1824). Four years later, the abridged edition appeared. In that same year Gibbs
received an appointment at Yale as lecturer in biblical literature and college librarian. In
1826 he was promoted to the rank of Professor of Sacred Literature at the Yale Divinity
School, a post that he occupied with distinction until the end of his career (Dexter, *Biographical Sketches* 6:250–56).
[18] Papers of the Board of Visitors, 23 September 1828.
[19] Ebenezer Porter, "Terms of Admission to the Theological Seminary, Andover," *American
Biblical Repository* 2 (July 1832) 592.

No wonder that so few in Europe ever pursue the study of the Hebrew to any great length, while the process of acquiring it is made so tedious; and while ... their studies are conducted on a plan, which makes the learner rather a *passive recipient* than an active agent. The human mind, from its very nature, cannot long follow such a course of study with much satisfaction.[20]

With this in mind, he arranged the *Hebrew Chrestomathy* around selected passages which he considered uncomplicated "and, in some respect or other, of special interest; and which may therefore serve at once to excite the student and to instruct him." The work began with "examples for praxis," simple examples of declensions and conjugations, designed to give the student a feeling for the word forms and changes, without grammatical complexities. These were to be used with the Old Testament readings, which Stuart divided into two parts: one hundred "easy sentences for beginners" and "select portions of the Hebrew Scriptures in prose and poetry," carefully arranged to move from the simple to the complex in vocabulary and grammatical structure. Following the selections were notes, mainly grammatical, though often with exegetical comments "to assist the beginner and make his progress more agreeable to him."[21]

Stuart did not entertain unrealistic expectations about the popularity of Hebrew studies. Still, with the publication of the *Hebrew Chrestomathy* and its companion works, he envisioned the day when increasing numbers of Americans would avail themselves of the opportunities these works afforded: "Hebrew is now accessible to all classes of people, who may wish to learn it. ... Private persons, for their own advantage and gratification, may study it." He noted that the language is easier to learn than Latin or Greek, that the "apparent difficulties" of the peculiar written characters are quickly overcome, and that other "imaginary terrors in which this language has been clothed" are more the fault of the "older books of instruction" than the nature of the language. "I do most earnestly hope," he concluded,

that the day is coming, when the subject of Hebrew study will be treated with more candour than it has been in our country, for a century past; and that the obscurity which has been thrown around it, by such treatises of former days as have invested it with confused and confounding mists, and the terrors also, which have been merely imagined to exist by such as are reluctant to make the exertion demanded of those who embark in the study of it, or have not enough of the energetic spirit of acquisition to urge them forward in such a study, will vanish away before the illuminating and enterprising spirit of the day, and never more make their appearance.[22]

[20] *Hebrew Chrestomathy*, iv.

[21] Ibid., v.

[22] Ibid., vii. An interesting though bizarre criticism of this work and of the *Hebrew Grammar* of 1828 appeared in a pamphlet by Roswell Judson entitled *Two Epistles of Free Stricture on the American Dictionary of Mr. Webster, on the Hebrew Grammar and Hebrew*

A second edition of the *Chrestomathy* appeared at Andover in 1832. Except for some rearrangement of material and the substitution of easier short phrases for eighty of the "one-hundred simple sentences," which students considered too difficult, the work remained substantially unaltered.[23]

Meanwhile the fourth edition of the *Hebrew Grammar* appeared in 1831. It retained the compact form of the third edition but was notable for another change in vowel classification, which had bothered Stuart almost from the beginning of his grammatical work. In this instance, Stuart omitted his *medial* classification:

> My convictions in regard to this subject remain as before, but the inconvenience of the division in question to the learner, and its disagreement with the division of vowels in other languages, united with a conviction that "the trouble is more than a balance for the advantage," have occasioned my return *practically* to the old theory of long and short vowels only.[24]

Again Gesenius was Stuart's main source, though this edition refers also for the first time to Heinrich Ewald (1803–1875). By 1831 Ewald was at the beginning of his career, but he was later to prove second only to Gesenius among the German Hebraists.[25] Stuart noted merely that he had consulted the "latest edition" of Ewald's Hebrew grammar. He made no further reference to him on this occasion.[26]

Chrestomathy of Mr. Stuart, and on the Manual Hebrew Lexicon of Mr. Gibbs (2d ed.; [New Haven, CT: The Herald, 1830]). Judson, a Stratford, Connecticut, lawyer was partially insane and alcoholic some years before his death in 1835. See Dexter, *Biographical Sketches*, 4:553–55. In this rambling and sometimes incoherent article, Judson was vehement against Stuart's "minutiae," obscure vocabulary, use of the vowel points, borrowings from Gesenius, and other less significant particulars. "I would as soon place a son of mine on a snowy arena of quail tracks to learn Greek," Judson cried, "as oblige him to wade and mire in the swamp of Hebrew minutiae lore of either Stuart's grammar or chrestomathy, containing as they do, all the *posse* of their linguistic hermeneutic *exegeses* and *epexegeses*, with their texts intermingling and blending linguistic glories unintelligible, unspeakable and inconceivable" (43). He noted further Stuart's "wrongful diminution of the labor necessary to acquire a knowledge of the Hebrew, purposely . . . to induce the sale of his books" and concluded with the belief that the *Grammar* and *Chrestomathy* "are the very worst things of the sort that I have seen, and in my opinion deserve least of the public's patronage and support" (57–58). It is evident that this unbalanced critique was taken for what it was worth, for it neither hindered the sale of the books nor evoked a response from Stuart or from anyone else, so far as can be discovered. Though some hoped for a more simplified approach to the language, Stuart indicated all along that his works were intended for the average, intelligent college and graduate student, and not as elementary primers.

[23] *A Hebrew Chrestomathy Designed as an Introduction to a Course of Hebrew Study* (2d ed.; Andover, MA: Flagg & Gould, 1832) v. A third edition was published in Oxford, England, in 1834.

[24] *A Grammar of the Hebrew Language* (4th ed.; Andover. MA: Flagg & Gould, 1831).

[25] Ewald, professor at Göttingen, had been a pupil of Eichhorn.

[26] The first Hebrew grammar of Ewald was published in 1827 under the title *Kritische Grammatik der hebräischen Sprache* (Leipzig: Hahn). Successive editions appeared in 1828,

Two more editions of the *Hebrew Grammar* appeared, the fifth in 1835 and the sixth in 1838, both published at Andover. In the former the changes were of a "subordinate kind," though Stuart again revised the section on the vowels, and noted that "it is the most difficult part of the grammar, so far as a satisfactory mode of representation is concerned. The dubious appearance of so many vowels makes the subject obscure to a tyro; and scarcely any labour which a grammarian can bestow upon it, will make it explicit at first."[27] The later work noted further consultation of Ewald's second abridged edition and "free and constant use" of the eleventh edition of Gesenius. Stuart also mentioned a third German source, the "distinguished" essays of Herman Hupfeld (1796–1866) which appeared in the *Theologische Studien und Kritiken*[28] and to which Gesenius professed himself "to be peculiarly indebted."[29] He observed once more that the section on vowels had been "for the most part, cast entirely in a new mold," along with corrections in the section on syntax, but he defended his right to make changes:

1835 (abridged), 1837, and 1844. The last in his lifetime was the eighth (1870). Like that of Gesenius, the work passed into numerous later editions and translations. Though Stuart followed Ewald's works, he never responded to him as he did to Gesenius. He looked upon Ewald as one who proposed change merely for the sake of change. He noted Ewald's "obsession at being different from other Hebrew scholars" and expressed his feeling that Ewald "has only brought before us *old* things with *new* names, or well known facts with new and sometimes ingenious theories to account for them." This, Stuart believed, was "the tendency of his whole grammatical work." For Stuart, the blatant example of this characteristic was Ewald's contention that "praeter" and "future" should be called modes, not tenses. Stuart took an opposite view, holding that Hebrew "has *tenses,* but has *modes* only secondarily and in an indistinguished manner." He scorned Ewald's habit of reducing "everything . . . to theory" and noted that therein lay his attraction "to a certain class of the German critics." He regretted that so many had followed Ewald's extremes to the detriment of Gesenius. "His grammar is, in the eyes of many, an absolute *nonpareil* of perfection. Gesenius, and all who have preceded or followed him, with the exception of Ewald, are tame, dull, old-fashioned writers, who have advanced no further than *agere actum.* It is the theory of this new adventurer, which has become in grammar, what the *Principia* of Newton became in philosophy. When one contemplates facts like these, how can he help thinking of what Madame de Stael has so characteristically said of the Germans: 'The Englishmen live on the water; the Frenchmen on the land; but the Germans — in the air'" ("The Hebrew tenses. Translation of Ewald's Syntax in the Second (abridged) Edition of his Hebrew Grammar, so far as Respects *the Use of the Tenses* in Hebrew, with Remarks on the Same," *American Biblical Repository* 11 [January 1838] 132, 149–52. See also *American Biblical Respository* 8:477–78, 483).

[27] *A Grammar of the Hebrew Language* (5th ed.; Andover, MA: Gould & Newman, 1835) iii.

[28] The articles, which appeared in numbers 2 and 3 of the magazine (Hamburg, 1830) were entitled "Kritische Beleuchtung einiger dunkeln und misverstandenen Stellen der Alttestamentlichen Textgeschichte." Hupfeld gained considerable fame in Germany as a Hebraist, first as a professor at Marburg where he was educated, and after 1845 as the successor of Gesenius at Halle.

[29] *A Grammar of the Hebrew Language* (6th ed.; Andover, MA: Gould & Newman, 1838) iii.

I have become more and more satisfied that all works of this nature must have imperfections, and as I cannot doubt that my own have them, I must still believe that the better way is to correct what we have found to be erroneous, and supply, if we can, what is found to be deficient. If such grammarians as Matthiae, Buttman, and Gesenius, have found it necessary to do this, it would be arrogance in me to claim an exemption from the like necessity.[30]

His last major work in Hebrew philology was his translation of the *Hebrew Grammar of Gesenius as Edited by Roediger, with Additions, and also a Hebrew Chrestomathy.*[31] In the preface, Stuart observed that the sixth edition of his own grammar was sold out and that with the appearance of Roediger's reworking of Gesenius — "the most complete representative of the present state of Hebrew philology, with which I am acquainted" — it seemed better to translate the new volume than to revise his work, now out of print. "My translation is designed to be a free one," he stated, "not in respect to modifying or changing the views of the writer, but merely as to the costume with which they are invested. It has been my design and effort to Anglicize the style, certain *technical* words alone excepted."[32] He added a page of paradigms of irregular verbs; the new *Chrestomathy* remained substantially the same as the earlier one.

Unlike Stuart's other Hebrew grammatical works, this one met with a negative public reaction. Stuart's carelessness — and, to some extent, indiscretion — contributed to the reaction, for the translation was "free" indeed. In some places it was simply inaccurate. The harshest review came from Thomas Conant, who published a fifty-three page pamphlet, *Defence of the Hebrew Grammar of Gesenius against Professor Stuart's Translation.*[33] Conant had published a careful English translation of Gesenius's eleventh edition in 1839, and at the time Stuart's work appeared he was about to issue a translation of the same Roediger edition. This element of competition, coupled with Stuart's seeming indiscretion of not consulting Conant,

[30] Ibid., iv.

[31] Andover, MA: Allen, Morrill & Wardwell, 1846. Two briefer articles by Stuart should also be mentioned: the scathing "Review of Roy's Hebrew Lexicon," *North American Review* 46 (April 1838) 487–532; and "Correspondence between Prof. M. Stuart and Dr. J. Nordheimer, on the Use and Omission of the Hebrew Article in Some Important Passages of Scripture," *American Biblical Repository* 6 (October 1841) 404–18.

[32] *Hebrew Grammar of Gesenius,* iii. Emil Roediger (1801–1874) was educated under Gesenius at Halle, where he taught for some time before accepting the post of Professor of Oriental Languages at the University of Berlin. The present work was based on the last edition of Gesenius's grammar to be published in his lifetime and constituted the fourteenth edition of the whole series.

[33] New York: D. Appleton & Company, 1847. Thomas Jefferson Conant (1802–1891) was a prominent Baptist biblical scholar and translator. A graduate of Middlebury College, he was variously professor at Colby College, Hamilton Literary and Theological Institution, and Rochester Theological Seminary. The later part of his life was spent in the employ of the American Bible Union.

who had made the standard translation of Gesenius, sharpened the critical tone of the review. The "defense" was scathing in its indictment of Stuart's incompetence as a translator, an indictment supported by evidence.[34] Conant showed that Stuart's translation not only distorted but also opposed the original text. Some of Conant's citations revealed no more than infelicity of style, but his testimony leaves no doubt that Stuart devoted little care to exactness and that his work was of questionable value. Conant found support in the *North American Review,* which noted "the incontrovertible evidence of the ... errors of Mr. Stuart"[35] and pointed to a possible cause for the dangerous slip:

> We suppose Mr. Stuart, in the pressure of other duties, and under the burden of ill health (it is wonderful how much labor he has accomplished, though an invalid for many years), hurried through his task with such rapidity, that these numerous mistakes wholly escaped him; if he had paused upon his steps long enough to look about him, he would inevitably have detected and corrected them; but failing to do so, he pays the penalty of haste (it is haste alone) in having his inaccuracies exposed by a skillful and accomplished rival.[36]

Whether marred by haste or by some other flaw, the work was below Stuart's earlier standards. He attempted a defense in *A Letter to the Editor of the North American Review, on Hebrew Grammar* (Andover, MA, 1847), but the writing failed to overcome the evidence against him. Public response supported the critics, for Stuart's work was quickly outdistanced by Conant's 1846 translation of the Gesenius–Roediger volume.

Greek Studies

Stuart's investigations of New Testament Greek were not as extensive as those of Hebrew. None of his Greek studies was as important as the *Hebrew Grammar* of 1821 or the first edition of the *Hebrew Chrestomathy.* Nevertheless, Stuart produced three Greek grammars and several smaller works. Much of his early interest developed out of the long controversy over the question whether New Testament Greek was pure "classical" or Attic Greek; or a distinctive language, largely Hebraic, unique to the biblical writings and divinely inspired; or a later Hellenic-Hebraic Greek, conforming in grammatical form and structure to classical Greek.[37]

Stuart expressed his view in his first Greek grammar, a translation

[34] Though it had no direct bearing on Stuart's work, Conant was further involved emotionally by the appearance at this time in England of a plagiarized version of his 1839 translation. See *Defence of the Hebrew Grammar of Gesenius,* appendix, vii–viii.

[35] "Review of Stuart's Hebrew Grammar as Edited by Roediger," *North American Review* 45 (July 1847) 256–59.

[36] Ibid., 258–59.

[37] For the history of this development through the nineteenth century, see Adolph Deissman, "Hellenistic Greek," *Schaff-Herzog Encyclopedia* 5:211–15.

made with Edward Robinson, Stuart's gifted assistant, of the *Grammatik des neutestamentlichen Sprachidioms als sichere Grundlag der neutestamentlichen Exegese bearbeitet* (1822) of Georg Winer (1789–1855), which they published in 1825 under the title *A Greek Grammar of the New Testament*.[38] Winer developed the grammatical principles of the moderates, who found a Hellenic-Hebraic Greek in the New Testament. By avoiding the extremes of the Hebraizing tendencies, without going over to the old "purist" school, Winer showed that it was possible to apply to the New Testament the principles of grammar which the classicist Gottfried Herman (1772–1848) had developed for classical Greek. Thus Winer put the New Testament language on a firm grammatical foundation without ignoring its Hellenistic and Hebraic characteristics.[39] His work was a pathbreaking achievement in New Testament studies, and although Stuart and Robinson added little to the grammar in their translation, their appreciation of Winer's principles reveals their own development.

Noting the difficulty of studying New Testament Greek with "common" grammars based on the Greek of "profane" authors, or with earlier New Testament grammars, the authors presented Winer's work as "new in its kind" and eminently deserving of "an introduction to the theological schools, and . . . colleges of our country."[40] Though Stuart and Robinson believed that Winer had not exhausted the subject and had not dealt adequately with prepositions—they regarded his theories "as rather ingenious than solid; as more savouring of *a priori* theory, than of sound practical experience"—they thought he had laid a foundation worthy of future improvement:

> There is, on the whole, so much which is good and useful in the work, that it will be found a help to the young interpreter of no small importance, in respect to the attainment of a discriminating knowledge of the New Testament diction. It may serve, at least, to turn the attention of the rising generation of the clergy and others to a subject, respecting which there is yet but little accurate knowledge in our country. If it should pave the way (as it not improbably will) to a more successful effort of the same kind, hereafter, among ourselves, it will not be in vain that it has been published. Everything which tends to promote an accurate knowledge of its language is worthy of the patronage of an enlightened and religious public.[41]

[38] Andover, MA: Flagg & Gould. Educated at the University of Leipzig, Winer became a professor of theology at that school in 1819, moving in 1823 to a professorship at Erlangen and finally in 1832 back to Leipzig, where he taught in the field of biblical languages until his death.

[39] G. Lechler, "Winer, Johann Georg Benedikt," *Schaff-Herzog Encyclopedia* 12:383–84.

[40] Stuart and Robinson, *A Greek Grammar*, iii, iv.

[41] Ibid., v. The grammar proper was divided into three sections: part I on the character and diction of the New Testament, part II on forms of words, and part III on syntax. Stuart translated all of parts I and II, and part III up to the syntax of the verbs. Robinson was responsible for the remainder, which constituted a little more than half of the whole work.

Moses Stuart

Aside from the little book entitled *Practical Rules for Greek Accents and Quantity*, a translation of two articles by Phillip Buttman and Franz Passow (1786–1833) that appeared in 1829,[42] Stuart offered no other work on Greek grammar until his own *Grammar of the New Testament Dialect*,[43] published at Andover in 1834. This work, too, drew from German scholarship, but Stuart placed his stamp upon the sources; and, although he admitted his indebtedness to German grammarians, he was careful to point out his free adaptation of their conclusions. "My purpose," he stated in the preface, "has been, *to bring together all the important forms and principles of Greek Grammar, in as short a compass as possible, and yet be perspicuous and satisfactory*."[44] Much was dictated by the needs of the Andover students. He noted the inconvenience of the European grammars which omit the "Formenlehre," stressing syntax at the expense of the word forms and inflections, and thus forcing the inexperienced student to consult two grammars. Uniformity and completeness were the norm for language helps, and they were difficult to achieve at an institution like Andover:

> Most individuals come to this Seminary with a very imperfect knowledge of the Greek; its flexions, therefore, are recalled with much labour and difficulty. They bring here the different grammars of our country, studied at the different institutions where they have been educated. The difficulty of bringing about a uniform method of linguistic discipline, thus becomes very great; and every teacher knows how desirable this is, with respect to any class which is under his care.[45]

Stuart took pains to overcome this deficiency, and he consulted a number of authors to complete the section on forms and inflections. The New Testament grammar of C. F. Matthiae (1744–1811) proved "exceedingly useful," as did the works of Phillip Buttmann, Heinrich Thiersch (1817–1885), and Hermann. Buttmann, he observed, provided the "leading principles" of the third declension, but Stuart developed his own mode of "exhibiting" that declension. He noted, moreover, that one part of the section on the syntax of the article was "entirely the result of my own labours."[46] The remainder of the section drew on the work of Winer, shortened for simplification.

[42] Andover, MA: Flagg & Gould.
[43] Andover, MA: Gould & Newman.
[44] *Grammar of the New Testament Dialect* (1834 ed.) vi.
[45] Ibid., v. Stuart also admitted that the Winer translation had a very poor sale and suggested that its weakness in the area of forms and inflections was the major factor in its failure (vii).
[46] Ibid., vi–vii. Stuart was not, however, completely at peace regarding the use of the Greek article, and in a long monograph entitled "Hints and Cautions Respecting the Use of the Greek Article," which appeared in the April 1834 issue of *American Biblical Repository* (4:277–327) concluded that much further study was needed on the matter.

Unlike the 1825 translation of the Winer grammar, Stuart's 1834 grammar was successful with the public,[47] and in 1841 Stuart issued a second, revised edition. In addition to Winer, whom he considered standard, Stuart consulted the latest foreign sources.[48] So much had been done, Stuart observed, "that not much further room is left for any improvements." Yet he was mindful that "the history of the past may well admonish us, not to exclude the hope of still further accessions to grammatical science."[49] His work was as complete as he could make it without complicating it beyond the ability of his students. Though the grammar comprised over three-hundred pages, Stuart observed that his work was shorter than "distinguished examples" of European works. In the long run it proved to be one of his most popular grammars, and it was reprinted in 1850 and 1857.

Except for his translation of Roediger, Stuart's grammatical works on the biblical languages proved useful. They show a surprising competence in a developing technical field, and though they were surpassed by the works of other American scholars—some of whom, like Robinson and Gibbs, Stuart himself had trained—they were not discredited. Together they constitute a lasting monument to Stuart's dedicated task of opening the scriptures to Americans. The fact that he even approached the goal would constitute his lasting reward.

[47] The *American Biblical Repository*, which at that time was published in Andover, gave the work a warm review ("Review of Stuart's Grammar of the New Testament Dialect," 5 [January 1835] 245). A British review of the 1838 London edition was less enthusiastic: "In the compilation of the present work, Mr. Stuart evinces a considerable acquaintance with the labours of the recent scholars of Germany. But he should have remembered, that the merits of those eminent philologists cannot be successfully emulated by the mere affectation of systematic accuracy. His book is too elementary to be acceptable to the scholar, while it is too minute and technical for the less ambitious students whose wishes do not extend beyond the acquirement of a moderate acquaintance with the language of the New Testament" ("Review of Stuart's Grammar of the New Testament Dialect," *British Critic and Quarterly Theological Review* [April 1838] 565.)

[48] Stuart noted that "the mention of a few of these may aid the reader, in forming some proper judgment of the zeal with which this object is pursued abroad. Among the most distinguished Essays may be named Kruger's *Grammatical Investigations;* F. Franke, *On the Negative Particles of the Greek;* Richter's *Specimens of Greek Anacolutha;* Reimnitz's *System of Greek Declensions;* Max Schmidt, *On Greek and Latin Pronouns;* Gotting's *Doctrine of Greek Accents;* Spitzner's *Guide to Greek Prosody;* Liscovius' *Pronunciation of the Greek Verb;* Merleker's *Greek Accentuation;* Eichhoff, *On the Inf. Mode;* Hartung, *On the Greek Particles;* the same, *On the Formation of Cases;* and above all, the masterly Greek Grammar of G. Kuhner" (*Grammar of the New Testament Dialect* [Andover, MA: Allen & Morrill, 1841] iii–iv.)

[49] Ibid., iii.

VII

THE PUBLISHED SCHOLAR:
CRITICAL WORKS AND COMMENTARIES

Stuart was busily engaged in the composing of commentaries and critical articles on the scriptures. His lecture series during his first decade at Andover revealed his interest in the critical problems of the Old Testament canon. The annual report to the Board of Visitors for 1824 notes further that he delivered twelve lectures on the book of Hebrews—presumably both introductory and exegetical—during the academic year.[1] Thus, by 1825 Stuart had amassed a considerable amount of material, and though preoccupied with grammatical studies, he was soon to devote his attention to extended exegetical works.

In his report to the Board of Visitors in 1826 Stuart mentioned that his commentary on the epistle to the Hebrews would soon be forthcoming.[2] The first volume appeared in September 1827 and the second, five months later. Thereafter came six more major biblical studies, the commentaries on Romans, Revelation, Daniel, Ecclesiastes, and Proverbs, and a general work on the Old Testament canon.[3] Stuart also published some twenty shorter exegetical or critical articles. A number of these he incorporated into the larger works or wrote as expansions of points made in the commentaries. Two are of special significance: a review in the *American Biblical Repository* of the first volume of Andrews Norton's *The Evidences of the Genuineness of the Gospels* (Boston, 1837), and the companion article, "Inquiry Respecting the Original Language of Matthew's Gospel, and the

[1] Papers of the Board of Visitors, 22 September 1824.
[2] Ibid., 27 September 1826.
[3] The full titles of these works are: *A Commentary on the Epistle to the Hebrews*, 2 vols. (Andover, MA: Mark Mewman, 1827–1828); *A Commentary on the Epistle to the Romans* (Andover, MA: Flagg & Gould, 1832); *A Commentary on the Apocalypse*, 2 vols.(Andover, MA: Allen, Morill & Wardwell, 1845); *A Commentary on the Book of Daniel* (Boston: Crocker & Brewster, 1850); *A Commentary on Ecclesiastes* (New York: Putnam, 1851); *A Commentary on the Book of Proverbs* (New York: M. W. Dodd, 1852); and *A Critical History and Defense of the Old Testament Canon* (Andover, MA: Allen, Morill, & Wardwell, 1845). Three works appeared in subsequent editions: the commentary on Hebrews (Andover, MA, 1833, 1854, and 1860; and seven London editions from 1828 to 1864); Romans (Andover, MA, 1835, 1854, and 1865; and six London editions from 1833 to 1865); and Ecclesiastes, which was edited and revised by Stuart's son-in-law, R. D. C. Robbins (Andover, MA, 1862).

Genuineness of the First Two Chapters of the Same: with Particular Reference to Mr. Norton's View of These Subjects as Exhibited in His Treatise
on the Genuineness of the Gospels."[4]

The Apologist

The report of the committee appointed by the Andover Trustees in
1825 to investigate German studies in the seminary[5] had not questioned
Stuart's critical soundness; but in the concluding paragraph the committee
inserted a pointed observation about his future labors:

> In conclusion, your Committee would remark, that from the ample
> materials already before the public, there might undoubtedly be com-
> piled a commentary on the sacred Scriptures, which, while it should
> embrace whatever is most valuable in the literature and criticism of
> German writers, should exclude their eccentricities and errors. Such a
> work cannot but be regarded as a desideratum. It would, under Divine
> blessing, accomplish much good and probably prevent much evil. To the
> theological students of this and other seminaries it would save an incalcu-
> lable amount of precious time. And it would exempt them from that
> habitual familiarity with error and sophistry which has sometimes proved
> fatal to common minds, and from which the strongest have not always
> escaped without essential injury.[6]

This suggestion was no doubt a stimulus for exegetical and critical labors
on Stuart's part. It also foreshadowed the apologetic tone of these labors.

Stuart's apologetics reflected his doctrine of inspiration. Stuart believed
that if a book was in the canon it was inspired, and it bore, despite minor
discrepancies, the authority of genuineness in all its parts. He was cautious
about making any speculation about the identity of any biblical author
when the internal evidence seemed contradictory or when it provided only
elusive hints or when the writer remained anonymous. He often accepted
external evidence for date and place, but internal evidence took precedence
when it named a particular person as writer, despite any counterarguments
based on external evidence. This was manifest especially in Stuart's New
Testament investigations, which required him also to consider apostolic
credence. Further, his conservative position on authorship tended to dictate
his conclusions about the dating, placement, and genuineness of the text—
again, often despite strong external arguments. Thus, the issue of inspiration
was crucial. On this hinged most of Stuart's answers to critical problems,
even though he found the German higher critics arrayed against him. It

---

[4] The full title of the first review was "Review of Professor Norton's Evidences of the
Genuineness of the Gospels," *American Biblical Repository* 11 (April 1838) 265–343. The
second review appeared in *American Biblical Repository* 12 (July 1838) 133–79 and was continued (October 1838) 315–56.

[5] Above, p. 65, n. 34.

[6] Woods, *History of Andover,* 178.

would be unfair to view Stuart as merely reacting against the Germans, for he learned much from them, but the conservative, apologetic strain remained dominant in his critical writings.

New Testament Criticism

His first commentary, on the epistle to the Hebrews, was in some respects the most defensive. Volume I he devoted entirely to critical matters. The book begins with a protracted discussion of the letter's destination, Stuart speculating that the epistle was written to a church in Palestine, probably Caesarea.[7] The date is near the time of the destruction of Jerusalem, for citations in the first epistle of Clement to the Corinthians show that Hebrews was in use by A.D. 96, the date Stuart assigned to Clement's writing.[8] By far the most pressing problem, however, was authorship. Here Stuart mustered his critical powers to establish that Paul was the author. He was aware that the church had never agreed unanimously, but he was convinced that tradition ascribed the letter to the apostle Paul and that his authorship could be supported by sound arguments. His investigation is pedantic to the point of exhaustion. In long, involved sections, he treats the internal evidence—especially the reference in 13:23 to "our brother Timothy," which he thinks clearly points to Paul—compares the thought with other Pauline letters, and examines patristic evidence. Most elaborate, however, is his treatment of arguments by Germans who dismissed the Pauline authorship on the basis of comparative philology. He summarized and attacked the studies of Leonard Bertholdt, David Schulz, Wilhelm M. L. De Wette, and Eichhorn,[9] which had tried to show that the language of the book of Hebrews is non-Pauline. Then in a bizarre, ironic effort, Stuart attempted to refute the Germans by examining First Corinthians, which no one denied was genuinely Pauline, and listing its "non-Pauline" phrases.[10]

The commentary on Romans appeared in 1832. In some ways, it was Stuart's best work, thorough, meticulous, and marked by moderate Calvinist theological balance. He achieved this position by a painstaking review of a long line of Reformed exegetes, beginning with Calvin and including Hugo Grotius, J. A. Turretin, J. F. Flatt, and F. A. G. Tholuck. One example of that moderate Calvinism, Stuart's interpretation of Paul on original sin, provoked a negative reaction from one quarter, but for Stuart the

---

[7] *Commentary on Hebrews*, 1:9–73.

[8] Ibid., 74–90.

[9] Bertholdt, *Historischkritische Einleitung in die sämmtlichen kanonischen und apokryphischer Schriften des alten und neuen Testaments* (Erlangen: Johann Jacob Palm, 1812); Schulz, *Der Brief an die Hebräer, Einleitung, Übersetzung und Ammerkungen* (Breslau: Holäufer, 1818); De Wette, *Lehrbuch der Historisch-kritischen Einleitung in die Bibel: Alten und Neuen Testaments* (Berlin: G. Reimer, 1826); Eichhorn, *Einleitung in das Neue Testament* (Leipzig: Weidmannischen Buch Handlung, 1810).

[10] *Commentary on Hebrews*, vol. 1:241–52.

overriding question in the commentary was not its theology but the unity
of the book, especially the relationship of the last two chapters to the rest
of the epistle.[11] Typical of those who questioned the unity of Romans was
Semler, who theorized that Paul addressed chap. 15 not to the Romans but
to those who took the letter to Rome.[12] Similarly, Semler believed chap. 16
to have been a brief recommendation to people along the way for those
carrying the larger text. The two chapters might be written by Paul, he
argued, but they were not part of the letter to the Romans. A related theory
that Stuart noted was that chap. 16 comprised fragments of some other
epistle of Paul, which were added piece by piece to the letter to the
Romans.[13] Stuart rejected each of these theories and concluded that neither
internal nor external evidence could be made to support such "extravagant
and incongruous suppositions."[14]

Though Stuart wrote no commentaries on the Gospels, his remarks on
Andrews Norton's *Evidences* indicate a lively and informed interest. Again
he stood decidedly against the German radicals, as did Norton, who wrote
his work to refute the proposal in Eichhorn's *Einleitung in das Neue Testament*
that the Gospels are the grossly corrupted reworkings of a lost "Original
Gospel" and only in a limited sense the works of the authors to whom they
are ascribed. Modern readers may well recognize here an early "source
theory" of the Gospels, but for Norton and Stuart, Eichhorn's view was
disturbing and unfounded.

Norton organized his argument under two propositions: that the Gospels remain essentially the same as they were composed, and that they were
ascribed to their true authors. He attempted to prove his first statement by
examining the manuscripts, which, he thought, showed remarkable agreement. He also investigated the "Original Gospel" and concluded that
nothing was ever spoken or heard of such a work in Christian antiquity.
Proof for the second proposition followed mainly from the first, but Stuart
strengthened it by an extended discussion of patristic evidence for the
genuineness of the Gospel accounts and by a refutation of lesser hypotheses
that assumed "primitive" accounts lying behind the Gospels.

When Stuart reviewed Norton's first volume, he had high praise for it.
At several points he noted an exact coincidence with his own studies,[15] and

[11] Although he did not give evidence for his opinions, Stuart believed the book to have been
written by Paul at Corinth, about A.D. 57, shortly before Paul left for Jerusalem (*Commentary
on Romans*, 38–42).
[12] *Dissert. de. dupl. appendice ep Pauli ad Rome*, passim.
[13] Stuart, *Commentary on Romans*, 46.
[14] Ibid., 47.
[15] "Review of Professor Norton's Evidences," 265–343. Stuart was delighted with Norton's
rejection of Eichhorn's position that the manner in which Justin Martyr quoted from the
Gospels indicated that he was using a source not corresponding to any canonical Gospel
(ibid., 287). See also Norton's discussion in *Evidences* (2d ed.; London: J. Chapman, 1847)
1:126–48.

he declared Norton free from any charge of being a "rationalist or a naturalist."[16] In one place, though, Norton, according to Stuart, had given in to "neological" thinking. The Gospel of Matthew, Norton had declared, was originally composed in Hebrew, with the first two chapters of the Greek text having been added from another source at the time of the translation into Greek.[17] Stuart believed this to be a dangerous admission on Norton's part, mainly because he saw in it the collapse of Norton's position against Eichhorn. In reply to the claim that Matthew was composed in Hebrew,[18] Stuart admitted that patristic testimony pointed to a lost "Gospel according to the Hebrews," but he cautioned against confusing this with the Gospel of Matthew and noted that when quotations from this book (gleaned from the Fathers, mainly from Epiphanius) are compared with Matthew, they suggest only an "interpolated and . . . spurious" copy of the Gospel. The Fathers may appear to quote from a Hebrew gospel of Matthew, but they were using only the spurious "Gospel according to the Hebrews."[19] Stuart supported his argument by observing that if a Hebrew original did exist, antiquity gives no clues regarding its fate. Certainly such a work would have been used by Judaizing Christians as a defense against the doctrines of Paul.[20] Finally, he observed, according to his own study, the present Greek text shows no evidence of being a translation.[21]

Norton's second point, that the first two chapters of Matthew were not part of the original writing, posed the more serious threat. For Stuart, though, its validity depended upon the argument for an original Hebrew text. If that could be shown improbable, one needed only to consider the history of the Greek text as it is known today. The evidence, Stuart believed, was conclusive: "*All Ms. copies of Matthew the world over, and all the ancient Versions without an exception, contain the first two chapters of Matthew,* and exhibit them as a part of his Gospel." Though he admitted the possibility that the text of the Ebionites, as reported by Epiphanius, did not contain the disputed chapters, this proved nothing "except the strength

[16] "Review of Professor Norton's Evidences," 287. With an eye to the prevailing party differences Stuart noted that "it would be difficult . . . to make out from his Treatise anywhere, that Mr. Norton is a Unitarian; although those who are much conversant with doctrinal statements might conjecture this, on the ground that every declaration of a positive nature, on this great subject is carefully avoided." But as far as Stuart was concerned this was a commendable characteristic. Norton had said nothing which could "justly offend" (288–89).

[17] Norton treated the subject only briefly in his main text (*Evidences*, 2d ed.; 1:15–18) but expanded the point in a long note in the appendix (196–210).

[18] "Inquiry Respecting the Original Language of Matthew's Gospel, and the Genuineness of the First Two Chapters of the same, with Particular Reference to Mr. Norton's View of These Subjects as Exhibited in His Treatise on the Genuineness of the Gospels," *American Biblical Repository* 12 (July, October 1838) 133–79, 315–56.

[19] Ibid., 135–60.

[20] Ibid., 165.

[21] Ibid., 169.

of prejudice in a particular party among early Christians." Further, he rejected the German theory that "the three Evangelists" composed their Gospels from an early "Protevangelium," a written source that did not contain the materials found in Matthew 1 and 2: "Of the Protevangelium no ancient writer of the church ever spoke, heard, or dreamed.... It is a phenomenon of Neology alone, first dreamed, I believe, among countless other like visions, by the great heresiarch Semler; and after him by others, whose imaginations were as lively as his."[22]

The remaining New Testament work to which Stuart devoted critical analysis was the book of Revelation. As early as 1839, he lectured on the entire work across the summer term.[23] It was not until 1845, however, that the published commentary appeared. It was cautious and conservative. Stuart believed that the book was written on the island of Patmos, as indicated in the first chapter, and he opposed critics who held that the reference was merely "a poetical fiction."[24]

He also favored the traditional belief that John, the disciple of Jesus, was the author, and he opposed such critics as De Wette, Ewald, and Lücke, who had held out for other "Johns" mentioned in the New Testament or in patristic literature. Questions about the date and style overlapped with the question of authorship, so Stuart gave them his attention. He held that internal evidence, particularly Revelation 6–11—which he took to be a prophetic description of the Roman conquest of Jerusalem in A.D. 70—pointed to a date previous to that event and therefore easily within the lifetime of the apostle. The tenor of the book also suggested to Stuart that the author and his Christian contemporaries were undergoing a persecution, so he placed the date during the reign of Nero, around A.D. 64.[25] In all of this, he was aware that many of the Germans preferred to view chaps. 6–11 as a description of a past event and suggested that the author lived through Domitian's persecution, late in the century beyond the life span of the apostle John. But for Stuart, a futuristic prophetic interpretation was wholly within reason, given the inspired character of the work. He used the claims for futuristic prophecy and apostolic authorship to support each other.

Regardless of the date, a number of the Germans had insisted that a comparative study of style precluded any supposition that the same writer

[22] Ibid., 317, 330, 331.

[23] See the notes from an anonymous student, "Professor Stuart's Lectures on the Apocalypse," 7 June through 30 August 1839, Dartmouth College Library.

[24] He particularly noted Eichhorn, who in his *Einleitung* held that there was nothing to substantiate the statement that John was banished to this place. Stuart noted Eichhorn's self-contradiction by citing Eichhorn's statement in *Commentarius in Apocalypsin Joannis* (Göttingen: Dietrich, 1791) that John was on Patmos (Stuart, *Commentary on the Apocalypse*, 1:257).

[25] Ibid., 76.

wrote the Gospel, the epistles of John, and the book of Revelation. Stuart acknowledged the language differences, but he attributed them to the poetic nature of the book. In no sense would he admit that the book of Revelation, when compared to the Gospel of John, was full of *"barbarism* or *solecism.* . . . Nearly all that is apparently irregular or unusual . . . we may vindicate by references to classical or to Hebrew-Greek usage. It is only the greater frequency of these things in the Apocalypse, to which any appeal can be made for establishing the charge of *peculiarity* in this book."[26] In fact, he sought to show a correspondence between the "Johannean" works in the Bible, though he was reluctant to press the similarity too far. And he proved to his satisfaction the uniformity of the writings.

A knottier critical problem was whether to follow the German "neologists," notably Wettstein, Semler, and Ewald,[27] who rejected the prophetic import of the work and treated it as an imaginative tract written for times of Roman persecution, or the larger group of apocalypticists and visionaries, including such older interpreters as Vitringa and Albert Bengel as well as "the recent millenarians of our own country,"[28] most of whom professed to see in the work an outline of the end of human history. Stuart rejected both extremes. He found the "generic theme" of the work to be "the final and complete triumph of Christianity over all opposition and all enemies, and the temporal and eternal glory and happiness to which this triumph leads the church." This "is a common theme of prophecy, both in the Old Testament and in the New."[29] Though he took care to affirm the apocalyptic character of the work, the richness of its imagery, the profuseness of its symbolism, and the epic quality of its poetry,[30] he was firm in his belief that inspired prophetic truths lay behind the literary form. "*Substantial facts* lie at the basis of the Apocalypse, . . . and . . . this basis is not a mere imaginary or poetic conception." So much for the "neologists," who had found in the Apocalypse "little else but the Roman conquest of Judea and Jerusalem, excepting the final erection of a new and spiritual kingdom."[31]

Yet Stuart's grammatical-historical hermeneutic prevented him from making the work a source book of prophetic imaginings applicable to any historical event from the time of Christ to the present. He insisted that the book had a specific meaning for the time and situation in which it was written. The setting was the persecution of the Christians under the Roman emperor Nero; and John's purpose was "to console the oppressed and

[26] Ibid., 255. For his investigation of the language and style of the book of Revelation, see 228–57.
[27] Ibid., 470–73.
[28] Ibid., 467–70; 473–74.
[29] Ibid., 155, 12.
[30] Ibid., 31–36, 131–49, 173–200.
[31] Ibid., 161. Among this class Stuart cited Hartwig, *Apologie der Offenbarung;* and Herder, *Maran Atha Oder das Buch von der Zukunft des Herrn* (1779).

anxious Christian" living in these times, not to give a "mere *Syllabus of History* . . . down to the end of the world."[32]

Stuart's critical analysis, therefore, sought the middle ground between "neologists" and literalists. This is seen in his treatment of the four great episodes or visions in chaps. 6–22. Stuart regarded the first section, chaps. 6–11, as a futuristic representation of the Jewish wars, culminating in the destruction of Jerusalem and the overthrow of the "Jewish persecuting power." Here, as in the next section, chaps. 12–19, which he classified as prophecies about the overthrow of Rome, Stuart found a remarkable correspondence between the visions and the first-century persecutions of Christians. The episodes, he concluded, had to be related to historic events in the early church, even though much of the prophecy was depicted in "outlines and mere sketches."[33] Exemplary of the correspondence were the symbols of the beasts in chap. 13, which according to Stuart depicted the civil and religious power of the Roman Empire, and the symbols of the wounded head, the forty-two months of power, and the number 666, which he saw as thinly veiled references to Nero.[34] In broad outline, he thought, the prophecies in these sections had been fulfilled. To look for the coming of the "two witnesses," or to identify a later empire with one of the beasts, or a ruler or pope with a head or horn of the beast was unwarranted.

The third episode, chaps. 20–22, begins with the binding of Satan and the resurrection of the martyrs and continues through the reign of one thousand years, the liberation of Satan, the invasion by Gog and Magog, the great catastrophe, and finally the general judgment. The concluding section depicted the New Jerusalem. All was prophecy, based on the great and awful facts of divine retribution and vindication; this much Stuart stoutly maintained. But it was also apocalyptic literature, and Stuart thought that the time of these happenings and the identities of the actors

---

[32] Ibid., 150–59. In one fine paragraph Stuart bore down on those who would make this interpretation: "It is time—high time—for *principle* to take the place of fancy, for exegetical *proof* to thrust out *assumption,* and for all men to call to mind, that the apostles did not occupy themselves with writing conundrums and charades. They wrote to be read and understood by those to whom they addressed themselves; and if they were understood it was by virtue of explaining their writings in a manner which accorded with the usual laws and principles of exegesis. These never could have given birth to a scheme of interpretation, which divests the Apocalypse of all present and proper regard to the churches, clothed as they then were in sackcloth, groaning under oppression, and often bathed in their own blood. To forget all this, and to engage oneself in the leisurely and fanciful employment of sketching traits of historical events in distant future ages, and many of these merely *civil* events—is not appropriate work for the illustrious exile wandering on the barren and seagirt rocks of Patmos" (161).

[33] Ibid., 76.

[34] Ibid., 2:272ff., 434–58. See also Moses Stuart, "The Number of the Beast in the Apocalypse," *Bibliotheca Sacra or Tracts and Essays on Topics Connected with Biblical Literature and Theology,* ed. Edward Robinson (New York: Wiley & Putnam, 1843).

lay outside the intent of the author.[35] Millenarian interpretations were idle speculation.

Old Testament Criticism

The commentary on Revelation appeared in 1845, the same year that Stuart published his first major Old Testament study, *Critical History and Defense of the Old Testament Canon*. The date itself is a matter of interest when one considers the long span of time between this work and the lectures on the Old Testament composed during his first years at Andover. Yet the *Critical History* is remarkably similar to the lectures in most of its conclusions. It reveals the same conservative interest manifested in all his critical studies:

> My intention is to confine myself, in the main, within the limits of a critical and historical view of the Jewish Canon of Scripture in the days of Christ and the apostles, and to show that this Canon, as received by the Jews at that time, was declared by our Saviour and his apostles to be of divine origin and authority, and was treated by them as entitled to these claims.
>
> If it can be shown that Christ and the apostles, as the commissioned messengers of God to establish Christianity, did receive, regard, and treat the Scriptures of the Jews as obligatory and of divine authority, and also that these Scriptures were the same books which belong to our present Old Testament, then two consequences must follow from the establishment of these propositions. The first is, that whatever doubts or difficulties any one may have about the critical history or origin of particular books in the Old Testament, still he must now acknowledge that they have received the sanction of an authority from which there is no appeal. . . . The second is, that the man who admits the divine origin and authority of the Christian religion, and that the New Testament contains a credible and authentic account or development of it by Christ and by the apostles, must be altogether inconsistent with himself and inconsequent in his reasonings, if he rejects the divine origin and authority of the Old Testament Scriptures.[36]

---

[35] Though Stuart believed that the symbols were to be interpreted in a figurative sense, this was not his opinion about most designations of time in the Apocalypse. He was opposed to those who would construe the "time, times and half a time" pattern in Revelation and Daniel (also appearing as "forty and two months," and in Daniel as "1260 days") as referring to anything other than a period of three and a half years. Stuart directed this especially against Lücke, who in his *Introduction to the Apocalypse* had given a figurative interpretation to this designation. However, Stuart believed the situation regarding the "thousand years" in chap. 20 to be somewhat different, noting that it is frequently used to designate a "period of time long and in its nature indefinite" (Stuart, *Commentary on the Apocalypse*, 1:212–15; *Commentary on Daniel*, 222–23; and "How are the Designations of Time in the Apocalypse to be Understood?" *American Biblical Repository* 5 [January 1835] 33–83).

[36] *Critical History and Defense*, 2–3.

The occasion of his statement was the publication in 1844 of the second volume of Andrews Norton's *Evidences,* which contained an extended passage asserting precisely the opposite of Stuart's convictions.[37] In brief, Norton contended that it was both impossible and unnecessary for a Christian to affirm the genuineness of all the Old Testament writings. The divine origin of the Jewish religion was indeed sanctioned by Christianity, observed Norton. "But Christianity has not made itself responsible for the genuineness, the authenticity, or the moral and religious teachings, of that collection of books by Jewish writers, which constitutes the Old Testament." Attempts to establish the genuineness and to account for the discrepancies of the Old Testament writings eclipsed their religious value. "A false character has been ascribed to them, which brings them into perpetual collision with the moral and religious conceptions of men of more enlightened times than those of their writers, with the principles of rational criticism in the interpretation of language, and even with the progress of the physical sciences."[38]

The threat of Norton's position was clear. Epitomizing the argument, Stuart noted that "in order to maintain the divine origin of the Jewish religion, as founded by Moses," Norton tried to show that Moses "did *not* write the Pentateuch" and that the prophets, "the true disciples of a true religion," could not be held responsible for "books . . . filled with incredible, or trivial or superstitious narrations and notions." If we follow Norton, Stuart continued,

> the best we can do, even with the prophets, is to select here and there a passage that accords with reason and sound judgment, to which we may give our assent as being worthy of the ancient dispensation, while the rest is to be placed under the same category as the fictions and extravagant accounts of all other nations, respecting their origin and their history in ages too remote to have been consigned to writing.[39]

The threat demanded a precise and thorough rebuttal. Proceeding on the principle that the Old Testament is divinely sanctioned by the New, Stuart examined the history of the canon as he had in his lectures, book by book, rather than by addressing the question of canonical integrity as a whole.

Stuart first considered the problem of the Pentateuch, and his main defense against Norton, though diversionary, was interesting. Norton denied that Moses was the author of the Pentateuch, because alphabetic writing had not been invented by Moses' time. Hence, he could not have written the first five books of the Bible. But Stuart charged that Norton was

---

[37] "On the Jewish Dispensation, the Pentateuch, and the other Books of the Old Testament," *Evidences* (2d ed.; London: J. Chapman, 1847) 2:402–512.

[38] Ibid., 402, 403.

[39] *Critical History and Defense,* 2.

simply behind the times and cited "the recent paleographic examinations in Egypt, Phenicia [sic], Persia, and Assyria" compiled by Gesenius in the thirteenth edition of his Hebrew grammar. "This preëminent paleographer" had been a "strenuous assertor of the *late* origin of the Pentateuch" for most of his life, but even he was finally compelled to admit that " 'alphabetic writing must have been in use among the Egyptians at least 2,000 years before the Christian era.'"[40] Ewald, who could never be accused "of any leaning towards orthodoxy," had also acknowledged the practice of writing among the Hebrew people as early as the time of Moses.[41] "Even De Wette, the coryphaeus of doubters," allowed the point.[42] Each scholar had been forced to retract earlier statements about the lateness of the Pentateuch. None would now claim, as had Norton, that it was written after the return from captivity.[43] "Our own countryman then, Mr. Norton, who so often speaks with not a little severity of the skepticism of the Germans, plainly outdoes the very leaders of dubitation among them, in the case before us."[44]

But this was a secondary problem, and Stuart turned to the more serious arguments of the Germans, who, regardless of their judgments about Moses' literacy, still denied the Mosaic authorship of the Pentateuch. After a long discussion of pentateuchal "source" theories from Semler through von Lengerke, Stuart remained firm in his conviction that whatever the sources Moses used, the Pentateuch is from his hand, as testified "by all the historians and prophets of the Old Testament; by the Apocryphal writers, by Philo, Josephus, and all the New Testament writers, and expressly and repeatedly by Christ himself.[45] And so it was with the remainder of the books of the Old Testament. Wherever Norton or the Germans[46] rose to deny the genuineness, authenticity, or unity of an Old Testament writing, Stuart rose to defend. Though he modified his arguments to meet the newer

[40] Ibid., 13–14.

[41] Ibid., 47. The work referred to is *Geschichte des Volkes Israel* (Göttingen: In der Dieterichschen Buchhandlung, 1843).

[42] *Critical History and Defense*, 47.

[43] *Evidences*, 2:436.

[44] *Critical History and Defense*, 48. Stuart believed this to be particularly dangerous in the light of Norton's professed stand against "that branch of the so-called Liberal Party," namely the transcendentalists, who, as Stuart describes, "have discarded the authority of both the Old Testament and the New; who doubt the personality of the Godhead; and who flatly deny the possibility of miracles." Though Norton would reject the party identification, Stuart perceived there was now little difference between the two (16).

[45] Ibid., 49, 48–60.

[46] Those most frequently cited were Ewald in the work already mentioned and Wilhelm M. L. De Wette in his *Lehrbuch Historisch-kritisch Einleitung in das Alte Testament* (Berlin: G. Reimer, 1817). Stuart had also read De Wette in the translation by Theodore Parker, and he reserved particular scorn for some of the statements Parker had made in this edition (*A Critical and Historical Introduction to the Canonical Scriptures of the Old Testament*, 2 vols. [Boston: Little & Brown, 1843]).

theories, his conclusions varied little from the ones he reached thirty years earlier.

There were a few exceptions. Although he continued to maintain that Job was a real person, Stuart had changed his opinion about the dating of the book. It now seemed clear, on the basis of style, that the book must be placed in the same age as Ecclesiastes or "in the Chaldean period of the prophets,"[47] rather than in the age of the patriarchs.

He flirted with the possibility of there having been several authors of Isaiah, though he felt the evidence still too inconclusive to abandon his older opinion. He admitted that as a theologian he would "have little to object to the *compound* nature of the book," but as a critic, he had "serious doubts whether recent criticism has yet made its way clear." "Most knots which we must now cut," he continued, "would easily be united" if it could be determined with certainty that another Isaiah lived and wrote at this time. But in the face of the complete silence of Jewish history on the matter, Stuart could not rely on such a theory.[48]

The authorship of Ecclesiastes now seemed clearer to Stuart. He had questioned the older opinion that Solomon was the author but had preferred to leave the matter open rather than defy tradition. It seemed certain now, however, that Solomon was not the author. A king at the "very summit of human greatness" would hardly have talked about the "emptiness and vanity of all earthly objects and pursuits." And since Stuart assumed that Solomon wrote part of Proverbs, he could not ignore the difference in style between Proverbs and Ecclesiastes: "Chaucer does not differ more from Pope, than Ecclesiastes from Proverbs. . . . It seems to be, when I read Coheleth, that it presents one of those cases which leave no room for doubt, so striking and prominent is the discrepancy."[49]

The dating of Ecclesiastes had not surfaced in the early lectures. Now Stuart treated it as highly conjectural and decided only on a date during the "Persian" age, because the book dealt with the toils and hardships typical of that period.[50] The "philosophy" of the book, Stuart believed, reminded one of the discussions on Socrates in the Dialogues of Plato. He observed:

> I cannot help thinking that the writer must have been a Hebrew who had resided abroad, where he had formed some acquaintance with the philosophic discussions of the Greeks. So *unique* is the tenor of his book, and so widely different from the usual circle of Hebrew thinking, that no very probable account can be given of these matters, without such a supposition.[51]

[47] *Critical History and Defense*, 147.
[48] Ibid., 109, 110.
[49] Ibid., 139.
[50] Ibid., 140–41.
[51] Ibid., 140.

This problem he pursued with more care in his *Commentary on Ecclesiastes* (1851), a work shorter than his previous commentaries, though every bit as useful. Here Stuart reversed his opinion about the Greek influences that he advanced in his *Critical History and Defense* six years before. To be sure, the book was philosophical, but whereas Greek philosophy was ontological and metaphysical, Ecclesiastes was practical: "All the reasonings are built on the results of experience; and all the precepts which accompany them are such as have regard, not to mere abstract truth, but to wary, considerate, and sober demeanor. The book begins and ends with one and the same theme; and this theme itself is the result of observation and experience." A Jew familiar with Socrates and Plato would have written an entirely different kind of work. The absence of Greek influences indicates a composition before the Hellenistic, or "Macedonian," period when the knowledge of Greek philosophy became widespread.[52] This position supported Stuart's argument in the *Critical History and Defense*, which dated the work in the "Persian" age.

Of more concern, however, were charges from the Germans that the author of Ecclesiastes was guilty of skepticism, fatalism, and Epicureanism. Speaking against De Wette and Umbreit, Stuart denied the charges. He admitted that some parts of the work seemed skeptical and fatalistic but not the book as a whole. Indeed, the preacher raised doubts merely to answer them. "The most natural account of the plan of the book seems to be this, viz. that the writer has given a picture of the struggle and contest through which his own mind had passed, when he set out on the road of philosophical inquiry." In this regard the author is no different from Paul or some of the psalmists. Further, Stuart cautioned against expecting too much from the writer. "Why would we demand that he should so far outstrip all his contemporaries and predecessors, as to make his book a gospel-treatise instead of an Old Testament production?"[53] As for the charge of Epicureanism, Stuart acknowledged that the book urges one "to eat, and to drink, and to enjoy the good of one's labor"; but "there is not one [passage] which savors of encouragement to drunkenness, or gluttony, or revelling. . . . In all this there is, or need be found, only a cheerful and thankful acceptance of the gifts of God."[54]

Stuart's two other commentaries on the Old Testament, the studies on Daniel (1850) and Proverbs (1852), reproduced the critical opinions of the lectures and the *Critical History and Defense*. In both commentaries, however, he expanded the critical sections.

In analyzing the book of Daniel, the critical concern was the identity

---

[52] *Commentary on Ecclesiastes,* 8.

[53] Ibid., 26, 28.

[54] Ibid., 29. Stuart's characterization of Epicureanism never went beyond this superficial generalization.

of the author. Stuart's commentary, his last elaborate work, continued to
defend his earlier view that Daniel was a historical person living through
the events described in the first six chapters. He criticized the opposing
views of such German liberals as E. F. K. Rosenmueller and von Lengerke,
especially the latter.[55] Again Stuart related his doctrine of inspiration,
especially that of prophetic inspiration, to critical questions. He was sur-
prisingly modern in his exegesis, for he saw, as no other American exegete
saw, that most of the events described in the prophetic portions refer to later
Jewish history. This much he gratefully received from the German "neologists." But the writer of Daniel, he thought, might have prophesied these
events at the time of Nebuchadnezzar, centuries earlier. In fact, Daniel,
having foreseen the rise and fall of eastern empires from Nebuchadnezzar
through Antiochus Epiphanes, seemed to Stuart a supreme example of the
inspired prophet. Thus, a historical interpretation of the passages, combined with a high view of inspiration, supported his original contention
about the historicity and genuineness of the work.

Stuart did give considerable attention to critical problems in the first
six chapters—the personal history of Daniel, the seeming irrationalities in
the narrative, and the apparent discrepancies between the book's names
and dates for Babylonian personages and external evidence about them.
But he thought that "neology" had failed to overcome the traditional belief
that Daniel had faithfully recorded events.[56] Stuart's critical approach
could be characterized as an eclectic apologia for divine inspiration.

A Commentary on the Book of Proverbs, his last full-length work, was
a simpler study, partly because it examined less complex critical problems.
Yet to the last Stuart fought the battle of the critical conservative. Though
he did not deny the composite authorship of the book, he remained convinced that Solomon had the major hand in composing it, despite Ewald's
contention that one part of the book was written two hundred years after
the death of Solomon.[57] Though Stuart admitted that the writing took
shape gradually, he maintained that it was completed around three hundred years after the reign of Solomon, sometime before the Babylonian
exile.[58] A number of peculiar words and phrases in the book might indicate
a later date, but these are few considering the book's length, and they
constitute no valid argument against Solomon as the main author.[59]

[55] The relevant works of these men were Rosenmueller's *Daniel* (Leipzig, 1832) and von
Lengerke's *Das Buch Daniel* (Königsberg, 1835).
[56] *Commentary on Daniel.* See particularly the excursuses, 19–170, passim.
[57] *Commentary on Proverbs,* 23–38.
[58] Ibid., 59.
[59] Ibid., 59–61.

Exegetical Aids and Method

Though Stuart was learned and productive in such critical matters as the date, place, author, and genuineness of the books in the Bible, his principal intention was to clarify the meaning of the texts. The investigation of critical problems was never an end in itself. Always he related them to the task of bringing to light God's revealed word as found in book, chapter, or verse of the scriptures. The biblical scholar, Stuart believed, was primarily a commentator.

Much of the framework of what we have to say about Stuart as a commentator was provided by Stuart himself in an article entitled "Hints Respecting Commentaries upon the Scriptures," which appeared in the *American Biblical Repository* in January of 1833.[60] The article presents Stuart's practical principles for writing a useful commentary. He noted that the aim of a commentary is to explain the words, phrases, and idioms of the text according to the rules of grammatical-historical interpretation. Such an aim requires (1) a clear and simple translation; (2) the philological analysis of doubtful or ambiguous passages; (3) the comparison of the words used in the passage with the use of the same words in other passages; and (4) an exegetical and descriptive paraphrase, wherein all "the difficulties of grammar, idiom, phraseology, peculiar style, geography, antiquities, history, etc." are made clear.[61] Next, the commentator should logically present the results. Each separate investigation should be related to the whole in a balanced and orderly method enhancing, not obscuring, the "economy" of the book. Finally, the commentary should be suitable to its intended audience. Specialized scholars and educated clergy need technical manuals that contain the steps and conclusion of philological and historical investigations. The public would best be served by practical, homiletical works in which the simple sense of the scripture is explained and applied.[62]

Each of Stuart's six commentaries illustrates that he took these aims seriously. The grammatical-historical method of investigation and interpretation is everywhere predominant, with special pains taken in translation. In his first commentary, on Hebrews, he noted the care with which he had chosen the words and remarked that he much preferred the "Saxon English

---

[60] Vol. 3, 130–85.

[61] Ibid., 173.

[62] Ibid. Stuart admitted exceptions to this principle. In particular, he noted that he knew of "no rule which would hinder a critical commentator ... to admit doctrinal discussions to a certain extent, provided they are conducted in a critical manner.... Nor can he be debarred from *preaching* some, if he chooses so to do.... Taste, and tact, and the times" will guide him in these respects, but always such excursuses should be "just as brief as the nature of the case permits" (176–77).

for a version of the Bible" and that he "purposely avoided substituting
Latinizing English in its room, unless a regard to the meaning of the original" compelled him to do it.[63] His translation of Hebrews occupied a special
place at the head of the second volume, and though after his commentary
on Romans the translation appeared in the exegetical sections, Stuart
always took care with the translations. In his last commentary, on Proverbs,
he could still note that he had "more often hesitated in order to find a Saxon
word which is not vulgar, instead of a word derived from the Latin or
Greek, than from almost any other cause."[64]

Two examples from familiar passages in Hebrews and Romans will
suffice as illustrations of Stuart's style. The brackets are his:

> Now faith is confidence in respect to things hoped for, [and] con-
> vincing evidence of things not seen. On account of this, moreover, the
> ancients obtained commendation.[65]

> What shall we say, then, concerning these things? If God be for us,
> who is against us? Even he who spared not his own Son, but freely gave
> him up for us all—how shall he not also, with him, freely give us all
> things? Who shall accuse the elect of God? It is God that justifieth; who
> is he that condemneth? It is Christ who died [for us]; yea rather, who is
> risen, and who is at the right hand of God, and who intercedeth for us.
> Who shall separate us from the love of Christ? Shall affliction, or anguish,
> or persecution, or famine, or nakedness, or peril, or sword? (As it is writ-
> ten: "For thy sake we are continually exposed to death, we are counted
> as sheep for the slaughter"). Nay, in all these things we are more than
> conquerors, through him who loved us. For I am persuaded, that neither
> death nor life, neither angels nor principalities, neither things present
> nor future, nor powers, neither height nor depth, nor any other created
> thing, shall be able to separate us from the love of God, which is in Christ
> Jesus our Lord.[66]

In his philological analysis Stuart was thorough to a fault. Frequently
one finds pages devoted to a single word, a debated point of syntax, or an
analysis of textual readings of a disputed passage. Illustrations abound
almost at random. His discussion of the word *hilastērion* in Rom 3:25 is
typical of his philological method. Nothing is novel or original in the treatment, and modern scholars might judge it strained or unbalanced, but his
plodding thoroughness is important to observe.[67] Stuart translated the Rom
3:25 passage to read "whom God hath set forth as a propitiatory [sacrifice]
by faith in his blood." *Hilastērion*, Stuart noted, is an adjective that may be
translated *propitiatory*, or *atoning*, after the usage in classical Greek,

---

[63] *Commentary on Hebrews*, 2:vi.
[64] *Commentary on Proverbs*, 7.
[65] Heb 11:1–2; *Commentary on Hebrews*, 2:26.
[66] Rom 8:31–39; *Commentary on Romans*, 22.
[67] The full discussion is found in *Commentary on Romans*, 164–66.

particularly in Homer. The main problem was Paul's "elliptical" use of the adjective and the identity of the missing noun to be supplied after the word. "Is it *epithema, cover;* or *thuma, offering* or *sacrifice?*" Evidence from the Septuagint would lean toward the first reading, as would evidence from Hebrew usage. Citing passages in Exodus and Leviticus, Stuart noted that here the Hebrew *"kaporeth,"* or *"covering,"* is the adjective, referring to the ark of the covenant, "the throne of Jehovah in his earthly temple, the place from which he uttered his oracles, and communed with the representatives of his people." Philo, in his *Vita Mosis,* supports the usage. It was this interpretation, Stuart believed, that could show *mercy seat* to be the proper translation of *hilastērion.* Such was the conclusion of "Origen, Theodoret, Throphylact, Oecumenicius, Erasmus, Luther, and others."[68]

"But was Paul necessarily limited to this?" Evidence from other Greek writings would show that the adjective suggested a second reading, *offering* or *sacrifice;* for example, Dio Chrysostom, *Orat.* II, "propitiatory offering"; Josephus, *Antiquities* XVI, "a propitiatory monument"; and 4 Macc 17:22, "propitiatory death." Christian interpreters whom Stuart cites for the second reading are Hesychius, Grotius, Le Clerc, Kypke, Turretin, Elsner, Flatt, and Tholuck. In addition, the second reading could be supported by evidence that they had not discovered—evidence within the text itself. In the phrase *en tō haimati autou* (in his blood), which followed *hilastērion,* the relationship of *haima* (blood) to *hilastērion* was "unnatural" if *mercy seat* be the meaning of the latter word:

> For then Christ would be represented as a mercy-seat, sprinkled with his *own blood;* an incongruous figure, if the analogy of the Jewish mercy-seat be consulted. But if [hilastērion] means a *propitiatory sacrifice,* then is the image altogether congruous; inasmuch as the blood was sprinkled round about upon the altar, where the sacrifice was laid, Lev. 1:5, 11. 3:8.[69]

Still another support was available for the second interpretation. This lay in the proper signification of *proti-thēmi,* another of the words in the phrase. Three meanings could be given the word: (1) *to lay before, to set before or propose;* (2) *publicly to expose or to hold up to view;* and (3) *to prefer.* Of these, Stuart pointed out,

> the second classical one seems plainly to be that which is best adapted to our text; for this best agrees with the *eis endeixin* and *pros endeixin*[70] which follow. *Hon proetheto ho theos hilastērion* may then be rendered; *whom God hath openly exhibited to the world as a propitiatory sacrifice.* But suppose now, that we construe *hilastērion* as meaning mercy-seat,

---

[68] Ibid., 164–65.

[69] Ibid., 165.

[70] Both phrases, the second of which appears in verse 26, Stuart translated *"in order to declare"* (ibid., 167).

then where is the *congruity* of the image? Was the *mercy-seat*, exhibited to the view of those for whom atonement was made? Never; the high priest only saw it, once in each year, on the great day of atonement. To avoid this evident incongruity, one must render *proetheto, constituit;* and then the evident reference made by it to *eis endeixin* and *pros endeixin*, is lost or obscured.[71]

Thus he concluded: "I see no congruous method of interpreting the passage before us, except by rendering *hilastērion, propitiatory* sacrifice." Thoughts about the sacrificial nature of Christ found in John 1:29; Eph 5:2, 1 Pet 1:19; 3:24; Heb 9:14; and 1 Cor 5:7 all support "the sentiment which this rendering exhibits."[72]

But not every passage was treated so exhaustively. Some could be interpreted by a simple paraphrase. A good example is Stuart's exegesis of the familiar fifth and sixth verses of Proverbs 5. The passage is quoted in its entirety:

> (5) Trust in Jehovah with all thine heart,
>   and lean not upon thine own understanding.

This inculcates humility, and stands opposed to pride and self-confidence.—['el], *to, toward*, so the Heb., but in our own we say: *lean upon*.

> (6) In all thy ways acknowledge him, and he will
>   make straight thy paths.

This verse connects intimately with the preceding one, and presents a good reason for following the advice there given.—[ra] with the suff. becomes [da ehu];—[hu] has an emphatic sense, and it is inserted for this reason. The meaning is, *he* and none else.—[yᵉvasher] is reg. Piel Imperfect.[73]

Any one of the commentaries would exemplify Stuart's second aim as a commentator—the logical "proportionment" of all the parts. For Stuart this meant that each book was a logical whole, that it was written with a purpose or theme in mind, and that all its parts contributed to the expression of that purpose or theme. The commentator must be faithful to the message of the author by treating each philological or historical investigation as a contribution to the main flow of thought, not as a series of isolated units of research. He observed that the Germans often forgot this principle, and in his article on commentaries he likened some of them to an antiquary digging among ancient temple ruins, so interested in a fragment that he

---

[71] Ibid., 166.

[72] Ibid. For another example of a protracted word study, of less theological interest than the one cited, see his treatment of Rev 2:17, and particularly the meaning of the "white stone" mentioned in that verse (*Commentary on the Apocalypse*, 2:77–79). This grew out of an article on the same subject, "The White Stone of the Apocalypse: Exegesis of Rev. 2:17," *Bibliotheca Sacra* (1843) 461–77.

[73] *Commentary on Proverbs*, 168.

cannot tell the size or shape of the building to which it belonged or its use in the structure.[74]

The exegetical sections of each commentary usually began with a one-sentence statement of the theme, followed by a two or three-page summary of the divisions of the book. Thus, the panorama of the "temple" appeared before the reader's eye well in advance of the individual "fragments." As the commentary proceeded, each chapter or logical subdivision was presented in a paraphrase outline, with the key verses highlighted and the transitions noted for readers who might be referring only to a specific chapter or verse. Though it was not uncommon for the exegesis of a difficult word or phrase to become complex and extended, any material that was not strictly philological occupied a separate excursus placed at the end of the commentary or inserted in the body of the work but labeled separately and printed in small type.

The third aim, adapting the commentary to the audience, proved easy for Stuart, because he wrote for serious interpreters like himself. He did not disparage the "practical" kind of commentary,[75] but it was not his vocation to publish such works. He wrote for preachers and scholars. "A commentary merely hortatory and practical, they should themselves be able to make."[76] Hence, although one finds philology at every turn, one finds little practical application to the Christian life.[77]

The Commentaries Reviewed and Criticized

Critical response to Stuart's biblical writings was positive, though a few negative reactions came from readers offended by Stuart's apparent subversion of a favorite theological or critical opinion. Princeton's Charles Hodge disliked Stuart's treatment of original sin in his commentary on Romans.[78] Criticism of another sort came from anti-Catholics who complained that Stuart was too easy on Rome. Notable here was Edward Beecher, pastor of the Salem Street Congregational Church in Boston and

[74] "Hints Respecting Commentaries Upon the Scriptures," *American Biblical Repository* 3 (January 1833) 146–47.

[75] He indicated in his "Hints Respecting Commentaries" that he believed the writing of practical commentaries to be a worthwhile pursuit, and if done correctly, one more difficult and time-consuming than philological work, since the practical commentator must cover the philology before making practical applications. (174).

[76] *Commentary on Proverbs*, 5. A similar sentiment is expressed in the preface to his *Commentary on Hebrews*.

[77] Such practical matters were, however, apparently a part of Stuart's classroom exegetical lectures. The notes the anonymous student made from Stuart's lectures on the book of Revelation record the whole of the final presentation as treating the subject "On the use that is to be made of the Apocalypse in preaching" ("Professor Stuart's Lectures on the Apocalypse," Lecture 39, 30 August 1839).

[78] Charles Hodge, "Stuart on Romans," *Biblical Repertory* 5 (July 1833) passim.

an anti-Catholic, who roundly criticized Stuart's commentary on Revelation for failing to take proper account of the prophetic references to the Roman Catholic Church and the struggles of true believers against the papal "beast."[79]

At the other end of the theological spectrum, the Unitarians criticized the commentaries not only for their trinitarian presuppositions but also for questionable conclusions on critical matters. Stuart's insistence on the Pauline authorship of Hebrews evoked a long, detailed rebuttal by Andrews Norton.[80] The Unitarians also leveled their guns against the *Critical History and Defense of the Old Testament Canon*. Andrews Norton, after all, had been the target of much of the book. Norton's colleague at Harvard, George Noyes, Hancock Professor of Hebrew and Dexter Lecturer, drafted the reply. He noted that Stuart left intact Norton's views of the Old Testament books and added that Stuart's work "abounds in loose and inconclusive reasoning."[81]

The positive reviews also reflected party spirit or pet critical or theological positions. One anonymous writer, replying to Andrews Norton with regard to the commentary on Hebrews, affirmed Stuart's insistence on its Pauline authorship. But more was on the reviewer's mind than that topic: "We think [Stuart] has risen in his strength, and snapped the cords with which the Philistines would have bound him." He has convinced "the friends of vital religion in all parts of our country, that evangelical sentiments have no more strenuous or intelligent advocates than exists near the tombs of the Pilgrims." What was even more important, the work had ferreted out the Unitarian view on scriptural inspiration, forcing the "Cambridge men" openly to admit what they had secretly believed all along— that "this epistle is a cheat, a deception, having no claim, nor shadow of a claim, to a place in the sacred Volume."[82]

Whether or not the reviewers agreed with Stuart, most concurred in hailing him as a biblical scholar of the first rank. Charles Hodge claimed Stuart to be "one of the greatest benefactors of the Church in our country," and paid him "unfeigned homage as the great American reformer of biblical

[79] "Remarks on Stuart's Commentary on the Apocalypse," *American Biblical Repository* 3d series, 3 (April 1847) 272–304. George Duffield, Presbyterian pastor in Detroit, continued the criticism of Stuart's un-Protestant views. But the greater portion of Duffield's review was devoted to proving that Stuart had erred in the dating of the book. Though he agreed with Stuart that the apostle John was the author, Duffield believed the work to have been written during the reign of Domitian, not Nero ("Review of Stuart on the Apocalypse," *American Biblical Repository* 3d series, 3 [July, 1847] 385–411).

[80] "On the Author of the Epistle to the Hebrews," *Christian Examiner* 4 (November, December 1827) 495–519; 5 (January, February 1828) 37–70; 6 (May 1829) 330–47. For a review that attacked Stuart's trinitarianism, see George W. Burnap, "Stuart on the Apocalypse," *Christian Examiner* 40 (March 1846) 161–94.

[81] "Stuart on the Old Testament," *Christian Examiner* 40 (January 1846) 76.

[82] "Review of Stuart's commentary on Hebrews," *The Spirit of the Pilgrims* 2 (February 1829) 83, 87, 97–98.

study, as the introducer of a new era, and the most efficient opponent of metaphysical theology."[83] George W. Burnap, pastor of the First Unitarian Church of Baltimore, noted Stuart's "truly German . . . patience of labor and . . . power of producing books," the long length of his active life, and the fact that "he is one of the most industrious men of our times." Burnap continued by observing that Stuart's *A Commentary on the Apocalypse* was not only "the ablest as well as the largest, of his works," but also "a decided improvement on anything that has appeared, to our knowledge, in the English tongue on the book of Revelation." So complete is the work that "the student of Scripture is enabled to make up his own opinion as to the origin and meaning of this production, even when it differs from that of Professor Stuart." "We are glad [the volumes] are published," he concluded. "They constitute some of the best Orthodox criticism we have had in this country."[84] *The American Monthly Review* regarded the commentary on Romans, with all of its theological "prejudice" and "diffuse" style as "a work of great merit on many accounts." Stuart's consulting of "*original* authorities" was appreciated; and the artistry of the translation, "couched in elegant language," was singled out for praise.[85] One of Stuart's own party, James Marsh, president of the University of Vermont, made the same point regarding Stuart's translation of Hebrews.[86]

Methodists and Baptists published laudatory assessments. Stephan M. Vail, professor of Hebrew at the Methodist General Biblical Institute in Concord, New Hampshire, noted Stuart's "immense learning, fervent piety, and clear, sound sense," and remarked that he had "long since come to be considered a Coryphaeus among Biblical scholars and interpreters, both in this country and in Europe."[87] At the time of Stuart's death in 1852, Alvah

[83] "Stuart on Romans," *Biblical Repertory* 5 (July 1833) 382.

[84] "Stuart on the Apocalypse," 161, 166, 193. The most interesting compliment that was paid to Stuart in this article was indirect. Lamenting the lack of similar productions among the Unitarians, the writer exclaimed: "Would that we could bear a larger part in creating the theological literature which is to form the religious opinions of the rising millions of our growing country!" (194).

[85] "Stuart's Commentary on Romans," 2 (November 1832) 392, 393.

[86] "Review of Stuart on the Epistle to the Hebrews," *Quarterly Christian Spectator* 2 (March 1829) 132. Marsh also remarked about Stuart's thoroughness, his aim "to exhaust his subject, to leave no inquiry unnoticed, and no objection unanswered. . . . This characteristic appears still more worthy of remark when we observe, that there are at the same time no digressions from the question at issue, nothing irrelevant to the subject. We have no French declamation, and no English dogmatizing" (126).

[87] "Review of Stuart on the Apocalypse," *Methodist Quarterly Review* 29 (January 1847) 5. The author disagreed with Stuart about verbal inspiration, believing Stuart to be wrong in not admitting "a full, plenary inspiration of the very words and imagery, as well as the thoughts of the sacred writers." Yet, he made it clear that in regard to Stuart's "main principles, in his views as to the general object of the book—*the coming and completion of the kingdom of God,* in his view of the catastrophes, we go with him heart and soul. His work is the most candid, most clear, most learned, and altogether the most satisfactory of any on the Apocalypse we have ever read" (21).

Hovey, then beginning a distinguished teaching career at the Baptist seminary in Newton Centre, Massachusetts, expressed similar sentiments. Noting Stuart's "high conception of the work of an interpreter, Hovey spoke of the comprehensiveness of Stuart's commentaries:

> Many and various topics deeply interesting to the Christian, the interpreter, and the theologian are elucidated in them. The sheaves garnered by other hands are used with a freedom becoming one who had earnestly toiled for himself in the great harvest field of knowledge. Along with the results of study on the part of European scholars, he has given us original and often sagacious comments of his own, upon a multitude of passages in the early Christian writers. The pages of his Commentary on the Apocalypse illustrate the wide range of his investigations; and the first volume of this work offers to the American information which is not otherwise very accessible. The Commentary upon Daniel takes up, one by one, the objections raised by the keen, learned and tireless ingenuity of skepticism, against that portion of the Sacred Record, and shows their futility. In his work on Ecclesiastes, we have, probably, an abler and truer development of the course of thought presented by the inspired Preacher, than can be found in any English author. It may be truly said, that all his commentaries deserve careful perusal for the true learning they embody. And this is high praise.[88]

Our own estimate of Stuart's work as a biblical interpreter can be added briefly. First, his commentaries and critical works are pervaded by a spirit of confidence in the excellence and authority of the scriptures. They catch a deep and solemn interest in everything the scriptures teach. The Bible was for Stuart a revelation from God, and its inspired content a pattern for the highest standard of duty. Second, the commentaries are comprehensive, particularly in their use of the grammatical-historical method, even though objectivity is sometimes weakened in the push of theological prejudice. It was indeed true, as Alvah Hovey remarked, that in Stuart "the judge is too often lost in the advocate."[89] But it is equally true that subjectivity can seldom be avoided, and that when Stuart was accused of pressing his own beliefs, his opponents' arguments were also subjective. Considering the earnestness of the times, the surprise is that we find no more of the "advocate" than we do. Third, we must concur with Stuart's reviewers about his style. Except for the briefer commentaries on Proverbs and Ecclesiastes, the works are repetitious, burdensome, and tedious. His pen seldom halted for revision or condensation; his points often lacked incisiveness and therefore appeared weak when they were strong. None of this, however, detracts from the overall worth of the books, and though advances in biblical study have made obsolete much of his effort, they have not diminished the exemplary quality of his work. Stuart's books remain solid monuments to the spirit of faithful and learned biblical scholarship.

[88] "Moses Stuart," *The Christian Review* 17 (April 1852) 288, 290–91.
[89] Ibid., 292.

VIII

THE BIBLICAL THEOLOGIAN:

ROMANS 5:12–19 AND THE

DOCTRINE OF ORIGINAL SIN

As a biblical commentator Stuart made technical critical and philological investigations and was content to let others draw the practical and theological conclusions. But he did not always leave the implications unpursued, especially when texts touched on theological issues before the public, though his arguments usually proceeded from the settled opinions to which he as a New Divinity Edwardsean subscribed. Yet through it all, and especially in the commentaries, his method was exegetical rather than discursive. Stuart sought clear biblical revelation through faithful philological and historical research.

Of the theological issues in his exegetical writings, that which best reveals his method and his intellectual environment was his discussion of Paul's concept of original sin in Rom 5:12–19.[1]

Stuart's Protestant audience could accept much of his exegesis and theological elaboration of Romans. On the point of justification by faith, his interpretation, for all of its philological detail, preserved the main outlines of Reformation theology, albeit slanted toward the Reformed tradition.[2] Rom 5:12–19, however, presented theological questions on which Stuart could hardly have expected agreement: the sin of Adam and the universal sin of the race. In brief, Stuart's position when he interpreted Paul

---

[1] Stuart's commentaries did occasionally address other theological matters under debate among his contemporaries, notably the Trinity, baptism, and millenarianism. In each of these issues Stuart's treatment reflected his moderate Calvinist Congregationalism. Discussions of the Trinity occur at several places in the commentary on Hebrews but without substantial change from the position developed in the earlier episodes of the Unitarian controversy. The exegesis of Rom 6:4 insisted that baptism must be interpreted in a moral or spiritual light not physical. The millennium referred to in Rev 20:3–4 would involve a limited resurrection in which only the saints would be raised from the dead, followed by the binding of Satan for a thousand years, but without a literal, physical reign of Christ on earth. See especially *Commentary on Hebrews*, 2:311–39; *Commentary on Romans*, 252–54, and an extension of this argument in "Is the Manner of Christian Baptism Prescribed in the New Testament?" *American Biblical Repository* 3 (April 1833) 288–390; and *Commentary on the Apocalypse*, 2:474–90.

[2] See especially his discussion of Rom 9:8, 13 (*Commentary on Romans*, 382–89).

was to admit that all persons are sinners but to deny that the sin or guilt of *Adam* was imputed to his posterity. Sin is a personal act of each individual and is committed only when a person makes moral choices. The *result* of Adam's sin, mortal death, misery, and suffering, but not the sin itself, has been transferred to his posterity.

Two points are clear in Stuart's stand. First, it opposed the federal or covenant theory by which the Westminster Confession sought to answer the problem of human sin, that is, that Adam and Eve, as the representative heads of the race, through their own violation of the original covenant of works made between them and God, caused "all their Posterity, descending from them by ordinary generation" to sin and fall.[3] Stuart's second position was but a restatement of a traditional New England criticism of the Westminster formulation. In Stuart's circle, the most astute revisionist was his friend and successor at New Haven's Center Church, Yale's formidable theologian Nathaniel W. Taylor. Like the more conservative Calvinists, Taylor did not deny natural depravity, but he did point out that he did not believe human nature to be in itself sinful or morally corrupt. Nor could he believe that sin was imputed to the human race through generic participation in Adam's first sin. All he would venture to say positively was that one's nature was the "occasion" or "reason" of one's sinning.[4] Taylor would not deny that Adam's first sin was related to the universal sin of his offspring, but how, he did not explain. Human consciousness, the Bible, and the history of the race gave him his proof. Sin, he believed, "*is man's own act, consisting in a free choice of some object rather than God, as his chief good; — or a free preference of the world and of worldly good, to the will and glory of God.*"[5] Notably absent is any reference to the Westminster view that the guilt of Adam's sin is *imputed* to his posterity.

As Stuart proceeded to the exegesis of Rom 5:12–19, it was inevitable that he would have to declare himself on this perplexing issue. From the outset, he was in agreement with his New Haven friend. Although he spoke with some disparagement about the difficulties created by "speculative minds, relative to the various topics on which the paragraph before us had been supposed to touch,"[6] he found it impossible to work in a theological vacuum. Though unoriginal, the result was important because of its exegetical thoroughness. His contribution was to provide the New Haven

---

[3] *The Westminster Confession of Faith*, 6:3, 4. See Philip Schaff, *The Creeds of Christendom* (New York: Harper & Brothers, 1877) 3:615.

[4] *Concio ad Clerum: A Sermon Delivered in the Chapel of Yale College, September 10, 1828* (reprinted in Sydney Ahlstrom, *Theology in America* [New York: Bobbs-Merrill, 1967] 211–49). See also Sidney Mead, *Nathaniel W. Taylor, 1786–1858* (Chicago: University of Chicago Press, 1942) 223–26; H. Shelton Smith, *Changing Conceptions of Original Sin* (New York: Scribner, 1955).

[5] Taylor, *Concio ad Clerum*, 217.

[6] *Commentary on Romans*, 201.

"liberals," Taylor chief among them, a solid exegetical ground for their speculative conclusions. Stuart saw the text addressing three questions: (1) Have human beings sinned in their proper persons or in Adam? (2) What is sin? (3) How does Adam's posterity suffer the consequence of his sin?

The answer to the first question was found in the interpretation of verses 12 and 19. Much hinged on the translation of the last clause of verse 12, which Stuart read "*because* that all have sinned" in preference to "*in whom* all have sinned." The latter reading, as Stuart noted, appeared in the Vulgate and in "Augustine, Beza, Calixtus, E. Schmidt, Calovius, Quenstedt, Raphelius, et alli."[7] But even if the reading was "because" rather than "in whom," Stuart had to elaborate on the question of "how" — that is, whether the phrase implies that human beings sin in "their *own proper persons*" or in Adam. Stuart was aware that many of the most respectable commentators had regarded the phrase *pantes hēmarton* "as meaning that all have sinned in Adam, or at least, that through him they have become sinners," and that verses 17–19 seem to support such a reading. "And it must be confessed," he added, "that there is no more ground for objection to the *sentiment* which the expression thus construed would convey, than there is to the sentiment in vs. 17–19."[8] A simple consideration of the context, however, forbids such an interpretation. Moreover, Stuart could see no philological reason why the ordinary meaning of *hēmarton* should not be received "unless there is a solid reason for departing from it; and all this added to the later part of v. 12 seems to make it unavoidable that *pantes hēmarton* should be here construed *all have sinned in their own persons or actually*."[9]

Even if verse 19 be structurally related to verse 12, which Stuart was willing to grant, the one no more suggested the Westminster doctrine of imputation than the other. The key word to Stuart was *katestathēsan*, which he translated "were constituted," a phrase that no doubt came easily to mind from its inclusion in the Andover Associate Creed to which as a professor on that foundation he was legally bound. *Katestathēsan*, he asserted, by comparing its usage in Jas 4:4 (*kathistatai*) and 3 Macc 3:5 (*katheistēkeisan*) need not be construed in the active voice which implies imputation but could be used in the passive and middle voices to mean *were constituted* or *became*. That this construction was pivotal becomes evident in the way Stuart concluded his analysis:

> No necessity is laid upon us, by the use of the word *katestathēsan* of understanding the apostle to assert that men *involuntarily*, or without the concurrence of their own free will, become sinners. Surely men may become sinners in consequence of the act of another, and yet be altogether voluntary in becoming so; as is clear from the fact, that men every

---

[7] Ibid., 210.
[8] Ibid., 212.
[9] Ibid., 212–13.

day yield to temptations offered by others to commit sin, and yet are altogether voluntary in thus yielding. Nothing then can be drawn merely from the use of the word *katestathēsan* to show that here the doctrine of imputation, in the strict and proper sense of this word, is taught.[10]

Nor does the whole phrase — "the many became sinners by the disobedience of Adam" — suggest that Paul was asserting an imputation theory. Paul himself denies this in Rom 7:5 by referring to "our sinful passions which were by the law." A similar thought is conveyed in verses 7 and 8 of the same chapter. In no way does this mean that the law is the "*efficient cause of our sinful passions*," for Paul notes in the same context that "the law is holy, and just, and good." Thus "it is impossible that any legitimate conclusions in favour of imputation in its strict sense, can be made out either from the particular words or the general phraseology of v. 19."[11]

Not content with the philological arguments, Stuart appended several excursuses suggesting philosophical objections to the doctrine of imputation. He argued that the doctrine contradicts the principles of our moral consciousness and the biblical principles of moral justice.[12]

Having denied the theory of imputation, Stuart considered the nature and cause of the "actual" sin which remains. Certainly heredity is not the cause: "How could [Paul] say this, when Adam sinned without it?" Nor is sinning to be considered as necessary "in the sense of being *compulsive.*" If the presence of the mere "*faculties to sin*" made human beings sinners, "Adam and the fallen angels were sinners before their first transgression."[13] Nor is temptation the "ground cause" for sin, for the man Jesus was tempted and yet did not sin. Nor can sin be laid to the possession of natural desires and appetites, "for they are essential to men as human beings, and our Savior possessed them: as did Adam before his fall."[14] In fact, the natural passions are accompanied by conscience, reason, judgment, and moral sense, all of which are designed by God to control and restrain the desires:

> Whatever then may be the degradation in which we are now born, (degradation compared with the original state of Adam), we are still born moral agents; free agents; with *faculties* to do good, yea, all the faculties that are needed. If we are born with passions and affections

[10] Ibid., 236–37.

[11] Ibid., 239. Four years later Stuart wrote a separate article entitled "Have the Sacred Writers Anywhere Asserted that the Sin or Righteousness of One is Imputed to Another?" (*American Biblical Repository* 7 [April 1836] 241–330), in which this same conclusion was reached for all the biblical passages from which imputation had been common derived. "It is altogether certain," he stated, "that NO CASE exists . . . in which the *sin or righteousness of one man is declared to be imputed or put to the account of another*" (262).

[12] *Commentary on Romans*, 239–42.

[13] Ibid., 540.

[14] Ibid., 541.

attached to our natures which may lead us to sin, we are also born having a *moral* man within us to remonstrate against the abuse of our passions.[15]

Beyond this, reason cannot venture. *That* human beings sin actually and in their own persons, Stuart could not contest. That this was somehow related to the first sin of Adam he also believed. But like Nathaniel Taylor, whose thought Stuart followed closely, he could not explain *how* the connection was established. It was, for Stuart, "a matter of divine sovereignty," altogether beyond our power to fathom. This did not mean that he would lay the cause to God, for our sins "are strictly our own." But the relationship remained a mystery. "We can speculate and reason about it, and wonder; but it becomes us to bow in humble submission."[16]

Not until Stuart addressed the matter of the moral nature of infants did he define what he meant by actual sin. His agreement with Taylor is unmistakable: Actual sin is *"the voluntary non-conformity of an intelligent, rational, moral, free agent."*[17] Until capable of rational and moral action, infants remain innocent of sin. To assume, as do "President Jonathan Edwards and the Symbols of the Reformation," that "before children have any knowledge at all, yea, while they are in the womb . . . they are not only sinners, but all the sin which is ever to be committed by them, is in them in embryo," is to accept the theory of "connate depravity," which not only fails to account for Adam's first sin but is "plainly at variance with the explicit declarations of the Scriptures . . . , and with the first dictates of our unbiased feelings and our reason."[18]

[15] Ibid.
[16] Ibid.
[17] Ibid., 542.
[18] Ibid., 543. Gardiner Spring, leader among the Old School Presbyterians in New York, issued a scathing attack upon these views in a ninety-three page essay entitled *Dissertation on Native Depravity* (New York: J. Levitt, 1833). The main force of Spring's argument was directed toward Nathaniel Taylor, but since Stuart shared Taylor's position on infant depravity, Stuart also came under fire (20; 35 n.; 38 n.; 75–76). To lack positive holiness, observed Spring, is to violate the law, which must be positively fulfilled. Thus Spring agreed that all sin is a voluntary action, but he maintained that infants, in not fulfilling the law, are actual sinners from the very moment of their creation. See also Smith, *Changing Conceptions,* 134–35.

Stuart did not answer Spring directly but resumed his discussion on the nature of sin and the accountability of children in an article entitled "What is Sin?" which appeared in successive issues of the *American Biblical Repository* (13 [April 1839] 261–94; 14 [July 1839] 26–71). The thought is essentially the same as that in the commentary on Romans, especially in the second article, which was largely a treatment of scriptural references. A somewhat novel element appeared in the first article, however, for there Stuart referred to the Dutch Calvinist Campegius Vitringa (1659–1722) in support of the argument that sin is actual. Vitringa, noted Stuart, had made much of the point that sin is not merely the absence of good, and supported the position that sin is the actual committing of an act. Daniel Dana (1771–1859), Presbyterian pastor at Newburyport, trustee of Andover, long friend of Stuart, but firm in his Old Calvinist ways, replied in a pamphlet entitled *Letters to the Rev. Professor*

There remained one more question in the passage: how *does* Adam's posterity suffer from his sin? Again the key verse was Rom 5:12. As *death* came to Adam by sin, so *death* comes to all people by their sins. Stuart did not deny that sin is universal or that the sins of humankind and their condemnation stand connected with Adam's first sin, but his accent was clearly on death and not on the act of Adam that brought death: "As Adam sinned and brought death upon himself, so death in all other cases is in like manner the inseparable attendant upon sin; and death is universal, because sin is so."[19] Inasmuch as Adam's heirs are born without holiness and in such a condition that whenever they become moral agents their passions will lead them to sin, his offense has brought death to all without exception.[20] Implicitly, then, a real, though unexplainable, connection exists between his penalty and ours.

Stuart concluded his discussion with a long study of the term *death* (*thanatos*), a word that implied not only the death of the body or temporal evil but also the whole *"penalty for sin in its full measure."*[21] Though Adam's sin cannot be imputed to his posterity, the consequences of that sin for the sinning race can be reckoned only in the most comprehensive terms. "Indeed," Stuart added, "I see no *philological* escape from the conclusion."[22]

Stuart remained, then, a theological conservative. Still, he broke from the strict orthodoxy that shaped the dogmatic norms of Andover Seminary and its constituency. Not only was he the earliest of the Andover professors to make this declaration, but he was also, with the publication of his commentary on Romans, the first American Calvinist biblical scholar to offer extended exegetical support for what was perceived to be a significant divergence from the received theological tradition.

Stuart, Comprising Remarks on His Essay on Sin (Boston: Crocker & Brewster, 1839). Dana objected in particular to what he believed to be Stuart's treatment of Vitringa, which represented him as supporting a doctrine of actual sin to the exclusion of original, imputed, habitual sin. More central to Dana's intent, however, as an anonymous review in the *Christian Examiner* (27 [November 1839] 281–84) pointed out, was his "personal appeal to the peculiar situation of Professor Stuart," who as an officer in a seminary established to defend the Westminster Catechism openly denied one of its most obvious doctrines (282).

[19] *Commentary on Romans*, 215.
[20] Ibid., 227.
[21] Ibid., 208.
[22] Ibid. Charles Hodge, Princeton's able biblical scholar and ardent supporter of the Westminster Catechism, roundly criticized Stuart's exegesis of the imputation passages of Romans by contending that Stuart missed the point altogether, namely, Paul's development of the analogous relationship between the justification of the sinner through the merits of Christ, and the condemnation of the sinner through the demerits of Adam. (See the unsigned article by Hodge, "Stuart on Romans," *Biblical Repertory* 5 [July 1833] 381–416.) Stuart replied in the second edition of the commentary on Romans, which appeared in 1835. Here the exegesis, as well as the theological excursus, is expanded but without substantive change. Hodge is mentioned only as a "critic in our own country . . . who could find nothing but contradictions and absurdities in this part of my work" (*Commentary on Romans*, 2d ed. [Andover, MA: Gould & Newmann, 1835] 618 n.).

IX

PUBLIC ISSUES

In contrast to many other evangelical Christians, Stuart remained outside the public arena. His philological and critical work crowded out participation in political and reform movements. Yet, Stuart was not so cloistered as to be unmindful of social issues, and he shared with fellow citizens the vision of an evangelical Protestant empire. Indeed, he supported their empire-building crusades.

He had a lifelong interest in local and national partisan politics. Both his 1799 bachelor's and 1802 master's orations at Yale were tendentious Federalist declamations against Jeffersonian republicanism, and the master's oration so pleased the Federalists that it eventually appeared in the *United States Gazette* of Philadelphia.[1] His political interest continued to the end of his life, and he enjoyed a long and loyal friendship with Daniel Webster, with whom he often exchanged gossip and advice. In 1843, after a brilliant speech by Webster at Andover, Stuart proposed to publish under his own name a newspaper article defending Webster's unpopular decision to remain in John Tyler's cabinet as Secretary of State following the untimely death of President Harrison. The article would include references to private details of the successful Webster-Ashburton treaty settling boundary disputes between the United States and Canada, which, both men thought, required Webster to remain in the cabinet.[2] After consulting, they decided to publish the material in a pamphlet, which appeared anonymously early in 1844, *Mr. Webster's Andover Address and His Political Course While Secretary of State.*[3] It remains even now compelling political journalism,

[1] It was not, however, favorably received by the Republicans, who noted in an 1803 communication to *The American Mercury* (6 October 1803) that the attendance at the recent Yale commencement "had been notoriously small because Republicans did not care to be insulted, as in some previous years . . . by offensive political haranges" (Dexter, *Biographical Sketches of Yale College,* 5:623. For Stuart's master's oration "On Credulity," see Andover Newton Papers).

[2] See Moses Stuart to Daniel Webster, 11 and 15 November 1843, Daniel Webster Papers, Library of Congress.

[3] Essex County, MA: Publication for Distribution. The publisher honored in the breach Stuart's half-hearted attempt to remain anonymous by noting on the title page that "The Publishers have no authority to designate the authorship of the following pages, but from various circumstances, they infer the probability, that they were written by PROF. STUART, OF ANDOVER."

with details both about the treaty and about relations with France, Hawaii, Spain, and China, as well as about domestic issues.

Stuart's political interests also included world peace and the American Peace Society. On its behalf he addressed Webster, who had been reappointed Secretary of State in 1850. Stuart pleaded for the Society's arbitration proposal that "all our Treaties with foreign powers [contain] an article pledging mutually that the parties will submit all matters in dispute to an arbitration such as the parties may agree upon, instead of resorting to war." If agreeable to Webster, Stuart added, "a petition for such an arrangement addressed to the President and yourself may be got up with some million of names."[4]

Stuart also supported church union; his name appears among the "Witnesses for the Unity of the Savior's Body," forty-four clergymen and educators who lent their names to Samuel S. Schmucker's bold *Fraternal Appeal to the American Churches, with a plan for Catholic Union on Apostolic Principles.*[5] He served as an officer of the new American Society for the Promotion of Christian Unity, organized to promote Schmucker's book and program.[6]

Temperance

The public issues that engaged Stuart's attention were those to which the scriptures seemed to give an authoritative word. Temperance was one such issue. Biblical evidence about "strong drink" in Jewish and Christian traditions was important to the temperance movement. Stuart was equipped to secure that evidence. He accepted the assignment with his usual industry, producing two works, exhaustive in critical detail, and supporting temperance.

Stuart joined the American Society for the Promotion of Temperance after it formed in Boston in 1826.[7] Four years later he published *Essay on the Prize Question whether the Use of Distilled Liquors, or Traffic in Them, is Compatible, at the Present Time, with Making a Profession of Christianity.*[8] His answer was no, and this conclusion hinged on the term "distilled liquor." That both wine and "strong drink were allowed to the Hebrews" Stuart

---

[4] Moses Stuart to Daniel Webster, 27 October 1850. Daniel Webster Papers.

[5] Samuel S. Schmucker (1799–1873) was a Lutheran clergyman, graduate of Princeton Seminary, and for many years Professor of Theology at Gettysburg Seminary. The *Fraternal Appeal* was one of the most forthright and practical ecumenical proposals produced in the nineteenth century. The first edition was published in New York in 1838. For a modern reprint, see the edition with introductory essay by Frederick K. Wentz (Philadelphia: Fortress, 1965).

[6] Wentz, *Fraternal Appeal*, 20–21.

[7] *First Annual Report of the Executive Committee of the American Society for the Promotion of Temperance* (Andover, MA: Flagg & Gould, 1828) 7.

[8] New York: John P. Haven, 1830.

admitted,[9] but he claimed that the unadulterated wines in scripture and the intoxicating wines of his day were different substances. Modern wines, he observed, appealing to "celebrated chemists in Europe," contain up to a quarter part alcohol. Not so with the wines of Palestine.[10] Indeed, intoxicating wine was known in biblical times as "mixed wine," and nowhere did the sacred writers mention it "with approbation, or even with tolerance," except as diluted with water or milk.[11] Such "mixed wine" was the preparation offered Jesus on the cross. Jesus refused it.[12] With only two exceptions, the scriptures disapprove "strong drink": Prov 31:6 allows it as a medicine, and
Deut 14:22–26 limits it to the annual day of thanksgiving. In neither instance, observed Stuart, is the allowance for habitual or common consumption.[13] Again, the drink itself differs from the harder liquors of modern time. Distilled liquors were unknown to the Hebrews: "Their strong drinks were made by fermenting grain, honey, and fruits, especially dates," and are not to be compared "in strength to our common alcoholic liquors" such as "brandy, rum, [and] gin."[14] Beyond all this, some classes—priests, Nazirites, princes, and kings[15]—were forbidden to partake of either wine or strong drink.

Certain passages would seem to offer exceptions. Paul urged Timothy to take "a little wine . . . for the stomach's sake" (1 Tim 5:23). But Stuart viewed Paul's advice as "medicinal" and therefore allowable.[16] The story of the wedding at Cana in John 2:1–10 posed more of a problem. The difficulty was the implication that the guests were drunk. Having consumed the host's good wine, they were in no state to judge the poorer wine. For Stuart, such a reading was unfounded: there is no evidence of drunkenness, and the presence of Jesus, his mother, and his disciples "utterly forbids the idea that the party were in a state of intoxication." Wine was served, but wine among Hebrews was like cider or ale among New Englanders.[17]

Stuart was prepared to yield on one point. He saw little harm in the moderate use of the "lower wines" and beverages. These he believed to be nonintoxicating and hence no cause for church discipline or exclusion:

> Unless we prescribe the use of cider ale, and everything of the same nature, we cannot hold him criminal who, sometimes uses with moderation the lower wines, or any wines, that come not within the pale of intoxicating liquors. That the public, or the churches, are not prepared

---

9 *Essay on the Prize Question,* 6.
10 Ibid., 23.
11 Ibid., 12–13, 23.
12 Ibid., 15.
13 Ibid., 15–16.
14 Ibid., 22.
15 Ibid., 18–20.
16 Ibid., 32.
17 Ibid., 31.

for such an extreme measure of proscription, it is my full persuasion. It is equally so, that such a measure ought not to be taken.[18]

With "intoxicating liquors," the matter was different. Only one conclusion could be reached from a scriptural investigation:

THE USE OF THEM IN EVERY FORM AND MANNER, SO AS TO OCCASION ANY DEGREE OF INTOXICATION, IS MOST FULLY AND ENTIRELY PROHIBITED. We may further say, that NO PRECEPT AND NO EXAMPLE CAN BE BROUGHT FROM THE SCRIPTURES, TO SHOW THAT THE HABITUAL USE IN ANY WAY OF LIQUOR PROPERLY CALLED INTOXICATING, IS ALLOWED.[19]

The natural law that alcohol disrupts human well-being supports the truth of revelation.[20] So church members "who consume intoxicating liquors, or who traffic in them [are] to be regarded as deserving of Christian animadversion and discipline," even though the scriptural sanctions refer only to those who sin "against their brethren, and wound their weak consciences, and SIN AGAINST CHRIST."[21]

The churches have a right to debar intemperate drinkers from membership. Several New Testament passages make it clear "that men may be, and that they must be, (if the New Testament be followed), excluded from Christian Churches for less heinous sins than the one in question."[22] Only on one point did Stuart urge leniency. Churches should debar intemperate drinkers but not excommunicate drinking members who only recently learned the facts about liquor, for "to use intoxicating liquors to a certain extent, and to traffic in them, was deemed no absolute immorality, a few years since, by any church in our land."[23]

Not until 1848 did Stuart publish his other temperance statement, a sixty-four page pamphlet entitled Scriptural View of the Wine-Question, in a Letter to the Rev. Dr. Mott.[24] The previous year Eliphalet Mott (1773–1866), Presbyterian president of Union College, had published his Lectures on Temperance,[25] in which he argued that the "wine" recognized by biblical writers and used at eucharistic services in the church was not even the "lower" wine that Stuart had allowed in his Essay on the Prize Question but rather a simple unfermented grape juice, devoid of alcohol. Stuart's new essay modified his philological argument; he decided that the

[18] Ibid., 34.
[19] Ibid., 35.
[20] Ibid., 36–42.
[21] Ibid., 50.
[22] Ibid., 59. Scripture passages referred to were 2 Thess 3:8; 1 Cor 5:10; 6:9, 10; Matt 18:15–17.
[23] Ibid., 60.
[24] New York: Leavitt, Trow, 1848.
[25] Albany: E. H. Pease, 1847.

biblical definition and usage of "wine" did support the total abstinence that Mott and others were urging.

Stuart claimed now that the common Old Testament words signifying liquor— *"ya-yin"* for wine, or the *"liquid which the fruit of the vine yields,"* and *"shay-cawr"* for "strong drink" — are *generic* terms and can mean either "fermented or unfermented, intoxicating or unintoxicating" beverages.[26] The liquors in both have a *"saccharine principle"* and therefore may become alcoholic. But they could be kept in a harmless unfermented state.[27] Although Stuart had contended that the approved "wines" of the Old Testament were weak, he had not denied that they were fermented. Now he changed his mind.

The proof he derived from the Old Testament. In Numbers 6:3, a Nazirite law, the first part of the verse prohibits *"ya-yin"* and *"shay-cawr"* in the generic sense. But in the sequel Moses prohibited *"fermented wine and fermented shay-cawr."*[28] Both fermented and unfermented wines were forbidden to the Nazirites, and the same terms were used in both prohibitions. In other passages, as well, *"shay-cawr"* can denote drunkenness but also refer to the comforts of life, offerings to God, and medicine. Was the *"shay-cawr"* mentioned as a drink offering in Num 28:7 and Deut 14:26 fermented or unfermented? Stuart believed that it was unfermented, for fermentation was considered leavening and leaven would be excluded from the drink as well as from the bread. "The Jews, the world over with few exceptions, have kept the passover with unfermented wine," Stuart noted. Reason would thus suggest that *"shay-cawr"* was unfermented.[29]

In like manner, Stuart noted the various meanings of *"ya-yin"* and concluded that whenever the term is approved either for ceremony or for comfort unfermented grape juice is denoted. In this conclusion, he also examined the word *"tee-roash"* (e.g., in Num 18:12; Deut 28:51). Differing with Gesenius, who held it to mean *"inebriating* liquor," he noted that: "The nature of the case, when all the examples of the use of the word are compared, shows with a good degree of certainty, that it either designates *new-wine,* or if not new, at least that which has been kept in an *unfermented* state." That the Hebrews were capable of storing unfermented wine Stuart had little doubt. Pliny had noted a similar ability among the Spaniards, and one of Stuart's New Haven friends, Chief Justice Zephaniah Swift, "a remarkably temperate man," testified about drinking such wine while traveling in the mountains of Spain. The judge had gone so far as to claim "that

---

[26] *Scriptural View of the Wine-Question,* 11. The transliterations are Stuart's.

[27] Ibid., 15.

[28] Here the Authorized Version reads *"vinegar* of wine and the *vinegar* of strong drink" (italics mine). This Stuart rejected, noting that "the *vinegar of wine* and the *vinegar of strong drink,* . . . were no more employed as drinks by the Hebrews, than vinegar of cider or wine is used for drink by us" (ibid., 16).

[29] Ibid., 20.

a gallon of it drunk at a time, if any man could swallow down so much, would not affect his head in the least degree."[30] If the Spaniards could store unfermented wine, why not the Hebrews? "This I look upon in the light of 'taking the citadel,'" exclaimed Stuart. And if stored wine was kept in such a way that it improved in taste and usefulness, which the word "*tee-roash*" seemed to imply,[31] "then I am ready to say we have attained to a position that will command the whole ground.[32]

The Old Testament urges temperance while counting both wine and "strong drink" among the blessings and comforts of life. But a "tropical interpretation" of the generic terms can determine a specific meaning and remove the apparent contradiction. And what could be said for the Old Testament could also be said for the New. In no instance did Christ or the church approve of fermented wine. Whereas Stuart had once intimated that Christ served weak wine, lightly fermented, at the wedding of Cana, now he felt assured that the miracle produced unfermented wine and that Jesus drank only unfermented wine at the Last Supper: "Scarcely a greater mistake in reasoning can be made, than to rest the use of alcoholic wine at the sacramental table, on the example of our Saviour and his disciples."[33]

Finally, Stuart appealed to the New Testament command of love. Some might unreasonably believe on philological principles that the scriptures do allow "the use of *alcoholic* wine as a common beverage." Nevertheless, the practice of drinking "in the present circumstances" offends "against the *great law of love*. . . . No believer in Revelation will venture to gainsay the authority of Paul when he says '*It is good neither to eat flesh, nor to drink wine, nor anything whereby thy brother stumbleth, and is made weak*' (Rom. 14:21)."[34] No matter what the force of his other arguments, this one he believed to be final. Certainly it is his most valid. He concluded:

> Conceding then that my ground, as taken in the preceding pages, is not tenable, yet the issue of the great questions, on another ground, viz. the one which I have just stated, is the same. It is a duty to abstain. No matter whether you put this on the ground of command and example, or of Christian expediency. The result is the same. IT IS A SACRED DUTY TO ABSTAIN.[35]

Total abstinence was not merely a desirable ideal; it was a mandate revealed in the word of God.[36]

---

[30] Ibid., 26, 45.
[31] Ibid., 28.
[32] Ibid., 44.
[33] Ibid., 54.
[34] Ibid., 60–61.
[35] Ibid., 61.
[36] One other temperance publication was issued under Stuart's name, a brief letter to the editor of the journal of the American Temperance Union, the national body that in 1836 absorbed the earlier American Society for the Promotion of Temperance. This appeared with

Slavery

Biblical clarity was not so discernible on the topic of slavery. It was not that Stuart lacked convictions about it. From his college days, he advocated the eventual emancipation of America's slaves. He aligned himself with the American Colonization Society; and with such Congregationalist leaders as Leonard Bacon of New Haven, and Leonard Woods and Ebenezer Porter of Andover, he supported its gradualist principles of ultimate emancipation and resettlement in Africa.

Only after the rise of the radical abolitionists did he make his thoughts public. Between 1830 and 1840, the emancipation movement gained momentum under an energetic radical party bent on immediate abolition at any cost. Led by William Lloyd Garrison and Theodore Dwight Weld, the group attacked both the program of the colonization movement and its gradualist principles by proclaiming slavery a *sin*. Not only the slaveholders but also advocates of conciliation and gradualism elicited their scornful denunciation. To the radical abolitionists, slavery was a sin *per se* or a *malum in se*, a sin in and of itself, with which no compromise could be tolerated.[37]

This assertion became the rallying point of the abolitionist attack; it was an appeal to Northern emotions and a weapon against Northern gradualism. But a gradualist Stuart remained until the end of his life. Hence, he had to defend his position against the recurring charge that slavery was itself a *malum in se*.

Stuart's views became clear during the dramatic "anti-slave rebellion" on the quiet campus of Andover Seminary in 1835. The students had supported gradualism through a local abolition society and sent delegates to the annual meetings of the American Convention of Delegates from Abolition Societies. With the advent of abolitionism, however, the professors refused to allow the students to organize around the radical program and passed rules in the seminary and the academy forbidding any antislavery society. The ostensible reason was a fear of bad publicity and of frightening away Southern students,[38] but the professors also had an intense dislike for

several similar writings in a pamphlet entitled *Letters from Professor Stuart, of Andover, Lucius L. Sargent, Esq., of Boston, Gen. Cocke, of Virginia, and Rev. Justin Edwards, D.D. on the Maine Liquor Law* (New York, 1851). The four were unrestrained in their enthusiasm for the Maine law—the first stringent state prohibitionary legislative measure—passed in June 1851 largely through the efforts of Neal Dow, mayor of Portland. Excerpts from Stuart's letter were also printed in an appendix to a published version of the law, which appeared in New York that same year. Stuart was also responsible for the framing of the Temperance Pledge of the Officers and Students in the Theological Seminary, 1836 (Andover Newton Papers).

[37] For the classic statement of this view see Edward R. Taylor, *Slaveholding a Malum in Se, or Invariably Sinful* (Hartford, CT: S. S. Cowles, 1839).

[38] Claude M. Fuess, *An Old New England School, A History of Phillips Academy, Andover* (Boston: Houghton Mifflin, 1917) 225–26.

abolitionist methods and personalities and looked with horror upon the radicals' divisive tactics.

The matter came to a head when George Thompson, a brilliant English antislavery orator whom Garrison had brought to America, visited Andover during a lecture tour of Massachusetts. Though Thompson met rough treatment from hostile mobs, his engagements aroused enthusiasm for his cause, and now, desiring to attack the professors in their household, he applied for permission to speak in the seminary chapel and in the town's South Parish Church. He was refused at both places. But supporters found a hall in town, and despite prohibitions by the school, a number of students attended the rally. The following Sunday at the evening chapel service Stuart excoriated the delinquents for their breach of discipline and forbade attendance at a lecture announced by Thompson for that evening: "I warn you, young gentlemen, warn you on the peril of your souls, not to go to that meeting tonight."[39]

More than warnings would be necessary if the professors expected to prevail. Thus, Stuart undertook in a lecture to the students shortly after the Thompson affair to defend the moderate position. Though slavery carries a possibility of great moral evil, he argued, it cannot be defined as a "sin in itself," since nowhere does the Bible declare it as such. In short, the lecture was a close and myopic review of the literal position of the Bible.

Stuart began by treating "the original principles on the theory of slavery," noting the New Testament admonition to "love our neighbours as ourselves" and the protective legislation for slaves in the Old Testament.[40] He made three deductions: first, "any form of slavery which dissolves or disowns conjugal or parental relations [is] inconsistent with the laws of our social being and/or our relative duties"; second, "any form which denies to slaves the right of Christian instruction [is] inconsistent with the great law of spiritual love"; third, the evils of slavery, "oppression, injustice, pollution, malignity, poverty, severe labour, etc. [are] all dependent on the *abuse* of power, temper, etc.," not necessarily on the institution itself. In theory, slavery must always be an evil because it invades "the great law of *equality*." All people are of "*one blood*." There is one God; "one Redeemer; one Sanctified. But there are many gradations of slavery; some of which amount practically to less evil than the relation of the poor operatives in England to the public, or their employers."[41] Slavery is wrong—this Stuart had always held—but he was making concessions to the status quo by viewing institutions as distinct from the people who control them.

With this much established, Stuart moved to his specialty and asked, "Does the Bible allow slavery in any form?" For the Old Testament the

---

39 Ibid., 226.
40 "Abstract on Lecture on Slavery." Moses Stuart Papers, Andover Newton.
41 Ibid.

answer is yes. The regulatory laws indicate that slavery was common among the Hebrews, and other passages also provided evidence. Stuart cited Lev 25:44–46, which granted the Hebrews permission to "purchase slaves *ad libitum* of the heathen, around them, who shall be 'boundmen forever.' . . . How can this be *malum in se* and yet thus be permitted?" he queried. The purchase of Hebrew slaves to serve for six years was also allowed (Exod 21:2; Deut 15:12). "Hence it follows, at least, that Moses did not regard all slavery as a crime; nor favour the doctrine of immediate abolition, either in theory or practice."[42]

"Has the Gospel changed these rules?" No precept in the New Testament has direct bearing on the subject, Stuart observed. "Our Saviour has said nothing *specific*. . . . It is only under the great *law of love*, that we can find the principle." He then cited New Testament passages containing precepts to slaves and masters. Here slavery was neither commended nor condemned. "The reasoning from all this is *not* that slavery is itself right and proper, and allowable on strict Christian grounds. By no means"; John the Baptist gave directions to soldiers without approving of war; and Moses made exceptions on divorce, "contrary to the original law of our nature." In like manner must slavery be treated. But granting that slavery is an evil "which the principles of the Gospel would remove when fully exercised," Moses and Paul still allow that "it may be *tolerated for a time*."[43] It is a "*malum prohibitam*," not a "*malum in se*"; therefore, people may honestly differ on "how long it can be tolerated in particular circumstances" or what the best means may be to bring it to an end, and "each may be conscientious in his views."[44]

Stuart guarded himself against any accusation that would link him with the Southern proslavery biblicists or with such Northern fellow travelers as Episcopal Bishop John Hopkins of Vermont or Dartmouth's president Nathan Lord, who agreed that the Bible justifies the "peculiar institution." He also disassociated himself from abolitionists. The Bible, according to Stuart, is neither for slavery nor for radical abolitionism.

Having added his weight to the side of moderation, Stuart fell silent. He returned to philology, grammar, and syntax, and let others defend the moderate point of view. Not until 1850 did he again take a public stand. The occasion was the debate on Henry Clay's compromise measures that dealt with slavery in the western territories. By granting concessions, the bills tried to appease both sides and thereby forestall and prevent disunion. As the Senate vote neared, the public uproar intensified. On 7 March, Webster rose to make his speech in favor of Clay's measures.

[42] Ibid.

[43] Ibid.

[44] Ibid. See also Stuart's private letter to Wesleyan University president Wilbur Fisk, which was published without Stuart's permission by William Lloyd Garrison in *The Liberator* 7 (30 June 1837) 106.

Reverberations from the speech rolled in from the whole nation. Unionists North and South hailed Webster as savior. The abolitionists said he had sold himself to the devil. They poured out a flood of scorn that would have overwhelmed a lesser man. As a senator from Massachusetts, an abolitionist region, he was vulnerable. But his friends circulated in the Boston area an address signed by nearly a thousand supporters who approved his conduct. Among the signatures, which included most of the faculty at Harvard and many of Massachusetts's social and commercial lions, appeared the name of Moses Stuart.[45]

The radicals rejoiced. They had smoked out the moderate pack. The storm of protest around Webster now engulfed the signers as well, and Stuart, a theological patriarch, was also vulnerable. He was now seventy, frail of body, but with mental powers as vigorous as ever. Never one to shrink from controversy, he set himself to a reply: *Conscience and the Constitution with Remarks on the Recent Speech of the Hon. Daniel Webster on the Subject of Slavery.*[46] Hardly Stuart's best work, it is his most disturbing, for he set forth his mature position and exposed its weaknesses.

The work repeated his earlier views, with further marshaling of textual proofs. Abolitionists had argued that the Mosaic law did not sanction slavery, and they had cited Exod 21:16: "Whoever steals a man, whether he sells him or is found in possession of him, shall be put to death." The parallel passage in Deut 24:7, however, plainly indicates "that this law, in its primary design, applied only to the stealing of Hebrews." Stuart was willing to admit that it might well be the spirit of the law ("now the partition between Jew and Gentile is broken down") to apply it to all kinds of stealing of persons; "but to quote these passages, as is every day done, to show directly the criminality of foreign slavemaking, is doubtless uncritical and unfounded, as it respects the original and main object of the Jewish law."[47]

More important was the controversy over Deut 23:15–16: "You shall not give up to his master a slave who has escaped from his master to you; he shall dwell with you, in your midst, in the place which he shall choose within one of your towns, where it pleases him best; you shall not oppress him." Was not this a directive to violate the fugitive slave law? Not so, reasoned Stuart. The passage refers to an immigrant slave escaped from a *heathen* master. If a slave escaped to the Hebrews, worshipers of "the only living and true God," they were encouraged to share the privileges of their higher faith. If the escaped slave were from a Hebrew master, "the case is

[45] Claude M. Fuess, *Daniel Webster* (Boston: Little, Brown & Company, 1930) 2:226–27. Webster was delighted with Stuart's support and wrote him a warm letter expressing his thanks (see *The Private Correspondence of Daniel Webster,* ed. Fletcher Webster [Boston: Little, Brown & Company, 1857] 2:367).
[46] Boston: Crocker & Brewster, 1850.
[47] *Conscience and the Constitution,* 28.

greatly changed," for the master could claim Hebrew rights and lawfully receive back his property.[48] After he established the logic, Stuart made the application:

> With this view of the matter before us, how can we appeal to the passage in question, to justify, yea even to urge, the retention of fugitive bond-men in our own country? We are one nation—one so-called *Christian* nation.... When a fugitive bond-man, then, comes to us of the North, from a master at the South, in what relation do we of the North stand to that Southern master? Are our fellow citizens and brethren of the South, to be accounted as *heathen* in our sight...? The Mosaic Law does not authorize us to reject the claims of our fellow countrymen and citizens, for strayed or stolen property—property authorized and guaranteed as such by Southern states to their respective citizens.[49]

The problem of conscience and the fugitive slave law Stuart would take up later. But he could find no justification in the Old Testament for setting the law aside.

Nor was the New Testament more helpful to the abolitionist cause. Christ himself abstained from meddling in matters that belonged to the civil power. Even if one granted the ethical imperative of the New Testament, neither Jesus nor Paul can be made out as abolitionists. Paul said: "slaves obey your masters"; radical abolitionists were saying the opposite. "An honest deist, if such a rarity can be found, might consistently ignore Paul. But this will not do for Christians." But in all of his statements about the New Testament, Stuart nowhere mentioned the Pauline "law of love" which he had applied in his temperance writings, nor did he attempt to explain the omission.[50]

The object of the pamphlet was a legalistic defense of the Constitution and of obedience to its laws. Chief among abolitionist contentions was that the higher law of Christian conscience demanded disobedience to the Constitution if it protected slavery. For Stuart such a position was false and dangerous; and his defense of the letter of the law in the face of his own best convictions about the moral evil of slavery shows the tragically ambiguous dimension of moderation. Dealing first with the clause that governed laws for fugitive slaves, Stuart sought refuge in states rights. The sovereignty of the states allowed such a provision in the Constitution, despite the affirmation in the Declaration of Independence that all are created equal. One state cannot decide for another. Virginia may do wrong, but it is not under Massachusetts's "supervision or jurisdiction; nor are we, in any degree, accountable or responsible for her errors or sins."[51]

What of the "higher law of conscience"? Stuart replied to the question

[48] Ibid., 30–31.
[49] Ibid., 31–33.
[50] Ibid., 48.
[51] Ibid., 59.

by asking another: What is this "conscience" that decides "that the Constitution should be disobeyed? . . . Is the conscience in question a *Christian* conscience?" Without recognizing the historical differences or admitting the possibility that Paul may have fallen short of Christian love, Stuart turned to the example of the apostle and Onesimus: "Paul's Christian conscience would not permit him to injure the vested rights of Philemon"; and this is a doctrine "very different from that of the abolitionists. Paul's conscience sent back the fugitive slave; theirs *encourages him to run away.*"[52] The so-called higher law then lies only in the "passions and prejudices" of those who urge it. "It is a conscience wholly *subjective.*" Any person moved by passion "can manufacture a conscience into any convenient shape."[53] But this is not the conscience that guided the "exalted and noble" framers of the Constitution. They would look with a "mixture of sorrow and of frowning" upon their abolitionist descendants exhorting their "countrymen to disregard and trample under foot the Constitution which [they] had so significantly helped to establish."[54] Stuart was upon the horns of a moral dilemma. Biblical literalism seemed the only possible escape.

Focusing on the 1850 compromise, Stuart defended Webster's stand on the territorial problem and the extension of slavery. Together with Webster he rejected the Wilmot Proviso as useless. Each new state under the Constitution can determine whether it will be slave or free, regardless of its status while under federal jurisdiction as a territory. On the same principle, Stuart expressed opposition to the 1845 act that admitted Texas to the Union but that prohibited the formation of slave states in Texas territory north of 36°30'. Yet although Webster opposed both bills in principle, Stuart hastened to add that he had never voted for the extension of slavery or slave territory. His record of opposition to the annexation of Texas and to the Mexican War was clear proof:

> Has he lost any of this feeling of repugnance and opposition to slavery? NOT IN THE LEAST. He declared, that bitter as the task may be, to allow of new slavery States, still he must lift up his hand to carry solemn contracts into execution, to keep the plighted faith of this nation. There is—there can be no *repudiating* of such contracts. Even a *bad* bargain must be kept. If not, who after this can ever trust the faith or honor of this nation?
>
> And is Mr. Webster to be maligned, and vituperated, and thrust out of the confidence of his fellow-citizens, because he will not vote to violate solemn compacts? If this must be done, such a day awaits this nation, as no politician has yet imagined, and no prophet yet foretold. . . . Patriotism,

---

[52] Ibid., 60–61.
[53] Ibid., 61.
[54] Ibid., 63. Here Stuart was making a reference to William Jay, descendant of John Jay, and presiding officer at a meeting of the "anti-slavery Society . . . recently held at New York."

integrity, firmness, sound judgment, lofty soul-thrilling eloquence, may
thenceforth despair of finding their reward among us.[55]

Stuart's legalism required him to criticize not only abolitionists but
also Southerners who violated the Constitution. He spoke with severity
about the South Carolina law that demanded the incarceration of free
Negroes entering the state as crew members on vessels. This statute "is *a
direct, a palpable, an open* violation of the Constitution of the United
States,"[56] but the law of Ohio, and the "hoped for" law of California
prohibiting the settlement of free Negroes was no better. "What difference
there is, now, as to *principle,* between this legislation and the Carolina law,
I cannot see." Ohio, "with her views, her light and her circumstances,"
should know better. The Northerners would do well to mind the beam in
their own eye before crying out at the mote in the eye of South Carolina.[57]
Nor was his stand clarified by the unctious enumeration of the evils of
slavery with which he closed his work. Only briefly did he indicate any
solution to the problem of emancipation and suggested again the old scheme
of colonization, either in Africa or in one of the territories, all financed by
the government, perhaps from the sale of public lands.[58]

Stuart's argument was weak. Moderation might have been valid had
its proponents put forth an effective program between slavery and immediate abolition. But the fanciful scheme of colonization was a panacea,
inadequate to a Christian ethic and utterly impracticable. The failure of
people like Stuart to give moral guidance to the moderate cause inhibited
the movement. The spiritual directives of the abolitionists squared up
against the religious injunctions of Bible-quoting slaveholders. The moderates were all but drowned out. At least Stuart could see that if either
extreme prevailed, catastrophe lay ahead. The future was indeed somber.
All he could envision was a South "turned to a desolate wilderness," the
Union lost, the few former slaves remaining free to walk the ruins of houses
and towns under which lie buried their former masters. "I wash my hands
of the guilt of my country's blood,"[59] he concluded. It was a despondent and
heartfelt cry but one that does not wholly absolve him.

Stuart's pamphlet failed to mollify the radicals. Such temporizing, they
said, was little better than slaveholding itself. One typical review noted
that the work would have been better titled "a plea for American slavery,
based upon Scriptural authorities, with expressions of admiration for Mr.
WEBSTER, the whole interspersed with arguments and declarations,
which over-throw all that is adduced in favor of slavery."[60] Even more

[55] Ibid., 81.
[56] Ibid., 87–88.
[57] Ibid., 95.
[58] Ibid., 112–15.
[59] Ibid., 117.
[60] Rufus W. Clark, *A Review of the Rev. Moses Stuart's Pamphlet on Slavery, entitled*

damning was the melodramatic poem by John Greenleaf Whittier entitled "A Sabbath Scene." The work describes a dream in which a fugitive woman fleeing into a church for protection is instead handed over to her pursuer by the parson himself, who, speaking to the villainous master, exclaims:

> Of course I know your right divine to own and work and whip her;
> Quick, Deacon, throw that Polyglot before the wench and trip her!

Stumbling over the Bible, the girl is caught and made fast. The poem continues:

> I saw the parson tie the knots, the while his flock addressing,
> The scriptural claims of slavery, with text on text impressing.
> "Although," said he, "on Sabbath day all secular occupations
> Are deadly sins, we must fulfill our moral obligations:
> And this commends itself as one to every conscience tender;
> As Paul sent back Onesimus, my Christian friends, we send her!"
>
> My brain took fire: "Is this," I cried, "the end of prayer and
>   preaching?"
> Then down with pulpit, down with priest, and give us Nature's
>   teaching!
> I woke, and lo! the fitting cause of all my dream's vagaries —
> Two bulky pamphlets, Webster's text, with Stuart's commentaries![61]

Stuart exhibited in his attitude toward slavery the viewpoint of a later liberalism. Evolution, not revolution, was Stuart's platform. Such a view, however, minimized the "Calvinist emphasis on God's immediate and final judgment upon man and his institutions,"[62] the kind of judgment the abolitionists carried to extremes. Although Stuart did not live to the next decade he shared some of the responsibility for the great tragedy that finally engulfed the nation. Sincere and fervent, nothing he said had moral power enough to displace the ardent spirit of immediatism that prevailed.

Conscience and the Constitution (Boston: C. C. P. Moody, 1850) 9. Stuart noted that his work had called forth "one large drawerful of pamphlets and newspapers abusing me in every possible shape—besides some impossible ones. I keep them all, for the future amusement of my children" (Letter to Daniel Webster, 20 July 1850, Daniel Webster Papers, Library of Congress). And three months later: "Not a week passes still without fresh abuse for my pamphlet. Poor little thing! It has been murdered 500 times—and yet, thank God, it is still alive . . ." (ibid., 27 October 1850).

[61] From the pamphlet *The Platform of the American Anti-Slavery Society, and Its Auxiliaries* (New York: American Anti-Slavery Society, 1853) 34–35. Also in *The Complete Poetical Works of John Greenleaf Whittier* (Boston: Houghton Mifflin, 1904) 385–86, altered to omit the last stanza. At least one essay appeared in support of Stuart, a lengthy unsigned article entitled "Civil Government," which appeared first in the *Princeton Review*, January 1851, and later separately under the same title (Princeton, 1851). The article is a detailed exposition of the Calvinist theory of government applied to the enforcement of the fugitive slave law. It is possible that the article was written by Stuart himself, though a direct reference to "the venerable Professor Stuart" (8) would seem to make this unlikely.

[62] Daniel Day Williams, *The Andover Liberals, A Study in American Theology* (New York: Kings Crown, 1941) 25.

X

THE END OF A CAREER

The ten years from 1826 to 1836 were happy and productive for Stuart. His fame as a writer and teacher was established, his financial position at Andover secure, and his health reasonably sound. In the academic year 1836–1837, however, a serious attack of typhoid fever brought him close to the grave, and for months he remained inactive, scarcely able to read, to say nothing of attempting to write or teach.[1] He never regained his strength and was stricken again during the fall and winter months of 1840 and 1841. His physicians had abandoned his case, he noted, but "through the blessing of God," he had, "with occasional interruptions," greatly improved during the spring. He was sufficiently improved by the summer term to resume his full teaching load and sustained four courses of lectures on biblical books. Three times a week he lectured on 1 Corinthians; once a week to the middlers on Hebrews; once a week and part of the time twice a week on Ecclesiastes to the whole seminary; and part of the time, by the special request of the juniors, he lectured on the messianic Psalms. Though he refrained from preaching during the summer, he spent the time not occupied with lecture preparation and delivery in work on the second edition of his *New Testament Dialect*, which left the press that fall.[2]

The pattern was typical of the later years of Stuart's teaching. When able to meet his classes regularly, he was productive in his teaching. Though relieved of his work in Hebrew exegesis when Bela Bates Edwards assumed the responsibility in 1843, he continued to carry most of the lecture and recitation load that he had shouldered since his first years at Andover. It was a heavy burden. In 1847, his last year of teaching, he took the junior class through hermeneutics, New Testament Greek, exegesis of the four Gospels, and 1 Corinthians. He lectured the middle class on Isaiah "in the absence of Professor Robinson and at the request of the Committee on Exigencies"; and because Edwards A. Park was ill, he also lectured on

---

[1] In his letter to the Board of Visitors dated 5 September 1837, Stuart remarked that the illness, "which was all but mortal," had kept him from his work from December through the following July (Papers of the Board of Visitors).

[2] Ibid., 1 September 1841.

homiletics and criticized senior sermons. In all, he missed "only one or two teaching exercises during the year."[3]

He was also busy writing. Altogether he issued nineteen works during the six-year period. Of these the most important were *Hints on the Interpretation of Prophecy* (1842), *A Commentary on the Apocalypse* (1845), and *Critical History and Defense of the Old Testament Canon* (1845). Twelve were shorter works—monographs, sermons and pamphlets—and four were revisions of previously published materials.

His declining health, however, was a source of discouragement. In August 1844 he noted that he had been "entirely disabled by sickness" during most of the preceding winter and spring. Although he had "spent the summer in constant efforts for the recovery of health . . . all had been unavailing. . . . Unless the coming autumnal weather shall raise me up," he continued, "my labours would seem to be at or near their close."[4] A year later he reported some improvement, having fulfilled almost all of his lecture assignments, but sickness of the previous summer had left him in a "very reduced and feeble state." Preaching and conference meetings had all been dropped, nor had he been able to attend public worship "but a small part of the time."[5]

In moderately good health from 1845 through the summer of 1847, he succumbed again to his maladies that fall. He wrote in December to his physician, James Jackson of Boston, to complain of influenza and of a "typhoidal" sickness that for four weeks had left him "between life and death." He spoke of having the "blues" and worried about his nervous system, which "is so affected with such a long and severe trial, that the shutting of doors, the crowing of cocks, and the barking of a neighbour's dog—even the buzzing of a fly, have become intolerable. Sleep—dreaming and constantly interrupted. All the evils of Pandora's box, without hope at the bottom! This poor worn out frame—is there enough left to set it up once more? Sometimes, I doubt; and then I say again, 'I have been more sick and yet got up in good measure. But—I was not then 67 years old.'"[6] Without any prospect of improvement, he submitted to the Board of Trustees the question of whether he should remain in office. The matter was placed under committee advisement, and the group reported on 23 June 1848,

---

[3] Ibid., 31 August 1847. In this same year he read all the tragedies of Aeschylus in order to detect idioms and allusions explanatory of the Bible (Park, *Discourse*, 45).

[4] Papers of the Board of Visitors, 24 August 1844.

[5] Ibid., 3 September 1845. Nathaniel Taylor frowned upon professors who gave up "the preaching habit. . . . There is Stuart of Andover, . . . He gave up preaching and even going to meeting. He lost his spirituality, but by constant preaching I have kept mine" (quoted in Mead, *Nathaniel W. Taylor*, 237). The judgment seems unfair, not to say vain, but it indicates one of the reasons why Stuart was sensitive about his preaching duties.

[6] Moses Stuart to James Jackson, M.D., 6 December 1847, Massachusetts Historical Society, Boston.

recommending that the Board advise his resignation and arrange provision for his future support. This the Trustees proceeded to do, granting full salary to the end of the term, and afterward "six hundred dollars per annum with the use of the house and lands now occupied by him, on condition that he shall keep the same in good repair to the satisfaction of the Trustees." His name was to be kept in the catalogue "as a token of the respect and regard cherished" for him.[7] The resignation was submitted and accepted on 1 August. At the same meeting the Trustees agreed to shingle his house and paint the barn. It was also voted to appoint Bela Bates Edwards his successor as Professor of Sacred Literature.[8]

Retirement brought no end to Stuart's scholarly work. Refreshed by the rest that the abandonment of teaching duties afforded, he was productive to the end. Fourteen more works appeared between 1848 and 1852: the last three commentaries (Daniel, Ecclesiastes, and Proverbs), the pamphlet on slavery, a pamphlet on temperance, and several shorter reviews and articles.[9] Stuart planned several other works. "I am meditating fresh labors," Stuart noted: "I think of a volume of Jonah, Habakkuk, and Nahum; and am balancing between this and the Epistle to the Galatians." Referring to new forms of skepticism, he added: "often do I weep in secret places over this prospect, and ardently long to do something more in defence of authoritative inspiration, our only charter and compass."[10]

All these plans, however, were cut short. In better health than he had been for some time, he was walking on an icy day, early in December 1851, when he was struck by a boy on a sled. The collision fractured his wrist. Enfeebled by the shock, he fell ill with a cold and influenza, which subsequently passed into a "typhoid fever." He still found enough strength to correct the proofs of his *Commentary on Proverbs*, the final pages of which were sent to the printer only two days before he died.[11] At one point during his illness, when his physician expressed hope that his sickness was not "unto death," Stuart replied: "Unto the glory of God—*but* unto death." He had no

[7] Minutes of the Trustees of Phillips Academy, 23 June 1848, Records, Phillips Academy, Andover Seminary, 1841–1890, p. 74 (Andover Newton Papers). Whether the annual sum was adequate is questionable. William Adams noted that in private conversations with his closest friends Stuart was deeply wounded at his treatment by the Board of Trustees in this regard and anxious lest he be unable to provide for his physical needs during the declining years of his life. (See Adams, *Discourse*, 53).

[8] Minutes of the Trustees, 74. Edwards served only four years, dying in office in 1852.

[9] Three articles appeared in the *Bibliotheca Sacra:* "Exegetical and Theological Examination of John 1:1–18" 7 (January, April 1850) 13–55, 281–327; "Doctrine Respecting the Person of Christ: Translated from the German of Dr. and Professor J. A. Dorner, with Remarks," 7 (October 1850) 696–732; and "Observations on Matthew 24:29–31, and the Parallel Passages in Mark and Luke, with Remarks on the Double Sense," 20 (April, July 1852) 329–55, 449–68.

[10] Quoted in Adams, *Discourse*, 51. Park notes that Stuart was also contemplating commentaries on Jonah, Job, and the Corinthian letters (Park, *Discourse*, 46).

[11] Ibid., 33.

no wish to remain longer. "Save for the sake of his family and the execution of a 'three years' work" in his favorite study, which he had already projected, his strong desire was to go as soon as God "should see fit to grant him release." His mind remained alert, however, and his spirits good. The family was not aware of any immediate danger. Early in January, he suddenly declined; and in the midst of a howling winter storm, at ten minutes before midnight on 4 January 1852, the first Sunday of a new year, he died. So swift was his passing that his family could not even be summoned to his room. The tolling of the chapel and village bells on Monday morning announced his death to the townspeople, many of whom did not know he had been ill.[12]

The funeral was held on Thursday, 8 January, in Bartlet Chapel before a large group of friends. Calvin Stowe, then of Bowdoin College, opened the service with an invocation and scripture reading. The funeral prayer was offered by Professor Ralph Emerson of Andover, followed by one of Stuart's favorite hymns, Doddridge's "Thine Earthly Sabbath's Lord We Love," which was sung by the seminary choir. Edwards A. Park preached the funeral sermon on 1 Sam 2:30 — "Them that honor me, I will honor." Another of Stuart's favorite hymns, Watts's "This Life's a Dream, an Empty Show," based on Psalm 17, concluded the service.[13] A newspaper account described the closing moments in melancholy tones:

> The religious services ended, a solemn and affecting scene followed. The lid of the coffin was raised, and friends came forward to take their final leave. First approached the venerable Dr. Woods, and looked for the last time upon the features of his late associate and brother; pupils, clergymen, friends, neighbors and thronging groups of young men followed, until the winter's sun approached his setting, and his slanting rays through the windows diffused a somber and fitting light over the lessening number within. A wide pathway had been shoveled through the deep snow from the chapel to the burial ground, and the procession followed the body to the grave. It was a sad and silent farewell that we gave as we passed one by one through piles of snow and frozen clods, and looked down upon the lowly bed of the Father of Biblical Philology.[14]

Three years later a suitably imposing obelisk tombstone was purchased by the Andover alumni. On one side they placed the following inscription:

> A meek and earnest disciple;
> a fervid and eloquent preacher;
> a generous and cordial friend;
> a lover of all good learning;
> versatile in genius, adventurous;

[12] Adams, *Discourse*, 5.

[13] Park, *Discourse*, 56.

[14] From an unidentified newspaper clipping found in the Andover Newton Papers. The chapel burial ground lies just over the crest of the Andover hill, behind the present administration building of Phillips Academy.

in research, quick in acquisition;
an enthusiastic and attractive teacher,
devoting himself with patient and
successful toil to the revival and
cultivation of Sacred Literature,
he is justly entitled to be called among
the Scholars of his native country,
The Father of Biblical Science.
The Word which he loved in life
was his light in death.
He now sees face to face.

The epitaph was a fitting tribute. Stuart's eulogists, however, were not altogether unmindful of his faults — his impetuousness and headstrong sense of urgency, his occasional lack of scholarly care, or his tendency to ground his opinions on subjective emotion. But they also knew the ultimate worth of his life. "He introduced among us a new era of biblical interpretation," noted Park;[15] and if he helped create the standards by which he himself was judged, this too spoke of his greatness.

If then, he lapsed here and there in sacred literature, who are the men among us that correct him? Chiefly, the men who are in some way indebted to him for the power to make the correction. Chiefly, the men who have received from him the impulses by which they have learned to criticise him. Chiefly, the men who would have remained on the dead level of an empirical philology, had they not been quickened to an upward progress by his early enthusiasm. If the eagle in his flight toward the sun, be wounded by the archer, the arrow that is aimed at him is guided by a feather from the eagle's own broad wing.[16]

Romantic and rhetorical as these words are, their assessment continues to ring true.

[15] Park, *Discourse*, 39.
[16] Ibid., p. 44.

BIBLIOGRAPHY

I. UNPUBLISHED MATERIALS

A. *Stuart Manuscripts*

Andover Newton Papers. Andover Newton Theological School. Microfilm copy, Yale Divinity School.
Edwards A. Park Collection. Yale University.
Everett Papers. Massachusetts Historical Society.
First Church of Christ and Ecclesiastical Society, New Haven. Records.
Jackson Papers. Massachusetts Historical Society.
Miscellaneous Stuart Papers. Yale University.
Pearson Papers. Yale University.
Webster Papers. Library of Congress.

B. *Other Manuscript Materials*

Papers of the Board of Visitors. Andover Newton Theological School.
Miscellaneous Papers. Dartmouth College.

II. PUBLISHED WORKS BY STUART

A. *Grammars and Chrestomathies*

A Grammar of the Hebrew Language. 3d ed. [of *A Hebrew Grammar* . . . , q.v.]. Andover, MA: Flagg & Gould, 1828. [4th ed., Andover, 1831; 5th ed., Andover, 1835, Oxford, 1838; 6th ed., Andover, Oxford, 1838.]
A Grammar of the New Testament Dialect. Andover, MA: Gould & Newman, 1834. [2d ed., Andover: Ailen & Merrill, 1841.]
A Hebrew Chrestomathy, Designed as First Volume of a Course of Hebrew Study. Andover, MA: Flagg & Gould, 1829. [2d ed., Andover, New York, 1832, Oxford, 1834; 3d ed., Andover, 1838.]
A Hebrew Grammar With A Copious Syntax and Praxis. Andover, MA: Flagg & Gould, 1821.
A Hebrew Grammar With A Praxis on Select Portions of Genesis and the Psalms. 2d ed., Andover, MA: Flagg & Gould, 1823.
A Hebrew Grammar Without the Points: Designed as an Introduction to the Knowledge of the Inflections and Idiom of the Hebrew Tongue. Andover, MA: Flagg & Gould, 1813.

Manual of the Chaldee Language, by Elias Riggs. Preface by Moses Stuart. Boston: Perkins & Marvin, 1832.

B. *Commentaries*

A Commentary on Ecclesiastes. New York: Putnam, 1851. [2d ed., edited and revised by R. D. C. Robbins, Andover, MA, 1862.]

A Commentary on the Apocalypse. 2 vols., Andover, MA: Allen, Morrill & Wardwell, 1845. [Also published in London, 1845, 1847, 1850, 1854, 1865.]

A Commentary on the Book of Daniel. Boston: Crocker & Brewster, 1850.

A Commentary on the Book of Proverbs. New York: M. W. Dodd, 1852.

A Commentary on the Epistle to the Hebrews. 2 vols., Andover, MA: Mark Newman, 1827–1828. [2d ed., corrected and enlarged, Andover, 1833; 3d ed., Andover, 1854; 4th ed., Andover, 1860. Also published in London, 1828, 1833, 1837, 1846, 1851, 1856, 1864.]

A Commentary on the Epistle to the Romans. Andover, MA: Flagg & Gould, 1832. [2d ed., corrected and enlarged, Andover, 1835; 3d ed., Andover, 1854; 4th ed., edited and revised by R. D. C. Robbins, Andover, 1865. Published also in London, 1833, 1836, 1851, 1853, 1857, 1865.]

C. *Miscellaneous*

Cicero on the Immortality of the Soul, or Quaestionum Tusculanarum Liber I, with notes and an appendix. Andover, MA: Flagg, Gould & Newman, 1833. [Volume 1 of a proposed series of "Select Classics."]

A Critical History and Defense of the Old Testament Canon. Andover, MA: Allen, Morrill & Wardwell, 1845. [Published also in London and Edinburgh, 1849.]

Exegetical Essays on Several Words Relating to Future Punishment. Andover, MA: Flagg & Gould, 1830. [Also published in Edinburgh, 1848.]

Essay on the Hieroglyphic System of M. Champollion, Jun., and on the Advantages Which It Offers to Sacred Criticism, by J. G. Greppo, Translated From the French by Isaac Stuart, With Notes and Illustrations. Boston: Perkins & Marvin, 1830. Preface by Moses Stuart.

Introduction to the New Testament, by Johann Leonhard Hug, Translated From the 3rd German ed. by David Fosdick, Jr. With Notes by M. Stuart. Andover, MA: Flagg & Gould, 1836.

Miscellanies: Consisting of: I. Letters to Dr. Channing on the Trinity; II. Two Sermons on the Atonement; III. Sacramental Sermon on the Lamb of God; IV. Dedication Sermon—Real Christianity; V. Letter to Dr. Channing on Religious Liberty; VI. Supplementary Notes and Postscripts of New Additional Matter. Andover, MA: Allen, Morrill & Wardwell, 1846.

Passages Cited From the Old Testament by the Writers of the New Testament, Compared With the Original Hebrew and the Septuagint Version; Arranged by the Junior Class in the Theological Seminary, Andover, and Published at Their Request, Under the Superintendence of M. Stuart. Andover, MA: Flagg & Gould, 1827

D. Translations

Elements of Interpretation, Translated from the Latin of J. A. Ernesti, and Accompanied by Notes and an Appendix Containing Extracts from Morus, Beck and Keil. Andover, MA: Flagg & Gould, 1822. [2d ed., London, 1822; 3d ed., Andover, 1838; 4th ed., Andover and New York, 1842.]

Dissertation on the Importance and Best Method of Studying the Original Languages of the Bible, by Jahn and Others, Translated from the Originals, and Accompanied with Notes. Andover, MA: Flagg & Gould, 1821.

A Greek Grammar of the New Testament, Translated From the German of George Benedict Winer, Professor of Theology at Erlangen. Andover, MA: Flagg & Gould, 1825. [A joint effort with Edward Robinson.]

Hebrew Grammar of Gesenius as Edited by Roediger, Translated, with Additions and Also a Hebrew Chrestomathy. Andover, MA: Allen, Morrill & Wardwell, 1846.

Practical Rules for Greek Accents and Quantity. From the German of P. Buttman and F. Passow. Andover, MA: Flagg & Gould, 1829.

E. Pamphlets, Tracts, and Sermons

Articles on the American Education Society. Extracted from the July and October Numbers of the Biblical Repertory. Philadelphia: James Kay Jun. and Company, 1829.

A Brief Sketch of the Life and Character of Mrs. Elizabeth Adams. Andover, MA: Flagg & Gould, 1829. [From a funeral sermon.]

Christ a Sympathizing Saviour. A Sermon Preached at the Funeral of Mrs. Abby Woods, Wife of Leonard Woods, D.D. Andover, MA: Allen, Morrill & Wardwell, 1846.

Conscience and the Constitution, with Remarks on the Recent Speech of the Honorable Daniel Webster. Boston: Crocker & Brewster, 1850.

Essay on the Prize Question Whether the Use of Distilled Liquors, or Traffic in Them, Is Compatible, at the Present Time, with Making a Profession of Christianity? New York: John P. Haven, 1830.

An Examination of the Strictures Upon the American Education Society, in a Late Number of the Biblical Repertory, Originally Published in That Work. Andover, MA: Flagg & Gould, 1829.

A Farewell Sermon. Preached at New Haven, January 28, 1810. New Haven: Sidney's Press, 1810.

Is the Mode of Christian Baptism Prescribed in the New Testament? Andover, MA: Flagg & Gould, 1833.

A Letter to the Editor of the North American Review, on Hebrew Grammar. Andover, MA: W. H. Wardwell, 1847.

A Letter to William E. Channing, D.D. on the Subject of Religious Liberty. Boston: Perkins & Marvin, 1830.

Letters From Professor Stuart, of Andover, Lucius M. Sargent, Esq., of Boston, General Cocke of Virginia, and Rev. Justin Edwards, D.D. on the Maine Liquor Law. New York: n.p., 1851.

Letters on the Eternal Generation of the Son of God, Addressed to the Rev. Samuel Miller, D.D. Andover, MA: Mark Newman, 1822.

Letters to the Rev. William E. Channing, Containing Remarks on His Sermon Recently Preached and Published at Baltimore. Andover, MA: Flagg & Gould, 1819. [2d ed., corrected and enlarged; 3d ed., both Andover, 1819. Also published in Belfast, 1825; Aberdeen, 1834, 1839; London, 1844.]

Mr. Webster's Andover Address and His Political Course While Secretary of State. Essex County (Mass.): Publication for Distribution, 1844.

Scriptural View of the Wine Question, in a Letter to the Rev. Dr. Nott. New York: Leavitt & Trow, 1848.

A Sermon Delivered Before His Excellency Levi Lincoln, Esq., Governor, His Honor Thomas L. Winthrop, Lieutenant Governor, the Hon. Council, the Senate, and the House of Representatives of the Commonwealth of Massachusetts. May 30, 1827, Being the Day of General Election. Boston: True & Greene, State Printers, 1827.

A Sermon, Delivered by Request of the Female Charitable Society in Salem, at Their Anniversary, the First Wednesday in August, A.D. 1815. Andover, MA: Flagg & Gould, 1815.

A Sermon Occasioned by the Completion of the New College Edifice for the Use of the Theological Seminary at Andover and Delivered September 13, 1821. Andover, MA: Flagg & Gould, 1821.

A Sermon Preached at the Dedication of the Church in Hanover Street, Boston, March 1, 1826. Andover, MA: Flagg & Gould, 1826.

A Sermon at the Ordination of the Rev. William G. Schauffler, Missionary to the Jews. Preached at Park Street Church, Boston, on the Evening of November 14, 1831. Andover, MA: Flagg & Gould, 1831. [2d ed., Andover, 1831; 3d ed., Boston, 1845.]

A Sermon Preached at the Ordination of the Rev. L. Punderson, October 26, 1809. Pittsfield, MA: n.p., 1809.

A Sermon Preached Before the Administration of the Lord's Supper to the First Congregational Church in New Haven, January 14, A.D. 1810. New Haven: Sidney's Press, 1810.

A Sermon Preached in the Tabernacle Church, Salem, November 5, 1818, at the Ordination of the Rev. Messers. Pliny Fisk, Levi Spaulding, Miron Winslow, and Henry Hubbard as Missionaries to the Unevangelized Nations. Andover, MA: Flagg & Gould, 1819.

Synoptical View of Lectures on the Literary History of the Epistle to the Hebrews. N.p., n.d.

Two Discourses on the Atonement by Moses Stuart, Associate Professor of Sacred Literature in the Theological Seminary at Andover. Published by Request of the Students. Andover, MA: Flagg & Gould, 1824. [2d ed., 1828.]

What is the Most Appropriate Age for Entering the Active Duties of the Sacred Office? Andover, MA: n.p., 1839.

F. *Journal Articles*

It was estimated at the time of Stuart's death that the combined effort of his occasional essays and articles which appeared in periodical form would fill two thousand octavo pages. The extent of the following list suggests the probable truth of that figure.

1. *American Biblical Repository*

"Are the Same Principles of Interpretation to Be Applied to the Bible as to Other Books?" 2 (January 1832) 124–137.

"Christology of the Book of Enoch; with Some Account of the Book Itself, and Critical Remarks Upon It." 15 (January 1840) 86–137. [One of the first introductions to the American public of the then recently discovered book.]

"Commentary on Isaiah 17:12–14. 18:1–7. Translated from the German of Gesenius by Professor William S. Tyler, with Remarks by Professor Stuart." 8 (July 1836) 195–220.

"Correspondence with Dr. Nordheimer on the Use and Omission of the Hebrew Article in Some Important Passages of Scripture." 18 (October 1841) 404–418.

"Creed of Arminius with a Sketch of His Life and Times." 7 (April 1831) 226–308.

"Critical Examination of Some Passages in Genesis 1; with Remarks on Difficulties That Attend Some of the Present Modes of Geological Reasoning." 7 (January 1836) 46–106. [Also published as *Philological Views of Modern Doctrines of Geology*, Edinburgh, 1836.]

"Examination of Rev. A. Barnes' Remarks on Hebrews 9:16–18." 20 (October 1842) 356–381.

"Exegesis of Isaiah XV. XVI. Translated from the German of Gesenius, by W. S. Tyler, Theological Seminary Andover, with Remarks and Notes by M. Stuart." 7 (January 1836) 107–160.

"Future Punishment as Exhibited in the Book of Enoch." 16 (July 1840) 1–35.

"Have the Sacred Writers Anywhere Asserted That the Sin or Righteousness of One is Imputed to Another?" 7 (April 1836) 241–330.

"Hebrew Lexicography." 8 (October 1836) 448–494.

"The Hebrew Tenses. Translation of Ewald's Syntax in the Second (abridged) Edition of His Hebrew Grammar, So Far as Respects the Use of the Tenses in Hebrew, with Remarks on the Same." 11 (January 1838) 131–174.

"Hints and Cautions Respecting the Greek Article." 4 (April 1834) 277–327.

"Hints on the Study of the Greek Language." 2 (April 1832) 290–310.

"Hints Respecting Commentaries Upon the Scriptures." 3 (January 1833) 130–185.

"How Are the Designations of Time in the Apocalypse to be Understood?" 5 (January 1835) 33–83.

"Interpretation of Psalm XVI." 1 (January 1831) 76–110.

"Interpretation of Romans 8:18–25." 1 (April 1831) 363–406.

"Inquiry Respecting the Original Language of Matthew's Gospel, and the Genuineness of the First Two Chapters of the same, with Particular Reference to Mr. Norton's View of These Subjects as Exhibited in His Treatise on the Genuineness of the Gospels." 12 (July 1838) 133–179.

"Is the Manner of Christian Baptism Prescribed in the New Testament?" 3 (April 1833) 288–390.

"Meaning of *Kyrios* in the New Testament, Particularly as Employed by Paul." 1 (October 1831) 733–775.

"Notice of Rosenmuelleri Scholia in V.T., in Compendium Redacta." 2 (January 1832) 210–214.

"On the Alleged Obscurity of Prophecy." 2 (January 1832) 217–245.

"On the Discrepancy Between the Sabellian and Athanasian Method of Representing the Doctrine of the Trinity, by Friedrich Schleiermacher, Translated with Notes." 5 (April 1835) 265–353, 6 (July 1835) 1–116.

"On the Meaning of the Word *plērōma* in the New Testament; and particularly on the Meaning of the Passage in which It Occurs in Col. 2:9." 7 (October 1836) 373–428.

"On the Use of the Particle *hina* in the New Testament, Translated from the Latin of Professor Tittmann of Leipsic, with Notes." 5 (January 1835) 84–112.

"Remarks on Hahn's Definition of Interpretation and Some Topics Connected with It." 1 (January 1831) 139–159.

"Review of Professor Norton's Evidences of the Genuineness of the Gospels." 11 (April 1838) 265–343.

"Remarks on the Internal Evidence Respecting the Various Readings in 1 Timothy 3:16." 2 (January 1832) 57–79.

"Samaritan Pentateuch and Literature." 2 (October 1832) 681–723.

"What Has Paul Taught Respecting the Obedience of Christ? Translated from the Latin of Tittmann, with Notes and Remarks." 8 (July 1836) 1–87.

"What is Sin?" 13 (April 1839) 261–294, 14 (July 1839) 26–71.

2. *Bibliotheca Sacra*

"De Wette's Commentary on Romans 5:12–19." 5 (May 1848) 263–283.

"Doctrine Respecting the Person of Christ: Translated from the German of Dr. and Professor J. A. Dorner, with Remarks." 7 (October 1850) 696–732.

"Exegetical and Theological Examination of John 1:1–18." 7 (January, April 1850) 13–53, 281–327.

"Hebrew Criticisms: Psalms 22:17." 9 (January 1852) 51–77.

"The Lord's Supper in the Corinthian Church: Remarks on 1 Corinthians 11:17–34." (1843) 494–531.

"The Number of the Beast in the Apocalypse." (1843) 332–360.

"Observations on Matthew 24:29–31, and the Parallel Passages in Mark and Luke, with Remarks on the Double Sense." 9 (April, July 1852) 329–355, 449–468.

"On the Manuscripts and Editions of the Greek New Testament." (1843) 254–282.

"Patristical and Exegetical Investigation of the Question Respecting the Real Bodily Presence of Christ in the Elements of the Lord's Supper." (February, May 1844) 110–152, 225–279.

"Sketches of Angelology in the Old and New Testament." (1843) 88–154.

"The White Stone of the Apocalypse; Exegesis of Rev. 2:17." (1843) 461–477.

3. *Christian Review*

"Letter to the Editor on the Study of the German Language." 6 (September 1841) 446–471.

4. *The Liberator*

"Letter to Wilbur Fisk." 7:106 (June 30, 1837).

5. *North American Review*

"Review of Gilfillan's Bards of the Bible." 73 (July 1851) 238–267.
"Review of Robinson's Greek Lexicon." 72 (April 1851) 261–293.
"Review of Roy's Hebrew Lexicon." 46 (April 1838) 487–532.

6. *Quarterly Christian Spectator*

"Review Reviewed." 2 (August 1821) 425–435. Stuart's answer to the *Spectator's* review of his *Letters to Channing*. . . .

7. *Quarterly Journal of the American Education Society*

"Examination of Strictures upon the American Education Society." 2 (November 1829) 79–104.
"Letter on the Study of the Classics." 1 (April 1828) 85–98.
"Postscript to the Examination." 2 (February 1830) 135–149.
"Sacred and Classical Studies." 3 (February 1831) 161–166.
"Study of Hebrew." 1 (April 1829) 193–204.

8. *Quarterly Review of the Methodist Episcopal Church South*

"Traits of History and Doctrine Peculiar to Christianity." 5 (April, July 1851) 169–195, 329–357.

9. *Spirit of the Pilgrims*

"Aion and Aionios." 2 (August 1829) 405–452.
"German Theological Writers." 1 (March 1828) 164–168.

III. SECONDARY WORKS

"Account of the Revival of Religion in New Haven." *The Connecticut Evangelical Magazine and Religious Intelligencer* n.s. 2 (March 1809) 96–104. [Colorful report of revivals in Stuart's church.]

Adams, Alice. *The Neglected Period of Anti-Slavery in America, 1803–1831*. Boston: Ginn & Company, 1908.

Adams, William. *A Discourse on the Life and Services of Professor Moses Stuart, Delivered in the City of New York: Sabbath Evening, January 25, 1852*. New York: G. F. Trow, 1852.

Ahlstrom, Sydney E. *A Religious History of the American People*. New Haven and London: Yale University Press, 1972.

Albright, William F. "Moses Stuart." *Dictionary of American Biography*. New York, 1928–1944. 18:174–175.

Allen, Joseph H. *A History of the Unitarians in the United States*. New York: Christian Literature, 1894.

Andover Theological Seminary General Catalogue, 1808–1908. Boston: Thomas Todd Printer, 1909.

Armistead, Wilson (compiler). *Five Hundred Thousand Strokes for Freedom, or Leed's Anti-Slavery Tracts.* London: W. and F. Cash, 1853. [Contains Stuart's "Letter to Wilbur Fisk."]

Bacon, Leonard. "A Commemorative Discourse" in Taylor, John Lord, *A Memorial of the Semi-Centennial Celebration of the Founding of the Theological Seminary at Andover.* Andover, MA: Warren F. Draper, 1859.

———. "Moses Stuart." *New Englander* 10 (February 1852) 42–45. [Unsigned.]

———. *Thirteen Historical Discourses, on the Completion of Two Hundred Years, from the Beginning of the First Church in New Haven.* New Haven: Durrie and Peck, 1839.

———. *Slavery Discussed in Occasional Essays, from 1833–1846.* New York: Baker and Scribner, 1846.

Bacon, Theodore D. *Leonard Bacon, Statesman in the Church.* New Haven: Yale University Press, 1931.

Bainton, Roland. *Yale and the Ministry: A History of Education for the Christian Ministry at Yale from the Founding in 1701.* New York: Harper and Brothers, 1957.

Baldwin, Alice. *The New England Clergy and the American Revolution.* Durham, NC: Duke University Press, 1928.

Barnes, Albert. "Examination of Professor Stuart on Hebrews IX:16–18." *American Biblical Repository* 20 (July 1842) 51–70.

Barnes, Gilbert Hobbs. *The Antislavery Impulse, 1830–1844.* New York: Appleton Century Company, Inc., 1933.

Beecher, Edward. "Remarks on Stuart's Commentary on the Apocalypse." *American Biblical Repository* 3rd ser. 3 (April 1847) 272–304.

Beecher, Lyman. *Autobiography, Correspondence, etc., of Lyman Beecher, D.D.* Ed. Charles Beecher. 2 vols. New York: Harper, 1865.

Berkof, Louis, *Principles in Biblical Interpretation.* Grand Rapids, MI: Baker Book House, 1952.

Billington, Ray. *The Protestant Crusade—1800–1860.* New York: Macmillan, 1938.

Blake, Henry T. *Chronicles of the New Haven Green From 1638 to 1862: A Series of Papers Read Before the New Haven Colony Historical Society.* New Haven: The Tuttle, Morehouse and Taylor Press, 1898.

Bodo, John R. *The Protestant Clergy and Public Issues, 1812–1848.* Princeton, NJ: Princeton University Press, 1945.

Briggs, Charles A. *General Introduction to the Study of Holy Scripture: The Principles, Methods, History, and Results of Its Several Departments and of the Whole.* New York: Scribner's Sons, 1899.

———. *The Higher Criticism of the Hexateuch.* New York: Scribner's Sons, 1893.

Brown, Jerry Wayne. *The Rise of Biblical Criticism in America, 1800–1870: The New England Scholars.* Middletown, CT: Wesleyan University Press, 1969.

Burnap, George W. "Stuart on the Apocalypse." *Christian Examiner* 40 (March 1846) 161–194.

Channing, William Ellery. *Discourses, Reviews and Miscellaneous.* Boston: Gray and Grown, 1830.

———. *A Sermon Delivered at the Ordination of Rev. Jared Sparks.* Baltimore. MD: J. Robinson, 1819.

———. *Sermon Preached at the Annual Election, May 26, 1830.* Boston: Carter and Jendee, 1830.

Clark, Rufus. *A Review of the Rev. Moses Stuart's Pamphlet on Slavery, Entitled Conscience and the Constitution.* Boston: C. C. P. Moody, 1850.

"Civil Government." *Princeton Review* (January 1851). [Later published as a pamphlet under the same title, again anonymously (Princeton: n.p., 1851).]

Christie, F. C. "Beginnings of Arminianism in New England." *Papers of the American Society of Church History.* 2d ser., 3 (1912) 153–172.

Cheyne, T. K. *Founders of Old Testament Criticism: Biographical, Descriptive, and Critical Studies.* New York: Scribner's Sons, 1893.

Clark, Joseph S. *A Historical Sketch of the Congregational Churches in Massachusetts, from 1620 to 1858.* Boston: Congregational Board of Publication, 1858.

Conant, Thomas Jefferson. *A Defense of the Hebrew Grammar of Gesenius, Against Professor Stuart's Translation.* New York: D. Appleton and Company, 1847.

Conybeare, J. J. *The Bampton Lectures for the Year MDCCCXXIV, Being an Attempt to Trace the History and to Ascertain the Limits of the Secondary and Spiritual Interpretation of Scripture.* Oxford: The University Press, 1824.

Cowles, John P. "Stuart on the Romans." *Quarterly Christian Spectator* 4 (December 1832) 661–676.

Cooke, George W. *Unitarianism in America: A History of Its Origin and Development.* Boston: American Unitarian Association, 1902.

Cornelius, (Mrs.) M. H. "A Chapter of Reminiscences: Moses Stuart." *New Englander* 32 (July 1873) 550–560. [Especially good for anecdotes from Stuart's later life.]

Cunningham, Charles E. *Timothy Dwight, 1752–1817.* New York: Macmillan, 1942.

Dana, Daniel. *Letters to the Rev. Professor Stuart, Comprising Remarks on His Essay on Sin Published in the American Biblical Repository for April and July.* Boston: Crocker and Brewster, 1839.

Danhof, Ralph J. *Charles Hodge as a Dogmatician.* Goes: Oosterbaan, 1929.

Davenport, John Gaylord. "Moses Stuart—The Man Who Unfettered Religious Thought in America." *Connecticut Magazine* 11 (1907) 111–124.

Davidson, Samuel. *Sacred Hermeneutics Developed and Applied; Including a History of Biblical Interpretation from the Earliest of the Fathers to the Reformation.* Edinburgh: L. T. Clark, 1843.

———. *Sacred Hermeneutics.* Edinburgh: L. T. Clark, 1843.

Day, Mills. *Proposals by Mills Day, New Haven, for Publishing by Subscription, an Edition of the Hebrew Bible From the Text of Van-der-Hooght, Prospectus.* New Haven: n.p., 1810.

DeWette, William M. L. *A Critical and Historical Introduction to the Canonical Scriptures of the Old Testament.* Translated by Theodore Parker. Boston: C. C. Little and J. Brown, 1843.

Dexter, Franklin B. "Student Life at Yale College Under the First President Dwight (1795–1817)." *A Selection From the Miscellaneous Historical Papers of Fifty Years.*

New Haven: The Tuttle, Morehouse and Taylor Company, 1918.

Duff, Archibald. *History of Old Testament Criticism.* New York: Putnam, 1910.

Duffield, George. "Review of Stuart on the Apocalypse." *American Biblical Repository* 3d ser., 3 (July 1847) 385–411.

Dwight, Timothy. *Sermons.* 2 vols. New Haven: Hezekiah Howe and Durrie and Peck, 1828.

———. *A Statistical Account of New Haven.* New Haven: Walter and Steele, 1811.

———. *Theology Explained and Defended in a Series of Sermons.* 5 vols. New Haven: Clark and Lyman, 1818.

Dwight, Timothy. *Memories of Yale Life and Men, 1845–1899.* New York: Dodd, Mead, 1903.

Edwards, Jonathan. *Original Sin.* Ed. by Clyde A. Hollbrook. New Haven: Yale University Press, 1970.

Eichhorn, Johann Gottfried. *Einleitung in das Alte Testament.* 3 vols. Leipzig: Weidemannischen Buchhandlung, 1810.

Evarts, Jeremiah. "Review of American Unitarianism by Jedidiah Morse." *Panoplist* 11 (June 1815) 24–272.

"Exercise at the Annual Examination of the Theological Seminary in Andover, September 23, 1818." *Panoplist* 14 (September 1818) 420–421.

Farrar, Frederick W. *History of Interpretation; Eight Lectures Preached Before the University of Oxford in the Year MDCCCLXXXV.* New York: E. P. Dutton, 1886.

First Annual Report of the Executive Committee of the American Society for the Promotion of Temperance. Andover, MA: Flagg & Gould, 1828.

Fisher, George Park. *Life of Benjamin Silliman.* 2 vols. Philadelphia: Scribner and Company, 1866.

Fitch, Eleazar T. *Two Discourses on the Nature of Sin.* New Haven: Treadway and Adams, 1826.

Foster, Frank Hugh. *A Genetic History of the New England Theology.* Chicago: University of Chicago Press, 1907.

Foster, Stephen S. *The Brotherhood of Thieves, or a True Picture of the American Church and Clergy. A Letter to Nathaniel Barrey of Nantucket.* Concord, NH: P. Pillsbury, 1884. [Contains excerpts from Stuart's "Letter to Wilbur Fisk."]

Fox, Early Lee. *The American Colonization Society, 1817–1840.* Baltimore, MD: Johns Hopkins Press, 1919.

Fuess, Claude M. *Daniel Webster.* 2 vols. Boston: Little, Brown and Company, 1935.

———. *An Old New England School, A History of Phillips Academy, Andover.* Boston: Houghton Mifflin, 1917.

Gambrell, Mary Latimer. *Ministerial Training in Eighteenth-Century New England.* New York: Columbia University Press, 1937.

Gannett, Ezra Stiles. "On the Meaning of the Expressions, 'Everlasting Punishment and Life Eternal' in Matthew XXV.46 — 'These Shall Go Away Into Everlasting Punishment But the Righteous Into Life Eternal.'" *Christian Examiner* 5 (November–December 1828) 441–453.

———. "Professor Stuart's Remarks on an Article in the Christian Examiner, Concerning the Meaning of the Expressions, 'Everlasting Punishment,' and 'Life Eternal,' in Matthew XXV.46.—A Letter from the Writer of That Article."

Christian Examiner 9 (September 1830) 20–46.

Gannett, William C. *Ezra Stiles Gannett*. Boston: Roberts Brothers, 1875.

Gibbs, Josiah Willard. *A Hebrew and English Lexicon of the Old Testament Including the Biblical Chaldee*. Andover, MA: Flagg & Gould, 1824.

Gillispie, Charles C. *Genesis and Geology*. Cambridge, MA: Harvard University Press, 1951.

Giltner, John H. *Moses Stuart: 1780–1852*. Ann Arbor, MI: University Microfilms, 1965.

———. "Genesis and Geology: The Stuart-Silliman-Hitchcock Debate." *Journal of Religious Thought* 23 (1966–1967) 3–13.

———. "Moses Stuart and the Slavery Controversy: A Study in the Failure of Moderation." *Journal of Religious Thought* 18 (Winter-Spring 1961) 27–39.

Goodrich, Chauncy A., "Narrative of Revivals of Religion in Yale College." *Quarterly Journal of the American Education Society* 10 (February 1838) 289–310.

Grant, Robert M. *The Bible in the Church: A Short History of Interpretation*. New York: Macmillan, 1948.

———, McNeill, John T., and Terrien, Samuel. "History of the Interpretation of the Bible." *Interpreter's Bible*. New York: Abingdon-Cokesbury Press, 1951–1956. 1:106-141.

Greenslot, Ferris. *The Lowells and Their Seven Worlds*. Boston: Houghton Mifflin Company, 1946.

Hall, Edwin. *The Ancient Historical Records of Norwalk, Connecticut, With a Plan of the Ancient Settlement and of the Town in 1847*. Norwalk, CT: J. Mallory and Company, 1847.

Haroutunian, Joseph. *Piety versus Moralism: The Passing of the New England Theology*. New York: Archon Books, 1932.

Hengstenberg, Ernst W. "On the Nature of Prophecy, trans. by James F. Warner from Christologie des Alten Testaments (Berlin, 1829–1835)." *American Biblical Repository* (January, July 1832) 138–173, 499–540.

Hitchcock, Edward. "The Connection Between Geology and the Mosaic History of the Creation." *American Biblical Repository* 5 (January, April 1835) 113–138, 439–451; 6 (October 1835) 261–332.

———. *The Religion of Geology and Its Connected Sciences*. Boston: Phillips, Sampson, 1851.

———. "Remarks on Professor Stuart's Examination of Gen. 1, in Reference to Geology." *American Biblical Repository* 7 (April 1836) 448–487.

Hodge, Archibald Alexander. *The Life of Charles Hodge, D.D. LL.D., Professor in the Theological Seminary, Princeton, New Jersey, by his son, A. A. Hodge*. New York: Scribner's Sons, 1880.

Hodge, Charles. *Commentary on the Epistle to the Romans*. Philadelphia: Grigg and Eliot, 1835.

———. "On Slavery." *Biblical Repertory* 8 (April 1836) 268–305.

———. "Stuart on Romans." *Biblical Repertory* 5 (July 1833) 381–416.

———. *Systematic Theology*. 3 vols. London and Edinburgh: T. Nelson and Sons, 1873.

Holmes, Oliver Wendell. *Pages From An Old Volume of Life: A Collection of Essays*. Boston: Houghton Mifflin, 1891. [Andover reminiscensces.]

Hovey, Alvah. "Moses Stuart." *Christian Review* 17 (April 1852) 288–296.

Jay, William. *Reply to Remarks of the Rev. Moses Stuart on The Honorable John*

Jay, and an Examination of His Scriptural Exegesis Contained in His Recent Pamphlet Entitled: Conscience and the Constitution. New York: John A. Gray, 1850.

Judd, Willard. *A Review of Professor Stuart on Christian Baptism.* New York: Baptist Mission Room, 1836.

Judson, Roswell. *Two Epistles of Free Stricture on the American Dictionary of Mr. Webster, on the Hebrew Grammar and Hebrew Chrestomathy of Mr. Stuart, and on the Manual Hebrew Lexicon of Mr. Gibbs.* 2d ed. New Haven: The Herald, 1830.

Keller, Charles Roy. *The Second Great Awakening in Connecticut.* New Haven: Yale University Press, 1942.

Kelly, J. Frederick. *Early Connecticut Meeting Houses: Being an Account of the Church Edifices Built Before 1830, Based Chiefly Upon Town and Parish Records.* 2 vols. New York: Columbia University Press, 1948. [Contains a description of the First (Center) Church New Haven meeting house during Stuart's pastorate.]

Kingsley, James L. "Remarks on a 'Critical Examination of Some Passages in Gen. 1: with Remarks on Difficulties that Attend some of the Present Modes of Geological Reasoning. By M. Stuart, Professor of Sacred Literature, Theological Seminary Andover.'" *American Journal of Science* 30 (January 1836) 114–130.

———. *Review of Stuart's Select Classics, Vol. 1 Containing Cicero on the Immortality of the Soul, or Quaestionam . . . .* Boston: n.p., 1833. [Highly critical of Stuart's classical scholarship.]

Kingsley, William L., editor. *Yale College, A Sketch of Its History, With Notices of Its Several Departments, Instructors, and Benefactors, Together With Some Account of Student Life, and Amusements, by Various Authors.* 2 vols. New York: Holt, 1879.

Koch, G. Adoph. *Republican Religion: The American Revolution and the Cult of Reason.* New York: H. Holt and Company, 1933.

Kraeling, Emil G. *The Old Testament Since the Reformation.* New York: Harper, 1956.

Krout, John Allen. *The Origins of Prohibition.* New York: A. A. Knopf, 1925.

Lloyd, Arthur Young. *The Slavery Controversy, 1831–1861.* Chapel Hill, NC: The University of North Carolina Press, 1939.

Long, Orie W. *Literary Pioneers: Early American Explorers of European Culture.* Cambridge, MA: Harvard University Press, 1935.

Marsh, James. "Review of Stuart on the Epistle to the Hebrews." *Quarterly Christian Spectator* 3d ser. 1 (March 1829) 112–149.

Maurer, Oscar E. *A Puritan Church and Its Relation to Community State and Nation: Addresses Delivered in Preparation for the Three Hundredth Anniversary of the Settlement of New Haven.* New Haven: Yale University Press, 1938. [A history of the First (Center) Church in New Haven.]

Mead, Sidney. *Nathaniel W. Taylor, 1786–1858.* Chicago: University of Chicago Press, 1942.

A Memorial of the Semi-Centennial Celebration of the Founding of the Theological Seminary at Andover. [Prepared by J. L. Tayer.] Andover, MA: Warren F. Draper, 1857.

Meyer, Jacob C. *Church and State in Massachusetts from 1740–1833: A Chapter in the History of the Development of Individual Freedom.* Cleveland, OH: Western Reserve University, 1930.

Miller, Samuel. *Letters on the Eternal Sonship of Christ: Addressed to the Rev. Professor Stuart of Andover.* Philadelphia: W. W. Woodward, 1823.

———. *Letters to Unitarians: Addressed to Members of the First Presbyterian Church, in the City of Baltimore.* Trenton, NJ: George Sherman, 1821.

Mitchell, Mary Hewitt. *History of the United Church of New Haven: Written in Commemoration of the Two Hundredth Anniversary, 1742-1942.* New Haven: The United Church, 1942.

Moore, Clement. *A Compendius Lexicon of the Hebrew Language.* New York: Collins & Perkins, 1809.

Morison, Samuel Eliot. *The Founding of Harvard College.* Cambridge, MA: Harvard University Press, 1935.

———. *Harvard College in the Seventeenth Century.* Cambridge, MA: Harvard University Press, 1936.

Morse, James King. *Jedidiah Morse, A Champion of New England Orthodoxy.* New York: Columbia University Press, 1939.

Mott, Frank L. *A History of American Magazines, 1741-1850.* New York: D. Appleton, 1930.

Norton, Andrews. *The Evidences of the Genuineness of the Gospels.* 2 vols. 2d ed. London: J. Chapman, 1847.

———. "On the Author of the Epistle to the Hebrews." *Christian Examiner* 4 (November, December 1827) 495-519; 5 (January, February 1828) 37-70; 6 (May 1829) 330-347.

———. *Statement of Reasons for Not Believing the Doctrines of Trinitarians Respecting the Nature of God and the Person of Christ; Occasioned by Professor Stuart's Letters to Mr. Channing First Published in the Christian Disciple.* Boston: Wells and Lilly, 1819.

Nott, Eliphalet. *Lectures on Temperance.* Albany, NY: E. H. Peace, 1847.

Noyes, George R. "Stuart on the Old Testament." *Christian Examiner* 40 (January 1846) 69-77. [Unfavorable review of Stuart's *Critical Defense*.]

Olmstead, Marian. *Wilton Parish, 1726-1800.* Wilton, CT: n.p., 1900.

Paradise, Scott H. *A History of Printing in Andover, Massachusetts, 1798-1931.* Andover, MA: The Andover Press, 1931.

Park, Edwards A. *The Associate Creed of Andover Theological Seminary.* Boston: Tappan and Whittemore, 1883.

———. *A Discourse Delivered at the Funeral of Professor Moses Stuart.* Boston: Tappan and Whittemore, 1852. [Contains the funeral sermon and the best contemporary summary and estimate of Stuart's life and work.]

Peabody, Andrew P. "Early New England Unitarians." *Unitarianism: Its Origin and History.* Boston: American Unitarian Association, 1890.

Phelps, Austin. "A Memorial of the Author." In Elizabeth Stuart Phelps (pseud. "H. Trusta"), *The Last Leaf from Sunny Side.* Boston: Phillips, Sampson and Company, 1853. [An account of the influence of Moses Stuart upon his gifted daughter.]

Pierce, Richard D. "The Legal Aspects of the Andover Creed." *Church History* 15 (March 1946) 28-47.

Porter, Ebenezer. "Terms of Admission to the Theological Seminary, Andover." *American Biblical Repository* 2 (July 1832) 592.

Purcell, Richard J. *Connecticut in Transition, 1775–1818.* Washington, DC: American Historical Association, 1918.

"Review of Dana's Letters to Stuart on Original Sin." *Christian Examiner* 27 (November 1839) 281–284.

"Review of Pamphlets on the Unitarian Controversy." *Quarterly Christian Spectator* 3 (March 1821) 129–149.

"Review of Stuart's Commentary on the Hebrews." *Spirit of the Pilgrims* 2 (January, February 1829) 15–47, 80–105.

"Review of Stuart's Grammar of the New Testament Dialect." *American Biblical Repository* 5 (January 1835) 245.

"Review of Stuart's Grammar of the New Testament Dialect." *British Critic and Quarterly Theological Review* 23 (April 1838) 565.

"Review of Stuart's Hebrew Grammar." *North American Review* 13 (October 1821) 473–477.

"Review of Stuart's Hebrew Grammar of Gesenius as Edited by Roediger." *North American Review* 45 (July 1847) 256–259.

"Review of Whitman's Letters to Stuart on the Subject of Religious Liberty." *Spirit of the Pilgrims* 4 (March 1831) 117–179.

"Revival of Religion in New Haven." *Panoplist* 7 (August 1811) 113–118. [A report of revivals in Stuart's church.]

Ripley, Henry Jones. *Christian Baptism: An Examination of Professor Stuart's Essay in the Biblical Repository on "The Mode of Baptism."* Boston: Lincoln, Edmans, 1833.

Robbins, Sarah Stuart. *Old Andover Days.* Boston: Pilgrim Press, 1908. [Personal reminiscences by another of Stuart's talented daughters.]

Robinson, William A. *Jeffersonian Democracy in New England.* New Haven: Yale University Press, 1916.

Rowe, Henry K. *History of Andover Theological Seminary.* Newton, MA: n.p., 1933.

Schmucher, Samuel S. *Fraternal Appeal.* New York, 1838. Reprinted with introductory essay by Frederick K. Wentz. Philadelphia: Fortress Press, 1965.

Schwab, John C. "The Yale College Curriculum." *Educational Review* 12 (June 1901) 1–17.

Selleck, Charles J. *Norwalk.* Norwalk, CT: n.p., 1896.

Senior, Robert C. *New England Congregationalism, and the Anti-Slavery Movement, 1830–1860.* Ann Arbor, MI: University Microfilms, 1975.

Silliman, Benjamin. "The Consistency of Geology with Sacred History." In Robert Bakewell, *An Introduction to Geology. Second American From the Fourth London Edition,* edited by Professor B. Silliman. New Haven: H. Howe, 1833.

———. *Outline of the Course of Geological Lectures Given in Yale College.* New Haven: H. Howe, 1829.

———. *A Sketch of the Life and Character of President Dwight: Delivered as an Eulogium, in New Haven, February 12th, 1817, before the Academic Body, of Yale College, Composed of the Senatus Academicus, Faculty and Students.* New Haven: Maltby, Goldsmith, T. G. Woodward, 1817.

Smith, John. *A Hebrew Grammar, Without the Points: Designed to Facilitate the Study of the Scriptures of the Old Testament, in the Original; and Particularly*

Adapted to the Use of Those Who May Not Have Instructors. Boston: D. Carlisle, 1803.

Smith, H. Shelton. *Changing Conceptions of Original Sin.* New York: Scribner, 1955.

Spring, Gardiner. *Dissertation on Native Depravity.* New York: J. Leavitt, 1833.

———. *Personal Reminiscences of the Life and Times of Gardiner Spring.* New York: Scribner, 1866.

Stephenson, George M. *The Puritan Heritage.* New York: Macmillan, 1952.

Stokes, Anson Phelps. *A Biographical Study of Student Life and University Influences During the Eighteenth and Nineteenth Centuries.* New Haven: Yale University Press, 1914.

Stowe, Calvin. "Letter on Moses Stuart." Pp. 478–81 in William Sprague, *Annals of the American Pulpit.* Vol. 1. New York: Carter, 1859–1869.

"Stuart's Commentary on Romans." *American Monthly Review* 2 (November 1832) 388–394.

Taylor, Nathaniel. *Essays, Lectures, etc., upon Select Topics in Revealed Theology.* New York: Clark, Austin and Smith, 1859.

———. *Concio ad Clerum: A Sermon Delivered in the Chapel of Yale College, September 10, 1828.* New Haven, 1828. Pp. 211–249 in Sydney Ahlstrom, *Theology in America.* New York: Bobbs, Merrill, 1967.

Taylor, Timothy A. *Memoir of the Rev. Oliver Alden Taylor, A.M. Late of Manchester, Massachusetts.* Boston: Tappan and Whittemore, 1853.

Thomas, Milton Halsey. "Joseph Stevens Buckminister." *Dictionary of American Biography.* New York: Scribner, 1928–1944. 3:233–34.

Todd, John. *The Story of His Life, Told Mainly by Himself. Compiled and Edited by John E. Todd.* New York: Harper, 1876.

Tyler, Alice. *Freedom's Ferment: Phases of American Social History.* Minneapolis, MN: The University of Minnesota Press, 1944.

Tyler, Edward R. *Slaveholding a Malum in Se, or Invariably Sinful.* Hartford: S.S. Cowles, 1839.

Vail, Stephan M. "Review of Stuart on the Apocalypse." *Methodist Quarterly Review* 29 (January 1847) 5–22.

Vogel, Stanley M. *German Literary Influences on the American Transcendentalists.* New Haven: Yale University Press, 1955.

Walker, George. *Some Aspects of the Religious Life of New England, with Special Reference to Congregationalists.* New York: Silver, Burdett, 1897.

Walker, Williston. *A History of the Congregational Churches in the United States.* New York: The Christian Literature Company, 1894.

———. *Ten New England Leaders.* New York: Silver, Burdett and Company, 1901.

Wayland, Francis, and H. L. *A Memoir of the Life and Labors of Francis Wayland, D.D., Ll.D.* New York: Sheldon and Company, 1867. [Contains a glowing tribute to Stuart as a teacher.]

Webster, Fletcher, ed. *The Private Correspondence of Daniel Webster.* 2 vols. Boston: Little Brown and Company, 1857.

Webster, Noah. "The Peculiar Doctrines of the Gospel Explained and Defended." *Panoplist* 5 (July 1809) 58–74. [Brief essay by one of Stuart's notable Center Church converts.]

Welch, Claude. *In This Name.* New York: Scribner, 1952.

Whitman, Bernard. *Two Letters to the Reverend Moses Stuart: on the Subject of Religious Liberty.* Boston: Gray and Bowen, 1830.

Whittier, John Greenleaf. "A Sabbath Scene." From the pamphlet *The Platform of the American Anti-Slavery Society, and Its Auxiliaries.* New York: American Anti-Slavery Society and Its Auxiliaries, 1853. Also in *The Complete Poetical Works of John Greenleaf Whittier.* Boston: Houghton Mifflin, 1904. (Altered.)

Wilbur, E. Morse. *A History of Unitarianism in Transylvania, England, and America.* Cambridge, MA: Harvard University Press, 1952.

Williams, Daniel Day. *The Andover Liberals: A Study in American Theology.* New York: Kings Crown Press, 1941.

Williams, George, ed. *The Harvard Divinity School: Its Place in Harvard University and in American Culture.* Boston: Beacon Press, 1954.

Woods, Leonard. *The Works of Leonard Woods, D.D.* 5 vols. Andover, MA: J. D. Flagg, 1850.

———. *History of the Andover Theological Seminary.* Boston: J. R. Osgood, 1885.

Woolsey, Theodore S. "Theodore Dwight Woolsey—A Biographical Sketch." *Yale Review* 1 (January, April, July 1912) 260–299, 453–470, 620–638.

Wright, Conrad. *The Beginnings of Unitarianism in America.* Boston: Starr King Press, 1955.

———. "The Religion of Geology." *New England Quarterly* 14 (June 1941) 335–358.

INDEX

Hovey, Alvah, 110
Hupfeld, Herman, 82

"Inquiry Respecting the Original Language of Matthew's Gospel . . . ," 89

Jackson, James, 132
Jahn, Johannes, 43
Jameson, Robert, 68
Jefferson, Thomas, 117
Jones, John T., 27
Josephus, 43, 99, 105
Judson, Adoniram, 27

Kant, Immanuel, 54
Kennicott, Benjamin, 20, 30, 43
King, Jonas, 27
Kingsbury, Cyrus, 27
Kingsley, James L., 73–74
Koppe, J. B., 39
Kypke, 105

language
  Arabic, 7–8
  Aramaic, 7, 16
  Chaldee, 7, 16
  figurative, 40, 61, 70, 97n.
  origen of Hebrew, 77
  Sanskrit, 8
  Semitic, 7
  Syriac, 7
Le Clerc, Jean, 30, 105
Lensden, Johannes, 30
"A Letter to the Editor of the NA Review on Hebrew Grammar," 84
"Letters on the Eternal Generation . . . ," 65
"Letters to the Rev. William E. Channing," 57, 60–66
Liffingwell, William, 12
literalism, 43, 47, 58, 68, 74, 95
Locke, John, 54
Lord, Nathan, 125
Lowth, Bishop Robert, 37, 39, 52
Luther, Martin, 105

Marsh, James, 109

Masclef, Francois, 15
Matthiae, C. F., 83, 86
Meyer, G. W., 64
Michaelis, Johann David, 42, 70–71
Miller, Samuel, 65
miracles, 41, 49
Morse, Jedediah, 14, 57
Mosaic authorship of Scripture, 9, 33–35, 43, 98–99
Mosaic chronology, 67
Mosheim, Johann L., 2
"Mr. Webster's Andover Address and His Political Course . . . ," 117
Murdock, James, 26
mystical, mysticism, 39, 44, 51

Neptunism, 67, 72
Nero, 94–96
Newcombe, William, 12–13
Newell, Samuel, 27
New Testament
  books of
    I Corinthians, 91–92, 106
    Ephesians, 106
    Hebrews, 106, 108
    James, 113
    John, 53–54, 94–96, 106
    Luke, 32
    Matthew, 93–94
    I Peter, 106
    Revelation, 94–95, 97, 122
    Romans, 92, 104, 114, 122
    Romans 5:12–19, 111ff.
    I Timothy, 19, 119
    II Timothy, 19
  criticism, 84–87, 91–97
  origen of Gospels, 92–94
  persons of
    John the Baptist, 126
    Onesimus, 128, 130
    Paul, 91–93, 101, 105, 111, 114, 119, 122, 126–128, 130
Noedin, 8
Norton, Andrews, 89, 92–93, 98–99, 108
Noyes, George, 108
numerology, 51

LaVergne, TN USA
27 March 2011
221773LV00002B/205/A